DATE DUE

MAR 1 2 2008	
JUN 1 0 2009	
MAY 1 0 2009	
MAY 1 7 2010	
SEP 1 0 2011	

BEYOND
PLUNDER

BEYOND PLUNDER

Toward Democratic Governance in Liberia

Amos Sawyer

LYNNE
RIENNER
PUBLISHERS

BOULDER
LONDON

Published in the United States of America in 2005 by
Lynne Rienner Publishers, Inc.
1800 30th Street, Boulder, Colorado 80301
www.rienner.com

and in the United Kingdom by
Lynne Rienner Publishers, Inc.
3 Henrietta Street, Covent Garden, London WC2E 8LU

Library of Congress Cataloging-in-Publication Data
Sawyer, Amos.
    Beyond plunder : toward democratic governance in Liberia / Amos Sawyer.
      p. cm.
    Includes bibliographical references and index.
    ISBN 1-58826-384-3 (hardcover : alk. paper)
    1. Liberia—Politics and government—1980–   2. Political culture—Liberia.
3. Democracy—Liberia.   4. Political violence—Liberia—History.   I. Title.
    JQ3925.S29 2005
    320.96662—dc22

                                                        2005010746

British Cataloguing in Publication Data
A Cataloguing in Publication record for this book
is available from the British Library.

Printed and bound in the United States of America

        The paper used in this publication meets the requirements
(∞)   of the American National Standard for Permanence of
        Paper for Printed Library Materials Z39.48-1992.

    5   4   3   2   1

To Vincent Ostrom and
to the memory of Abel, my father,
Dudley, my brother,
and all who lost their lives in a quarter-century
of violent upheavals in Liberia

Contents

Preface: An Outlook from a Scholar-Activist

F OR MUCH OF MY ADULT LIFE, I HAVE STRUGGLED TO UNDERSTAND THE COMPLEX patterns of social institutions in Liberia. My efforts to understand the dynamics of state building, changing patterns of property rights, and the emergence of presidential autocracy, among other concerns, have made for engaging scholarship. But Liberia has been more than a scholarly interest of mine. Quite frequently, as a citizen, I have also intervened to help shape the course of these patterns. Thus, for more than thirty years, I have been driven by a scholar's curiosity to "understand what's happening" and an activist's passion "to do something about it." Obviously, this blend of scholarship and activism has had implications for both. Nonetheless, I have endeavored over these years to be guided by David Hume's admonition to let my quest for scientific understanding be accompanied by a desire to act.

The collapse of the Liberian political order and the decade and a half of violence that resulted from it have posed for the Liberian people and for scholars and practitioners a huge challenge. This tragedy built upon a decade of intermittent violence that characterized the period of Samuel Doe's rule. The situation was made extraordinary by the fact that Liberia became the epicenter of a system of conflict in the wider Mano River Basin area that includes Sierra Leone and the forest regions of Guinea. Feeding on a combustible environment created in these areas by years of government predation, repression, and governance failure, violent breakdowns in Liberia spawned a conflagration in the neighborhood. How do we understand this breakdown and the violence resulting from it? And how do we approach the task of reconstituting order? These questions have been central to discourse on Liberia for several years now. They have become even more critical to the discourse since the fall of the Taylor regime. This book attempts to make a contribution to that discourse.

A book that strives, at this time, to address the Liberian tragedy and the challenge of reconstituting order must direct its message to diverse audiences.

Of course, Liberians generally and the Liberian "attentive public" more specifically are important audiences; so also are scholars, policy analysts, and international development practitioners, among others. Shaping a message for the appreciation of such varied audiences can be risky business. Some practitioners may find this book not sufficiently prescriptive; some scholars may find it not sufficiently analytical or theoretical; and many Liberians may find it jargon-laden. I have attempted to straddle a course that in my judgment enables me to communicate the book's main message: that institutional arrangements of governance in Liberia have been inherently flawed and have been a structural source of breakdown and a significant contributor to violent conflicts; and that to reconstitute order, there is a need for a new constitutional paradigm and a new institutional design that depart significantly from those that have failed.

Every governing order faces constitutional dilemmas from time to time. Many of these dilemmas are addressed typically through rule changes within the extant constitutional paradigm. However, there can be junctures in the history of a country at which the constitutional paradigm itself becomes the problem. Liberia has arrived at such a juncture. The vision, mission, and institutional arrangements that characterize its body politic have been outpaced by the capabilities, potential, and aspirations of its people and the challenges presented by changed regional and international orders.

I would not have written this book at this time had it not been for two experiences I had in 2000. One was sad and destructive; the other was pleasant and offered opportunities. Wearing my activist hat, I had been involved in pro-democracy initiatives during the repressive regime of Samuel Doe and in the search for peace after Charles Taylor launched an invasion of Liberia in December 1989. For close to four years (August 1990 to March 1994), I served as head of the interim government of Liberia, which was charged with the responsibility of bringing belligerent parties into an agreement to end hostilities and restore peace. My efforts did not succeed. Several interim governments were subsequently organized following several failed peace agreements. Under the Abuja Agreement of 1996, snap elections were held and Charles Taylor was declared president. Like many war-weary Liberians, I attempted to reorganize my life, which had been deeply affected by repression and violent plunder, and to contribute to rebuilding our society. Again like many war-weary Liberians who attempted to rebuild during Charles Taylor's presidency, my efforts were not only thwarted but my life was put at risk. On November 28, 2000, security officers broke into the Center for Democratic Empowerment (CEDE) in Monrovia, where I served as chair and maintained an office, ransacked the premises, broke down doors, destroyed computers and other office equipment, and physically assaulted my colleagues and me. Sources close to Taylor confided later that this assault was meant as a warning and strongly advised me and other senior colleagues of CEDE to leave the country.

The Workshop in Political Theory and Policy Analysis at Indiana University has been my intellectual haven since 1986, when, under similar circumstances during the Doe regime, I was forced to leave Liberia. Vincent Ostrom's telephone call of December 2000 had been one of several he had made to me since my service in the interim government ended in 1994. This time, I was ready to return to the Workshop and to immerse myself in an effort to further deepen my understanding of Africa's governance dilemma generally and the Liberian tragedy particularly. Returning to the Workshop, I brought a new experience. Having served as head of the interim government of Liberia, I had seen the powers of the Liberian presidency at close range—albeit those powers had been truncated by state failure and violent conflict. I had seen how presidential approbation was the single most valuable asset sought after in Liberian society, and how laws and norms reinforced each other to uphold its value. Well-trained professionals conceded their expert views to adjust to what they thought the president wanted to hear. Older men ended their letters to the president with such complimentary closings as "your obedient servant." Aggrieved wives brought complaints against their husbands to the president. Much of this existed a half-century ago under Tubman. Not much seemed to have changed in spite of tremendous advances in education, distribution, and social integration. I had also interacted with leaders of other African countries during this period and had seen a similar phenomenon at work in some of those countries. Moreover, I had participated in the activities of regional and international governing bodies at the highest levels and had seen how the state, as an international legal entity, struggles to stand supreme and frequently unrestrained in affairs of humanity. I had also seen how leaders, claiming to be the embodiment of the state, often projected their ambitions and personal agendas. These experiences have affected my perceptions and to some extent have influenced the views expressed in this book.

I could not have wished for a more appropriate place from which to reflect and write the book. The Workshop in Political Theory and Policy Analysis is a community of scholars from various disciplines and regions of the world. It offers opportunities for collegial contestation, rigorous analysis, and exploration of the links between theory and practice. I have greatly benefited from the intellectual stimulation this community has provided, as well as from its financial and other material resources; I thank Vincent and Elinor Ostrom for making all of this possible. I also thank them along with other Workshop participants and colleagues for their diligent review and incisive comments on drafts of this work. Vincent Ostrom read several drafts of every chapter, and Elinor Ostrom, Michael McGinnis, Barbara Allen, and Sheldon Gellar read the entire manuscript twice. Their comments and suggestions were invaluable. I also want to thank Marilyn Hoskins, Sam Joseph, Sujai Shivakumar, Fillipo Sabetti, James Wunsch, Shittu Akinola, and other Workshop-affiliated colleagues who critiqued the manuscript and offered helpful suggestions during the Workshop's annual Thanksgiving week manuscript review in 2003. Marco Janssen, Milindo Chakrabarti, and Minoti Chakravarty-Kaul offered useful ideas, which I appreciate. For several years now, I have participated in the

Workshop's year-long seminar in institutional analysis and development and for the last three years have taught or co-taught the second semester version of the seminar. I thank participants of successive seminars who read and commented on various chapters of the book. I also thank Charlotte Hess, Laura Wisen, and the staff of the Workshop's library and information services along with Verlon Stone and his team of the Liberia Collections Project; they were exceedingly helpful in finding documents I needed. Kunle Oyerinde tracked down several references for me, and Ray Eliason, Hasan Cakir, and Lee Carlson relieved many anxious moments by helping me cope with and avoid computer glitches. Patty Lezotte, Sarah Kantner, and David Price were very helpful in preparing the manuscript for the publisher. I thank them immensely. I also thank Gayle Higgins, without whose organizational skills I would not have been able to carry out my other assignments at the Workshop while writing this book. Linda Smith, Nicole Todd, Jackie Schofield, and Carol Buszkiewicz have been most generous in helping me in various ways and at various stages of the project. I deeply appreciate their help.

Outside the Workshop and Indiana University, I have had the support of many others. Conmany Wesseh, Ezekiel Pajibo, Samuel Ajavon Jr., and the staff of CEDE were a base of support. Samuel Ajavon read the entire manuscript and helped me double-check historical dates and other facts. Gediminar Flomo, Krubo Kollie, Anthony Kesselly, Abdul Dukule, Michael Jebboe, Louis Kamara, and Archie Sawyer helped in compiling and verifying information; Anthony Tobi kept my computer working at home; Alfred Kulah and Tiawan Gongloe were my constant sounding boards; and both also read portions of earlier drafts and made valuable comments. Collegial contestations with Byron Tarr, Svend Holsoe, and Joyce Mends-Cole have been most rewarding. I am particularly grateful to Byron Tarr for his helpful comments as I revised the manuscript. Peter Schwab encouraged me in this undertaking and I am indeed grateful to him.

I am deeply thankful to Lynne Rienner and the staff of Lynne Rienner Publishers: to Shena Redmond, who handled this project, Dorothy Brandt, whose copyediting made the manuscript more readable, and all the others who are responsible for bringing this publication to fruition.

I want to thank the United States Institute of Peace for a generous grant (USIP-030-01S) in support of this project.

Special thanks to my wife, Comfort, who is always there for me, and to other members of my family for being a reliable pillar of support. Responsibility for views and errors in this book is, of course, exclusively mine.

BEYOND
PLUNDER

CHAPTER 1

Liberia's Path to the Present

THIS BOOK IS ABOUT THE CHALLENGE OF RECONSTITUTING ORDER IN LIBERIA FOL-lowing the collapse of its governing institutions and a tragic period of pillage, plunder, and carnage. It is neither a work of theory nor a practical manual. It is an effort to explore new ways of establishing constitutional foundations upon which peace can be sustained through democratic governance. Though focused on Liberia, and to some extent the Mano River basin area that includes Sierra Leone and Guinea, it speaks to many other parts of Africa where governing orders established at independence, frequently on colonial foundations, have broken down with serious, often tragic, consequences for ordinary people; or where reform efforts have offered patterns of change insufficient to alter the fortunes of peoples. While it shows how individual agency and institutional failure have wreaked havoc, it argues that institutions that are differently configured and that are organized through processes of decisionmaking characterized by informed discourse among the people of a society can become their vehicles to a better future.

Numerous publications about Africa have shown how individual excesses are a cause of Africa's underdevelopment and a source of repression. Leaders take liberties, destroy nascent institutions, and strive to exercise autocratic control. More recently, since the end of the Cold War, stories of domination, plunder, and carnage describe the plight of human beings in many parts of Africa. These occurrences, although not a post–Cold War phenomenon, seem in some cases to be more intensive; and they also seem to have gained greater visibility since the Cold War ended. During the Cold War, international actors often supported this situation in order to advance their own agendas.[1]

The destructive consequence of individual agency is a consistent theme that runs through most contemporary publications on Liberia. The havoc caused by armed groups, Charles Taylor's repressive rule, and the excesses of Samuel

1

Doe are among the horrors graphically described. There is also considerable finger pointing and name calling as Liberians and others seek to understand what went wrong in that society. Tubman is blamed for establishing a benevolent dictatorship, Tolbert for being tight-fisted and nepotistic, and the so-called radicals of the 1970s for trying to shape the debate and bringing the system down. Even if one accepts the view that the roots of the Liberian tragedy lie wholly in a sustained crisis of leadership and embraces the "bad man" theory of history, one must still see such crises through the prism of history and, at least, as a project of many accomplices, internal and foreign, witting and unwitting. For example, it is not possible to speak of recent bloodletting in Liberia without mentioning the postcoup military and economic support given by the United States that bolstered the confidence and capacity of the Liberian leadership to rampage against real and perceived enemies during the years immediately before the ending of the Cold War—or the abrupt withdrawal of that support on the eve of the fall of the Berlin Wall. One could not explain Taylor's plunder without the subplot of his escape from a U.S. prison and his relationship with influential African leaders, European business interests, and numerous others.

Looking at deeper roots of the Liberian tragedy and the role of human agency, one cannot assess the actions of settler-founders of Liberia without appreciating their circumstances at that time. The founding of Liberia by the American Colonization Society (ACS) and the mode of governance the ACS established posed a predicament that those who became Liberia's leaders had not only to endure but to address. Conceived as an alternative to abolition in the early decades of nineteenth-century America, Liberia never attracted massive immigration or adequate support. Its settler-leaders, upon taking over from the ACS, strove to shape a governing order that would reflect the contemporary ideals of human freedoms while ensuring Liberia's survival as a distinct and superior political order, much as did the imperial orders of the day.[2] These leaders cannot be judged as "bad" people solely bent on domination and control no more than should judgment be brought upon those indigenous leaders who cooperated or resisted the establishment of Liberia as a settler-dominated political order. This is not to deny the role of individual agency but to stress the importance of analyzing individual actions within the context of institutions or rules.[3] And this is what this study has set out to do.

■ Institutional Analysis and the Story of Liberia

Institutional analysis helps us to better understand how individuals craft rules and organize the rule-ordered relationships in which they live their lives. This approach to scientific inquiry, often referred to as "new institutionalism," is within the broader tradition of political economy. The specific variation used in this work draws from the Institutional Analysis and Development (IAD) framework, shown generically in Figure 1.1, developed over the years by Vin-

Figure 1.1 A Framework for Institutional Analysis

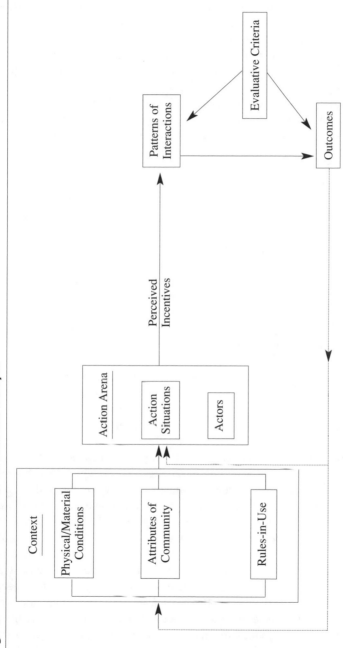

Source: Adapted from E. Ostrom, Gardner, and Walker (1994, 37).

cent Ostrom and Elinor Ostrom and colleagues at the Workshop in Political Theory and Policy Analysis at Indiana University.[4] As a tool of analysis, the framework helps to deepen understanding of how ecological conditions, cultural and other attributes of a community, and rules structure patterns of interaction among individuals. It helps us understand how institutions structure incentives and influence choices within ecological and social environments. Much more is said about these concepts in the course of this analysis (especially in Chapter 5).

The study of institutions provides a useful framework for understanding governance in Liberia since its founding a century and a half ago by freedmen and former slaves from North America; the causes and dynamics of the violent collapse of the country's governing institutions; the untold human sufferings people have endured; and, of particular importance to this book, the possibilities for reconstituting order differently. Understanding the biophysical conditions of Liberia—its Atlantic coastline dotted with mangrove swamps and lagoons, the treacherous undertow of its costal waters, its sand-clogged estuaries, and its eight rivers that are not navigable beyond twenty miles—helps us appreciate the pattern of initial settlement of coastal clusters up the banks of rivers not more than twenty-five miles from the coast. These physical features partially explain why, in the face of poor communications and transportation, a "confederal" governing arrangement was emerging in the early and mid-nineteenth century but could not be sustained by the settlers in the face of European imperial expansion and resistance from indigenous communities. Analysis of attributes of the settler communities, such as their sense of a "civilizing mission" to Africa, deepens understanding of core elements of their identity and of the nature of the relationship they sought to establish with local indigenous communities. We can further understand why the potential for conflict with settler communities existed where indigenous concepts of property rights precluded the alienation of land, and why acephalous indigenous communities could not be easily incorporated under state control during processes of state building. Thus, we can begin to see why Liberian state-building activities among the various indigenous communities were fraught with challenges.

Institutional analysis also helps us understand how, by the middle of the twentieth century, with new income from the exploitation of natural resources, the authority of the president was further strengthened. The dominance of that authority had already been established at an earlier juncture, where European imperial pressure and indigenous resistance had strengthened the perceived need for strong leadership to ensure state survival and settler community cohesion. It also helps us understand the strategies of control by the state under the authority of the president, the adaptive responses of various indigenous communities, and the way the expansion of educational opportunities, among others, led to increased demands for institutional reforms. Understanding these issues is important to appreciating how Liberia reached a point of violent collapse and what possibilities exist for reconstituting order differently.

In a previous effort, I sought to deepen understanding of how an autocratic governing order was constituted in Liberia and how it collapsed (Sawyer 1992). Many others have given accounts of state building and of developments leading to state collapse in Liberia.[5] There is a growing body of research on the subsequent decade and a half of violent conflicts.[6] These developments, though not the focus of this book, are taken as a point of departure.

In this book, I address the challenge of reconstituting order in Liberia after state collapse and violent conflict. I explore the possibility of establishing institutional arrangements that would avoid the overcentralized and predatory state model that has been a source of autocracy and repression and of building upon self-organizing capabilities that would allow Liberians to more fully utilize their human and material resources for democratic governance and development. Because such analysis must draw upon an understanding of the nature of Liberia's emergence as an overcentralized state, I provide in the sections that follow a brief account of Liberia's road to autocracy and also intersperse aspects of that account in the analysis presented throughout the book.

■ Recurrent Themes

In using institutional analysis to illuminate the challenges and opportunities of creating a self-organized democratic system of governance in Liberia, I highlight throughout the book the following interrelated themes.

Employing a Theory of Limited or Shared Sovereignty and Polycentric Governance

The first theme is the proposition that Liberia's prospects for attaining lasting peace will become brighter if its governing order is reconstituted on the basis of a theory of limited or shared sovereignty and not on a theory of unitary sovereignty as has been the case for over 150 years. To achieve this, processes of constitutional choice or constitutional rule making that are appropriate for crafting institutions for democratic governance must be established and sustained. Two issues concerning what should be considered the appropriate processes of constitutional choice are discussed or inferred: (1) how the processes of constitutional choice for democratic self-governance are essentially about how people self-organize to solve problems or otherwise address social dilemmas; and (2) how ordinary people engage in informed and enlightened discourse about making rules for choosing and ordering those who are to govern their society.

These processes do not presume the existence of a limited number of pre-conceived patterns of order, such as presidential and parliamentary models of government, from which a society must choose. Limiting choice to preconceived patterns unduly underestimates the variety of governance arrangements people in a given environment may be capable of constructing to meet their needs and circumstances. Similarly, the view that federal arrangements are more suitable for countries with large land mass, such as the United States, and not for small countries such as Liberia—a view held by some Liberian academics and other trained professionals during the constitutional drafting debates of the early 1980s and subsequently—disregards the fact that democratic governance arrangements must be designed by people to meet their needs and circumstances and not to conform to prescribed assumptions. Governance arrangements based on a theory of shared sovereignty reflect polycentric institutional forms. Unlike monocentric governments, which are underpinned by theories of unitary sovereignty, polycentric governance admits of heterogeneity and provides a variety of institutional forms capable of addressing diversity while ensuring equity and justice.

Understanding Extant Social Patterns

The second theme recurrently made throughout the book is that the task of constituting democratic governance must begin with a clear understanding of the variety of social patterns extant in society and how these patterns are constituted and configured. Understanding how people have resolved conflicts over time and what possibilities they have for strengthening or reconstituting such institutions requires reliance on local knowledge as a starting point. We must understand how ethnic communities, such as the Loma and Mandingo, have resolved their conflicts over the years if we are to craft institutions for conflict resolution appropriate for all Liberians. We must understand the meaning of citizenship in Kwa societies if we are to appreciate the nature of the freedoms ordinary people of southeastern indigenous Liberian communities expect to exercise. Local knowledge constitutes the initial building blocks or points of departure.

Equally important is knowledge about how communities elsewhere and in a variety of other circumstances have patterned order and addressed social dilemmas. Processes of constituting order do require drawing from wider epistemic systems and adapting from the experiences of others where necessary and as relevant. The process of creating a Liberian democratic order should not preclude drawing lessons from experiences elsewhere or adapting arrangements used elsewhere to address a particular dilemma. However, a deep understanding of such other orders is vital. For example, although Yoruba societies are considered to be patterned in hierarchies, certain communities in Yorubaland, such as those of Abeokuta and Ibadan, have succeeded in developing institutions that differed markedly from those of Ile-Ife, which seemed to project the control of the *ooni* (king) of Ile-Ife (Ayo 2002). Understanding the Yoruba experience in its variations and those of others could be helpful in widening the possibilities for adaptation in reconstituting order in Liberia. Constitutional patterns of South Africa, Switzerland, and other societies whose governance arrangements are designed to appreciate and build upon diversity can be a valuable resource from which to appropriately and relevantly draw.

Importance of an Open Public Realm and Enlightened Citizens

The third theme that runs throughout this book underscores the importance of an open public realm as a platform for ongoing discourse essential to sustaining systems of democratic self-governance. The open public realm provides opportunities for contestation, which is critical to public enlightenment and responsible decisionmaking. The mass media, town hall meetings, and other forums are necessary venues for open discourse. However, meaningful participation can be hampered without literacy and education. An individual's possibilities of acquiring the capabilities to fully exercise the prerogatives of citizenship are greatly reduced without literacy and education; that is why literacy and education must be considered among the fundamental public policies to be pursued in Liberia and elsewhere where autocracy has prevailed. Civic education must be considered among the country's highest priorities; therefore, written constitutional rules must be accessible to all who are literate and have a basic education. Civic education can become a difficult undertaking when constitutional rules are written in technical legal language that is inaccessible to most people.[7] Moreover, civic education cannot be seen as abstract teachings of constitutional rules and patriotic sentiments. It must lead to the empowerment of citizens to become knowledgeable and effective participants in the bodies and forums of decisionmaking. Thus, literacy is fundamental to that process of empowerment. Liberia and other African countries cannot hope to establish democratic governing orders without literate populations. These issues are discussed in various forms throughout the book (but especially in Chapter 8).

The Challenge of Entrepreneurship

The fourth theme often repeated has to do with the role of entrepreneurship in crafting and sustaining governance arrangements. Human beings are artisans—to use Vincent Ostrom's terms—and human institutions are artifacts created through human artisanship. The cultivation of entrepreneurial skills in problem solving—that is, the ability to identify or create opportunities—is fundamental to human progress. Unfortunately, entrepreneurship can be put to harmful purposes, such as organizing for destructive conflict as is discussed later (especially in Chapter 2). The importance of the entrepreneurial role of scholars and community development practitioners is highlighted at several points in the book. Processes of constitutional choice in Liberia are likely to be less meaningful if not grounded in sound knowledge and a free flow of information. Liberian scholars must be able to generate that knowledge through appropriate research. They must sharpen skills in the methods of scholarly research and apply them to attain deeper *scientific* understanding of Liberian social patterns, ecological regimes, dynamic processes of change over time, and the consequences and implications of those developments for that society and the wider West African subregion. They must do comparative analyses so as to more deeply understand experiences in social ordering else-where in Africa and other parts of the world and must strive to contribute to the development of governance approaches that build upon the Liberian experience while departing from the system of overcentralization that has yielded predation and tragedy. If there is an element of advocacy in this book, it is about the responsibility of scholars in society faced with the challenge of reconstituting order. Variations of these themes are at the core of the arguments advanced in succeeding chapters.

■ Terms and Contexts

Language is used to convey meaning, but because it is so imprecise, we struggle to adequately transmit a thought with all its nuances. This book struggles to convey specific meanings of some common terms, which are used here in the context of institutional analysis. Therefore, some preliminary explanations are required, since some of the terms may become clearer only as the analysis proceeds.

   Governance is used by the World Bank and other intergovernmental organizations engaged in socioeconomic development activities in developing countries to refer to the management of public affairs by the state and to denote the creation of an enabling environment for market economies. More recently, the concept of *good governance* has come into usage to embrace civil society and the private sector as partners with government in the management of public affairs.[8] As used in this book, the concept of governance draws from institutional analysis and refers to the conduct of public affairs by citizens of a country through an array of diverse institutional arrangements designed for making and implementing constitutional rules and a variety of policy and operational rules at various levels or scales. This mode of order is more precisely referred to as *self-governance* and is manifested through polycentric institutional arrangements. Self-governing institutions are crafted through processes of constitutional choice and are designed for problem solving by people themselves. Self-governance arrangements consist of a configuration of institutions that include centralized institutions but differ from the notion of "the government," which conveys the sense of a single set of institutions—in the case of Africa, typically dominated from the center—designed to run society.[9] Throughout the book, I use the terms *self-governance, democratic governance,* and *self-governing democracies* interchangeably but distinct from "the government," or *good governance.* I use the term *good governance* with specific reference to the formulations offered by the Bretton Woods institutions and the United Nations Development Programme (UNDP).

Development is typically used in the development literature to convey a meaning of transforming people and society from a state of "backwardness" associated with local traditions and lifestyles to a state of "modernity." I rely on Amartya Sen (1999) and see "development as freedom" as empowerment: the cultivation of capabilities to remove the major sources of "unfreedom"— such as inequality of opportunity and tyrannical and repressive governments. I use the term *self-reliant development* as a companion to self-governance to connote a self-generated and self-sustaining transformatory process that obtains through self-governance.[10]

Participation, like the term *democracy,* is often used to convey a variety of meanings. The mobilization of cheering squads as seen in certain political forums and decisionmaking assemblies in Africa and elsewhere is often considered indications of popular participation. Perfunctory involvement of people where their mere presence is calculated statistically to indicate a degree of participation can be misleading. I use *participation* or *meaningful participation* in this book with reference to the inclusion of individuals in situations that involve contestation, learning, and making choices. These are core elements of processes of constitutional choice and self-governance.

Constitutional choice, or how people put together systems of governance, is of profound importance to how they live their lives. As stated above, every time human beings establish or are able to sustain patterns of relationships among themselves, they engage in processes of constitutional choice. Constitutional choice for democratic governance involves the challenge of a people arriving at a theory of governance suitable to their circumstances and establishing governance institutions based on that theory. It is a process by which the people of a society, through enlightened discourse oriented to problem solving, make fundamental rules to address their governance dilemmas. Knowledgeable contestation in an open public realm is essential to successful processes of constitutional choice. Processes of constitutional choice for democratic governance have to be ongoing; they are processes of review and adaptation, trial, error, and correction as circumstances require. Because constitutional choice for self-governance provides ongoing opportunities to make constitutional rules, it is critically important that such processes are undergirded by strong normative principles as well as solid ideas of how to overcome social dilemmas. Alexis de Tocqueville ([1835] 1969) posited principles of freedom and equality as the bedrock of democratic association that should always be protected—including from the tyranny of the majority. Respect for the humanity and dignity of others and the acceptance of others as equals are salient values constitutive of normative principles essential to democracy. That is why a set of core and immutable principles must remain entrenched and protected in all systems of democratic governance, though constitutional rules established to project them may vary according to place and time.

Level and *scale* are terms often used interchangeably in contemporary scholarly literature. In the language of institutional analysis as used in this book, the term *level* is used with reference to decisionmaking or rulemaking, and *scale* with reference to spatial jurisdiction or domain. Three levels of decisionmaking are conceptualized: constitutional, collective choice or policy, and operational. Constitutional level is the level at which foundational or constitutional rules are made. Collective choice rules or policies are made at a level that is nested within the constitutional level, and operational rules are made within the framework of collective choice rules. The term *scale* is used with reference to a range of jurisdictions or domains such as household, neighborhood, local community, provincial, national, and supranational scales. However, these terms are not always used precisely in contemporary scholarship. I have not tried to change the terms when used by other scholars or in the context of their work. At times, I have also used them interchangeably, except where specifically noted. Nonetheless, I do think there is coherence to thinking about levels of decisionmaking within different sizes or scales of jurisdictions.

*   *   *

As a study that explores possibilities of establishing patterns of governance that are different from the highly centralized governmental arrangement that brought Liberia to a quarter-century of violence and misery, this book begins with a brief discussion of the foundations of oligarchic rule in Liberia. The remainder of this chapter is devoted to that discussion. Chapter 2 describes the breakdown—the nature and magnitude of the violence, plunder, and death, and the misery these visited upon the majority of Liberians and their neighbors; it also examines the key actors and the regional and international environments within which they operated. Chapter 3 discusses how Liberians survived. It shows how self-organizing capabilities were deployed to enable people to cope with their circumstances and the potential of this social capital for building a new order that strives to be a system of democratic governance. These chapters provide a point of departure. Chapter 4 makes the case for a new constitutional paradigm and new institutions of governance for Liberia. It examines the trajectory of the Liberian government under a theory of unitary sovereignty, discusses previous institutional reform initiatives attempted in Liberia—including the decentralization and good governance agenda promoted in Liberia by the Bretton Woods institutions and other external actors, and then makes the case for a new conception of governance and a new institutional design.

Chapter 5 focuses more specifically on how institutional analysis can be used as a tool to further the possibility of constituting a new Liberian order. It presents a framework for constitutional choice and discusses guideposts essential to the construction of a system of democratic governance or polycentric governments based on a theory of limited or shared sovereignty as an alternative to monocentric government derived from a theory of unitary sovereignty. Considering the book's focus on the reconstitution of order in a post-conflict situation, Chapter 6 addresses questions concerning the security environment and the nature of transitional peacebuilding, which are forerunners of, if not foundations for, processes establishing democratic governance in Liberia. Chapter 7 takes us from theory to practice and lays out an institutional design for polycentric governance in Liberia. Chapter 8 deals with the question of sustaining democratic governance and, in this light, discusses the importance of nurturing citizens and establishing an appropriate system of education as vital undertakings for sustaining a Liberian self-governing democracy. Chapter 9 concludes with a brief comment on Liberia's prospects for democracy and development.

■ Foundations of Centralization in Liberia

Liberia emerged as a highly centralized unitary state as a result of choices made at critical junctures in its history. Understanding these junctures and the institutional choices provides an appreciation of the foundations of centralized government in Liberia and key landmarks on Liberia's road to tragedy. Though not exhaustive, a chronology of events is provided to assist in this effort (see Appendix 1).

Early Settlement and ACS Sovereignty

The circumstances surrounding the founding of Liberia profoundly affected its early experiences with constitution making. Founded as an alternative to abolition in early nineteenth-century America, Liberia was initially a possession of the American Colonization Society, a philanthropic organization that received some support from the American government. A "compact" to establish order was created in 1820 even before the first group of emigrants set sail from the United States for West Africa.[11] The "Elizabeth Compact" and subsequent constitutions established the agent of the ACS as the unchallenged authority in Liberia and the board of managers of the ACS as the source of laws.[12] Subsequent compacts were also essentially rules reposing authority in the ACS. English common law as modified for use in the United States was further adapted to regulate interactions among the emigrants. It is important to understand that for a group of emigrants for whom settlement in unknown Africa was their best escape from servitude at that time, Liberia, as Claude Clegg (2004) put it, offered a site for identity formation where evolving meanings of slavery, freedom, race, and colonialism intersected in patterns characteristic of Atlantic cultures of the nineteenth century. Yet, given the nature of the times, emigrant negotiations with the ACS about the terms and conditions of governance could hardly yield immediate processes of self-determination; therefore, it is not surprising that Liberia's constitutional order reflected patterns of command and control dominated by the ACS, its founder.

It is also important to point out that at its founding in the 1820s, Liberia was an exclusive settler society situated amid a mix of indigenous African coastal communities that were members of three larger language communities. Principles of organization underlying these communities varied such that there were hierarchical and heterarchical orders and acephalous communities, engaged in fluid patterns of interactions that included the formation of confederations and shifting alliances (d'Azevedo 1971). All of these indigenous African communities subscribed to principles of property rights that precluded alienation of land. Early patterns of interactions between settler communities and indigenous communities were about commodity trade, slave trading, and the alienation (rather than the use) of land. Although these interactions involved violent conflicts and strategic cooperation between settler communities and various indigenous communities, the overriding goal of settler society was to maintain its cohesion and dominance in the area. Thus, the seeds of a system of domination and control were planted at the founding of Liberia.

Merchant Formation and Attempted Shared Sovereignty

Over the early years, as settlement patterns within the coastal environment shaped entrepreneurial opportunities for settlers, new relationships needed to be established among the settlers themselves, with the ACS, with surrounding indigenous African communities, and with the imperial powers (the British and French) that operated so vigorously in the area. At this historical juncture, the emergent settler merchant class, scattered among clusters of coastal communities, could no longer operate under the absolute sovereignty of the ACS, given the encroachment of imperial powers and the ambiguous relationships with surrounding indigenous communities. New patterns of order had to be defined. The constitution of 1839 was an attempt to constitute a new governing order. Under that constitution, clusters of settler communities sought to establish a quasi-federal arrangement sharing local government authority with the ACS.[13] This arrangement, called the "commonwealth constitution," could not provide the institutional capabilities to curtail British and French imperial encroachment in coastal trade or ensure indigenous communities' compliance with settler trade regulations, including port of entry laws. With these as their pressing needs, settler elites and the ACS grew increasingly dissatisfied with the commonwealth constitution feeling a need for more effective mobilization of capabilities to confront the challenges posed by the imperial powers and by unsustainable patterns of cooperation with indigenous communities.

Political Independence and Central State Sovereignty

Independence was thrust upon Liberia. By 1846, as imperial intrusion intensified, Liberian leaders found themselves at a significant historical juncture. They perceived two viable options to preserve the integrity of the settlements and to protect settler trade. The first and preferred option was to secure U.S. government guarantees of Liberian territorial integrity. This, however, was not forthcoming. The United States was not prepared to adopt Liberia as a colony or take actions beyond making occasional appeals to the British and French to respect Liberian efforts to survive and providing occasional military support. The second option was to declare Liberia an independent and sovereign state and, as such, to seek recourse in international law for the protection of its sovereignty. In this move, settler communities would internalize sovereign authority and project it through the symbols and structures of the Liberian state.

With a declaration of independence as the available means of ensuring its continued existence, Liberian leaders held a constitutional convention and debated the constitutional arrangements to be adopted. The proposal to form a unitary state, put forward by leaders from Monrovia and supported by the ACS, was hotly contested by representatives from the coastal settlements, especially from Bassa. Those opposing the establishment of a highly centralized system argued mainly for a constitutional arrangement that would cede some degree of local autonomy to the counties and for curtailment of the control the ACS exercised over certain portions of land. Despite substantial opposition from coastal settlements and questionable voting returns, Liberia's declaration of independence as a unitary sovereign state was considered adopted in a referendum held in September 1847 (Huberich 1947, 1:845–846).

Declared in a situation of crisis, the Liberian sovereign state was rejected by some indigenous communities with whom it was in conflict over trade, and recognized by several European countries, including Britain, France, and the governments of the Hanseatic German Confederation. The United States did not recognize Liberia's claims to sovereignty until after the American Civil War. European recognition of Liberia's independence, however, did not mean acceptance of all of its territorial claims. Thus, one could argue that from its founding, Liberian leaders have had to shape the contours of governance institutions in response to exogenous factors; and quite frequently, as was the case during the age of imperial expansion, international demands thrust upon

Liberia have required strong centralized control. Is this likely to change in the twenty-first century?

Postindependence and the Consolidation of Central State Sovereignty

Liberian leaders now faced the challenge of demonstrating effective occupation and control of claimed territories. Meeting this challenge essentially required the extension of the Liberian state authority over territories and among peoples beyond those hitherto considered a part of settler communities. Failing to achieve this, Liberian sovereign claims would remain limited to the three clusters of enclave trading communities, situated at the promontory of estuaries along the tropical coastline amid intensifying European imperial scramble.[14]

Opting to establish control over nearby territories, Liberian leaders faced a further choice of whether to strive to establish mechanisms of subordination and control, as the European imperial powers were doing, or rather to build an inclusive nation-state through processes that would involve the extension of prerogatives of citizenship to indigenous communities. For half a century, this question was at the core of the debate about the mission and vision of Liberia. The costs of pursuing either option were potentially high. Establishing effective control required putting in place coercive and administrative capabilities that were far beyond the means of the Liberians. But integrating indigenous communities as full-fledged members of the new Liberian community would radically and dramatically transform the character of settler society, undermine the espoused mission of Liberia, and possibly immediately overwhelm its leaders.

Most settler-leaders struggled to implement a third option, which was to establish relationships of tutelage with surrounding indigenous communities with the view to gradually incorporating individuals from those communities into the Liberian body politic, as such individuals would have been seen to have acquired the qualities to be considered "civilized." These qualities included acceptance of the Christian religion and the cultural traits and social practices of settler society. Pressured by aggressive European colonial expansion, the resistance of several indigenous communities, and declining economic fortunes, Liberian leaders, by the turn of the twentieth century, could not rely on this approach alone. They decided to develop the administrative and coercive capabilities essential for establishing state control over these communities. By the early 1920s, the Liberian government had organized a military force called the Liberian Frontier Force and incrementally established a bureaucracy to administer the indigenous communities. Both organizations were placed under the direct control of the president, resulting in a dramatic increase in presidential authority. Thus, the imposition of taxes in the form of labor, money, and in-kind on inhabitants of indigenous communities through the instrumentalities of the interior bureaucracy and the Liberian Frontier Force was the crucial element of a strategy of control provided in a new constitutional arrangement designed to consolidate central state sovereignty.

Indigenous communities adopted a variety of strategic responses to the attempt to impose Liberian state authority. Some communities accepted Liberian government authority as a means of protection against more powerful and threatening neighbors; others sought accommodation to protect their trading interests; yet others staunchly resisted. For many political communities, the imposition of state hierarchies was most difficult to accommodate. In some parts of the interior, as Liberian state expansion proceeded in the face of British and French colonial expansion, indigenous communities were put under added pressure. Under this pressure, some decided to become a part of the Liberian state.[15]

Post–World War II and the
Establishment of Presidential Sovereignty

Even though the establishment of the interior bureaucracy and the Liberian Frontier Force increased the capability of the central government to exercise control over the country, that control was weak due to communications and transportation difficulties and constant resistance of some indigenous communities, among other things. Because central government's instructions could not be easily communicated across the country, leaders of counties were able to exercise subproprietary control over their counties. District commissioners operated like local lords as the president struggled to rein them in. There were numerous problems of principal-agent relationships. By the end of World War II, this situation was to change substantially. The availability to the government of new revenues derived from property rights in natural resources and not through the interior bureaucracy strengthened the powers of the central government, especially those of the president. Through concession agreements, partnerships, and other arrangements, revenues from natural resources flowed directly into the public coffers and came under the control of the president. In addition to this, Liberia's involvement in the postwar African independence struggles made the president an important figure in pan-Africanist developments, thereby projecting the image of the president abroad and strengthening presidential authority at home. Moreover, with increased revenue, the president now had the capability to establish a patronage network that extended deep into interior communities. He could also expand educational opportunities, which in turn led to increased demands for inclusion.

By the mid-1950s, William V. S. Tubman, the quintessential Liberian president of the twentieth century, had transformed that office into a personal domain. A folksy figure and a Monrovia outsider, he broke the hold of the

Monrovia elite on the presidency by creating a new political base of settlers of low status, indigenous chiefs, and members of the Monrovia elite who had become disaffected with their own inner circle. He doled out public monies to buy loyalty, established an elaborate and greatly feared security network, crushed those members of the opposition whose loyalty he could not buy, and rammed through legislation and a constitutional amendment removing presidential term limits. He died after twenty-seven years in office, having transformed the presidency into a personal cult.

Inadequate Constitutional Responses to Pressure for Popular Sovereignty

Despite Tubman's wiliness, demands for inclusion increased steadily with increasing educational opportunities and with every effort of his to mobilize political support among indigenous chiefs. These pressures were responded to largely through constitutional reordering. Between the mid-1940s and mid-1960s, several constitutional amendments and legislative statutes were promulgated related to the extension of suffrage incrementally to women in settler communities and then to members of indigenous communities.[16] As a result of rapidly expanding educational opportunities in the interior, more individuals from indigenous communities got employed in the state bureaucracy and in government-participating economic joint venture establishments.

However, in addition to the expansion of suffrage, the most significant response during this period was the constitutional reform of the mid-1960s establishing new county jurisdictions and setting interior jurisdictions on par with settler-dominant coastal jurisdictions. It was this specific reform coupled with the expansion of educational opportunities that energized the quest by ordinary people for greater democratization and more meaningful participation in political decisionmaking processes. No other reforms since have had such impact. Liberia's contemporary crisis is underpinned by the fact that despite rising demands for a more participatory governing arrangement, there has not been fundamental constitutional reform to address these demands since the mid-1960s.

In the nearly twenty years between the constitutional changes of the mid-1960s and the military takeover in 1980, rapid expansion of education continued; primary and community health care delivery systems were introduced in earnest; and the network of roadways was expanded considerably. During this period, especially after the death of Tubman in 1971, the professionalization of the public service was initiated by William Tolbert, resulting in the recruitment of large numbers of qualified young professionals, especially from indigenous communities, into the state bureaucracy and parastatals.

However, the process of democratization did not keep pace with the rapid expansion of education, as rising expectations were also partially encouraged by the steady co-optation of professionals into technical positions and by the government's own rhetoric of reform. Despite enormous progress in physical infrastructural development and in human resource development, the Tolbert regime vacillated at an hour of historic choice, when the key to stability was to be found not solely in the expansion of socioeconomic infrastructures but also in the expansion of opportunities for democratic political participation. Liberia had arrived at a historical juncture requiring constitutional choice, and its leadership could not discern the meaning of the moment and appropriately respond to its challenges. Demands for the introduction of a multiparty democratic political process, including electoral reform, peaked in the late 1970s at a time of economic decline, which was caused in part by external factors such as the high cost of petroleum imports, by extravagant government spending, by highly skewed patterns of personal accumulation, and by a failed attempt to reform the ruling party, among other factors.

The involvement of my colleagues and myself in the political process in 1978, when I became a candidate for mayor of Monrovia as an independent, was one element of a broader movement for democratic reforms. The oligarchy's ultimate acceptance of multiparty reforms in 1979 and its partial promulgation of a decentralization initiative that same year came too late. The disintegration of the body politic had already begun.

Military Repression and an Attempted Constitutional Response

Coups have occurred so frequently in Africa that any coup is now perceived as yet another change of regime. Many Liberians and others in the international community did not fathom the true meaning of the coup d'état of 1980 that brought Sergeant Samuel Doe to power (see Appendix 1 for a chronology of events). Even many of those who saw it as the end of an era did not truly appreciate its more profound implications. For Liberia, the military takeover of 1980 completely uprooted the system of governance and brought to an end a century-old oligarchy. Moreover, and of profound significance, it brought to an end a distinct system of patrimonial rule. This system of patrimonial governance had, over the years, molded and incorporated indigenous governance institutions that were a mixture of lineage-based institutions and other clientele arrangements organized around specific principles and dominated by the oligarchy (Liebenow 1987; Sawyer 1992). The control of the levers of government by the Americo-Liberian elite masked the configuration of relationships that was constitutive of the entire governance arrangement. Thus, the total social order, not only the settler-dominated regime, unraveled with the downfall of the government and the takeover by noncommissioned officers of the Liberian military.

Settler patrimonial order was of a distinct character. In a sense, the ideology of patrimony that underpinned the oligarchy was based on a conception of patrimony rooted in settler history, a history that perceives Liberia as the patrimony of black American settlers. Transforming that sense of heritage to cover a more inclusive polity was its historic challenge. That is why one of the sources of its downfall can be found in the halting pace of democratization and inclusion amid rapidly changing circumstances. But as a patrimonial order, the protection of the patrimony, no matter how narrowly or broadly defined by its leaders over the years, was the motive force of its history, and the projection of black "sovereignty and civilization" was both its motif and mission.[17]

Not only were the noncommissioned officers who dislodged the oligarchy in the bloody coup unschooled in the traditions and methods of patrimonial rule in Liberia, they hardly had any vision of an alternative order. Though of indigenous background, most of them were schooled neither in the traditions and cultures of indigenous societies nor in what is broadly considered Western culture. Many had grown up in the shanties of Liberia's urban and periurban communities. After taking over, they embarked on a course of brutal repression within both the military and the larger society. The new military regime came under siege immediately by successive violent purges within its ranks and evolved into an ethnic-based dictatorship of monstrous proportions (Sawyer 1987a; Dunn and Tarr 1988; Liebenow 1987). In my monograph on the era of military rule, I attempted to underscore the profound significance for Liberia of the imposition of a brutal military dictatorship. I wrote:

> The greatest threat which the military dictatorship has posed to the Liberian society is not the abuse of human rights, as intensive and excruciating as these have been; neither is it the impoverishment of the Liberian people, as harsh and demeaning as their economic conditions are. The greatest threat posed by the military dictatorship to the Liberian society lies in the introduction of the military itself as a factor in Liberian political life in the future. The fact that a master sergeant could have hijacked political authority, instituted a repressive military dictatorship, promulgated decrees at will—sometimes backdating them, hire and fire civilian politicians, professionals and technocrats at will, lie to the Liberian people in open radio broadcasts and then deny the lies in subsequent broadcasts . . . [has] implanted in the military a dangerous disdain for the Liberian people, a feeling of invincibility and overlordship, and a view that the correct path to power is through gangsterism. (Sawyer 1987a, 35)

The assaults of the military dictatorship on vital institutions of society were extensive, reaching down to the level of the village where chiefs were replaced, elders of competing quarters and towns intimidated and disgraced, and fundamental principles of social organization such as reciprocity and standards of fairness scoffed at and ignored. The fact that the oligarchy had been overthrown was not the alarming issue, because many keen observers could see it disintegrating; the failure to create new institutions or repair old ones was the real tragedy of the Liberian situation after the 1980 coup.

After settling in as a military leader and purging the military of his opponents, Samuel Doe began to lay the foundations for a new patrimonial order, this time with a predominantly indigenous constituency resting on Krahn ethnic foundations. By stressing the attempts to replicate settler patrimonial order, I refer to initiatives to reinforce the mission of projecting Liberian sovereignty, replete with all the trappings introduced by the settler oligarchy. For example, he sought to restore and dominate the Fraternal Order of Masons, once a bastion of settler control; had himself declared head of the Poro (secret men's society; see Chapter 3) with the title *tarnue* (leader); and he sought honorary degrees from any source and pressured the authorities of the University of Liberia to organize a special graduate degree program that was conducted for him from the executive mansion.

He also built a multiethnic political support base, drawing largely from the ranks of professionals and political operatives who had felt underappreciated by the deposed Tolbert government, and he allowed his closest associates to draw from the public treasure and accumulate wealth as best they could. For himself, he appropriated the timber industry of the country and took charge of the accounts of the forest resource establishment. He promulgated decrees stifling freedom of the press and of association, and he issued orders banning individuals from participation in public affairs.[18] The plunder, pillage, and carnage that characterized his rule seemed legendary at that time but later paled when compared to the excesses of Charles Taylor's regime, as discussed in the next chapter.

Doe's mode of control of Liberia came close to classical warlordism as seen in imperial China (Sheridan 1966; Pye 1971); but his brutal repression did not go unchallenged. Students, religious leaders, his fellow military officers, and many others resisted by speaking out even as they were targeted. Many were murdered, imprisoned, or forced to flee the country.

Calls for the establishment of a timetable for return to civilian rule was a popular response to the brutal excesses of the Doe regime. In a massive demonstration staged one month after the coup, the Liberian National Student Union called for such a timetable. The United States and other key international actors also began pressing for a return to constitutional rule. The establishment of a national constitution commission was one of the regime's direct responses to the growing pressure to leave. The establishment of the constitution commission may have been seen by some in the military leadership more as a means of keeping at bay those who pressured for early return to civilian rule than as an initiative to design a new governance arrangement for a fresh start. My appointment as the commission's chairman was due in part to the fact that I had written several memoranda advocating the need for constitutional reform as a central part of a transitional process. Further efforts by myself and others to ensure the integrity of the commission's work and the subsequent electoral processes drew violent responses from the Doe regime, including my imprisonment and that of many others.[19]

Nonetheless, the emphasis on constitutional reform was meant to address the problem of unitary sovereignty in which the president had been strengthened through the incremental concentration of authority over time: the presidency had been transformed into a personal cult under Tubman and into a brutal dictatorship under Doe, each change bringing increasingly tragic consequences for the people of Liberia. Doe was able to manipulate the transition process, engineer the revision of the draft constitution to suit his purposes, and transform himself into a constitutionally elected president while continuing his repressive rule. Liberia had again missed a historic opportunity for democratic reforms.[20]

The Collapse of the Overcentralized State

The Doe regime was supported by a core ethnic base and was as widely known for its ruthless pursuit of its opponents as it was for the corruption that was widespread within its ranks. Doe, like Mobutu of the former Zaire, was kept afloat largely by external actors because his regime was considered to be of strategic importance in the global security arrangements of the Cold War. As could have been predicted, persistent internal resistance, combined with the withdrawal of U.S. support following a dramatic change in the international order at the fall of the Berlin Wall, led to the collapse of that regime, the killing of Doe by rebel forces, and a decade and a half of continued violent conflicts. The nature and consequences of these conflicts are discussed in the next chapter.

The origins of Liberia's violent conflict can be found in part in the constitutional choices made at critical historical epochs. For more than a century and a half (1821–1990), institutions of government in Liberia, built upon a theory of unitary sovereignty, have been shaped by responses to changing historical experiences. Constitutional choices made over this period yielded a short-lived "federal-like" experiment in 1839; an emergent central state, from 1847 to the early 1900s; a consolidated centralized state with increasing presidential powers, from the early 1900s to the Second World War; and a presidential autocracy (in the post–World War II era, 1945–1979) that was transformed into a brutal dictatorship in 1980 and collapsed in violence in 1989–1990.

Against the backdrop of such tragic experience, what lessons have we learned? One lesson is that the task of reconstituting governing institutions requires a careful study of past failures and a serious and systematic effort to reconstruct institutions differently. Are there alternative constitutional arrangements that can establish foundations for peace and support a system of democratic governance in Liberia? How can these arrangements be formulated? This book seeks to explore the prospects of establishing a democratic alternative to the overcentralized state whose failure has been a source of considerable human sufferings in Liberia and elsewhere in West Africa. A brief discussion of the nature and consequences of the violent conflict in Liberia provides an appropriate point of departure for this exploration.

■ Notes

1. Peter Schwab (2004) has provided a rather provocative argument that counterbalances this view by stressing the failure of Africa's leaders at independence to design viable governance arrangements.

2. This argument appears several times in Carl Burrowes's (2004) book.

3. Jeremy Levitt's (2005) recent book illuminates this question by showing how laws established by the ACS were designs for domination and control and thus for violent conflicts right from the start.

4. A substantial number of publications have been produced at the Workshop during the course of the development of the institutional analysis and development framework. In addition to the seminal works of Vincent Ostrom (1987, 1974, 1997) and Elinor Ostrom (1990, 2005), an appreciable portion of this work can be found in three volumes edited by Michael McGinnis (1999a, 1999b, 2000).

5. Among important historical accounts are those of Huberich (1947), Jones (1962), d'Azevedo (1962, 1969–1971), Liberty (2002), and Clegg (2004). Brown (1981), Clower et al. (1966), and van der Kraaij (1983) have provided economic analyses of Liberia; and Liebenow (1987), Dunn and Tarr (1988), and Chaudhuri (1985), have contributed to the political history of the 1970s and 1980s.

6. See, for example, Huband (1998), Berkeley (2001), Adebajo (2002), Jaye (2003), Pham (2004), and Williams (2002).

7. The constitution of Sierra Leone is one such example.

8. See, for example, the World Bank's governance website, www.worldbank .org/wbi/governance/programs.html.

9. Using the analytic approach of Alexis de Tocqueville, Sheldon Gellar (2005) has done a fascinating study of patterns of governance in Senegal that goes beyond the typical state-centered analyses.

10. See Shivakumar (2005) for a deeper understanding of development as a process of self-organization and self-governance.

11. Huberich (1947, 1:145) refers to some of the provisions of what was called the "Elizabeth Compact," bearing the name of the vessel in which the first group of settlers set sail for Africa in 1820.

12. See Huberich (1947), especially volume 2, *Appendix of Laws*, for subsequent constitutions, including the constitution of 1825.

13. For details of the constitution of 1839, see Huberich (1947, 1:chapter xvii).

14. By 1839, Liberian communities had been established in three clusters along the Atlantic coast. Each cluster contained a principal coastal city situated at or near an estuary and several "upriver" communities located near or along the banks of rivers almost always within twenty-five miles of the coast.

15. For example, as Samouri Touré and other leaders of the political communities he headed resisted French colonial expansion, many Loma communities opted to join

the Liberian state rather than the French or Touré's disintegrating confederation. See Suret-Canale (1964) and d'Azevedo (1969–1971).

16. For example, in 1946, suffrage was extended to women in settler communities and to other groups within indigenous communities incrementally as of 1946.

17. This is why the question of landownership as linked to citizenship remained a sensitive issue for both old guard settler-leaders and tribal chiefs and elders of historical standing. Both perceived themselves as custodians or caretakers of the patrimony. For them, the productive value of land or what de Soto (2000) designates as active capital, as opposed to asset or dead capital, was not as important as its symbolic value signifying an individual's standing in society; it was a mark of belonging, ownership, citizenship. An economic development strategy that involved the transfer of landed property rights in the form of twenty-year leases and ninety-nine-year concessions to foreign-owned enterprises is consistent with this conception of landed patrimony and its oligarchic order.

18. One such order declared Conmany Wesseh, then a student leader, a dangerous person, a confusionist, and a threat to public peace and directed the public to stay clear of him.

19. After seven weeks in prison, I was released and subsequently banned from participation in all public affairs, including interacting with the press. The constitution commission's records that had been stored in the public archives for a year were dug up and a new audit of its accounts ordered by Doe, despite the fact that an audit was completed prior to the dissolution of the commission. Many others who, like me, opposed Doe's effort to derail the transition process were not so lucky. Several colleagues of mine were sent to Belle Yalla, a notorious prison, and were severely tortured.

20. Relevant details of that initiative for constitutional reform are explained in various parts of this book and summarized in Chapter 4.

CHAPTER 2

The Legacy of
Predation and Violence

A S THE BERLIN WALL CAME DOWN AND THE "END OF HISTORY" AND THE "TRIUMPH of capitalism" were proclaimed (Fukuyama 1992), Liberians were facing arguably their worst tragedy since the consolidation of the central state in the early decades of the twentieth century. Scholars and public entrepreneurs will spend many years searching through the history of Liberia to fully understand the causes and nature of the conflict and how it could have raged on for a decade and a half in a large portion of the Mano River basin area of West Africa. In the previous chapter, I summarized Liberia's path to overcentralized and predatory government as a guide to understanding the structural underpinnings of the conflict. In this chapter, I discuss the conflict itself: the nature of the entrepreneurship that ignited it, the fuel that sustained it, the larger environment within which it flourished, the initial efforts made to end it, and the toll it has had on society. I discuss these issues as the legacy of government predation, repression, and governance failure.[1]

■ Military Roots of Violent Conflict

The violence applied to remove the dictatorship of Samuel Doe, which went beyond excising its essential core, was driven mainly by greed for power and wealth. It is not possible to fully understand the nature of the armed groups that perpetrated such violent conflict without understanding the transformation of the Liberian military and its role as the core instrument of violent conflict.

Transformation from "Patrimonial" Military to "Lumpen" Military

The Liberian military was constituted as a part of the patron-client network that was an important instrument of state consolidation. Its rank and file was

23

drawn from indigenous lineages and was linked to the Monrovia oligarchy through indigenous governance arrangements. Most soldiers had grown up in the traditions of their indigenous communities, experienced the rites of passage required in those communities, and remained active members of their local communities while in the military. As members of the military, they served as household hands, messengers, and watchmen for members of the oligarchy and performed duties as tax collectors and labor recruiters for the state. After years of service, many would return to their hometowns and villages where they would be considered among the elders of their communities; many became chiefs. For all practical purposes, the Liberian military was itself a patrimonial organization linked to both the Monrovia-based ruling oligarchy as well as to the indigenous social order.

With the rapid growth of the industrial (extractive) economy in the 1950s, especially the mining sector, and with the rising demands for democratization and inclusion, the security challenges facing the Liberian government could no longer be effectively handled by a patrimonial military force. Participation in African regional peacekeeping also became an obligation of leading African actors during the Congo crisis in the early 1960s. Thus, patterns of recruitment to the military dramatically changed when a military academy was established in the late 1960s. Chiefs and elders of indigenous communities ceased to serve as recruiters, and rural villages no longer supplied recruits. Desiring a military of mainly literate young men, the government now recruited heavily from among the growing pool of unemployed and unskilled literate and semiliterate young men of urban and periurban communities in the hope of both building a professional military and reducing urban unemployment.

Although members of this group typically have roots in rural communities, most of them are molded by the culture of the urban "lumpen proletariat." It is from this pool of the lumpen military that Samuel Doe and other noncommissioned officers who led the military takeover of 1980 came. Tempered by the harshness of urban poverty and lacking strong attachments to indigenous communities, this group turned out to have no loyalty to Liberia's governing institutions or to the norms that underpinned them. In other words, lacking property rights in both indigenous and "Western-oriented" societies, members of this group could become easily mobilized for plunder of both rural villages and for mayhem in cities. It was members of the lumpen military and others from the same social pool from which it was drawn that constituted the core of not only the security forces of the Doe regime but also those of Charles Taylor and other armed groups in the Liberian conflict. Both Fanthorpe (2001) and Abdullah (1998) have observed similar social features of the Revolutionary United Front (RUF) of Sierra Leone.

As Doe purged the military of his opponents, many Gio and Mano members of this pool fled the country and settled in cross-border Gio and Mano communities in Côte d'Ivoire and Guinea. It was from among ethnic Gio and

Mano of this pool that Taylor recruited his "commando unit" of about 120 young men that trained in Libya and became the small band of guerrillas, called the National Patriotic Front of Liberia (NPFL), that invaded Liberia from Côte d'Ivoire on December 24, 1989. Correspondingly, it was from among ethnic Krahn of the lumpen military and other Krahn individuals of this social pool that Doe sought to mobilize to repel the invasion. Both armed antagonists wreaked havoc on ordinary people.

From Lumpen Military to Armed Gangs

How did Taylor's group of about 120, trained as a commando unit, turn into an expanded gang? Taylor's men were trained in Libya at the Mathabat under the auspices of the Libyan organization called Maktub Tasdir al-Thawra—literally, bureau for the export of the revolution (Simons 1993; Mattes 1995). Ideological training in Colonel Muammar Qaddafi's principles of African revolution seemed inadequate if not inappropriate for Liberian circumstances. More importantly, whatever sense of discipline instilled by such training must have been undermined by the NPFL's leadership's exhortation to "capture what you can" and "keep what you capture." Thus, a gang-style ideology was introduced right from the start. In the absence of a proper ideology, the hunt for booty served to give some cohesion to the group and establish personal loyalty to its leader. As the conflict progressed, children became the more vulnerable victims of this form of control. NPFL commanders became their surrogate uncles and the *papay* (Taylor) became their father.[2] Children were the most loyal among those recruited, always ready to do the bidding of their superiors and consequently always called upon to become cannon fodder and to commit the most vicious crimes.

Furthermore, confronted variously with a breakaway faction, several other armed groups, and the Economic Community of West African States Monitoring Group (ECOMOG), as the peacekeeping force was called, Taylor's NPFL needed to swell its ranks more quickly than had been expected;[3] therefore, it resorted to indiscriminate recruitment and forced conscription. General conditions of conflict strengthened by the ruthless response of the Doe government on the people of Nimba County worked to assist Taylor's recruitment efforts.

Thus, whatever Taylor's original plans were, there seemed to have been a rapid transformation of what was said to be a well-trained commando unit into unruly armed bands, which included large numbers of children, that terrorized local populations. By 1992, about 40 percent of the population had sought security in Monrovia, 30 percent escaped to refugee camps in neighboring countries (mainly Côte d'Ivoire, Guinea, and Sierra Leone), and about 30 percent remained in towns and villages, including hamlets deep within the rain forest. For fifteen years, hundreds of thousands of Liberians from villages and towns throughout the country were to remain displaced.

■ The Irony of Taylor's Entrepreneurial Role

The nature of the leadership of the NPFL deserves closer examination if we are to gain an understanding of the true character of the conflict. The NPFL was designed and sculpted by Charles Taylor to serve his personal purposes; understanding his perceptions and ambitions, to the extent possible, can contribute to a better comprehension of the conflict. Unlike Doe, who sought to become the leader of a new Liberian oligarchy and to simply be respected in West Africa and abroad, Taylor's ambitions seemed to have been more grandiose. He not only wanted to exercise total control over Liberia and all of its resources, but he also wanted to be the leader of the Mano River basin area that includes Guinea and Sierra Leone. He is among a diminishing group of Liberians who see their country as the historic leader of the Mano basin area and its president as primus inter pares in the area and would like to return to the days of glory when President Tubman, a founder of the Organization of African Unity (OAU), now the African Union (AU), was one of Africa's leading statesmen. This ambition became clear after he became president of Liberia, but signals could be found in his behavior early in the conflict.

Training in Libya gave Taylor the opportunity to constitute a multinational rebel force by encouraging Sierra Leoneans, Gambians, and other West Africans who were also training there at that time to join him, with the understanding of receiving reciprocal assistance.[4] His launching of an invasion of Sierra Leone in 1991, long before he could claim to have accomplished his objective in Liberia, was not simply a tactical or strategic military move, nor was it a rush for diamonds. To him, Foday Sankoh was as much a political vicegerent as he was an economic agent. While many authors have emphasized the role of natural resources as an incentive for the conflict ignited by Taylor, it is important to also stress that Taylor's vision of a *pax Liberiana* was an equally strong incentive driving the conflict once he got started. His intervention in the Ivorian conflict in support of General Robert Guei, the military leader, was telling. After Guei's death, he continued to back those who had been associated with Guei and to cultivate low ranking officers in the Ivoirian military (Global Witness 2003).

Although Taylor and Qaddafi seemed to have been involved in a collaborative venture in West Africa, they were pursuing different objectives. While Qaddafi sought to establish an ideological foothold in the Mano River basin area to undermine what he perceived as the imperialist hold of the United States, Britain, and France, Taylor took advantage of Qaddafi's zeal and sought to establish a sphere of political and economic control in that part of West Africa. This ambition was his driving force up to his ouster in August 2003.

But the political control Taylor sought to establish was quite unlike that established by classical warlords. Even his most sympathetic supporters have had difficulty explaining why, in seven years of control of vast stretches of territory and natural resources prior to becoming president, he did not establish a single school or clinic in areas he controlled. The same can be said of the other armed bands whose leaders claimed to have been interested in ousting Taylor but whose behavior seemed largely to have been inspired by him.[5] Similarly, after becoming president, Taylor still did not turn his attention to reconstruction; instead, he continued to pursue the conquest of the Mano River basin area.

The Appropriation of Struggles for Change

While it is true that widespread repression amid growing economic decline under Doe created a conducive environment within which entrepreneurs like Taylor could recruit from among the lumpen youth and lumpen military and launch an ostensible "people's uprising," there is still the question as to how such revolutionary uprising became legitimized as an acceptable form of change initially supported by large segments of Liberian society. Put differently, in what ideological context did Taylor situate his quest for power? Taylor seized opportunities provided by two developments: first, he rode the crest of the progressive movements that began in the 1970s; and, second, he posed as heir to the legacy of Thomas Quiwonkpa, who was one of the noncommissioned officers who overthrew the Tolbert government in 1980. Quiwonkpa came from Nimba County.

Invoking Quiwonkpa's Name

As commanding general of the armed forces of Liberia after the coup, Quiwonkpa was considered one of the more powerful members of the ruling council and quickly became one of the council's most popular members among civilians. He fell out with Doe in 1983 and was killed after a failed coup led by him in 1985. In the recrimination that followed the coup attempt, hundreds of his Mano and Gio ethnic kinsfolk had to flee to sanctuaries in Côte d'Ivoire. Canvassing recruits among dispossessed Liberian youth in the villages of western Côte d'Ivoire near the Liberian border, Taylor presented himself as the heir to the struggle begun by Quiwonkpa. Not only was the Quiwonkpa connection his entry to Gio and Mano communities, it was also his link to those members of the military and others who followed or admired Quiwonkpa.

Adopting the Rhetoric of the "Progressives"

Elwood Dunn and Byron Tarr (1988) have referred to the decade of the 1970s in Liberia as "the extraordinary seventies," mainly because of the momentous events it brought forth. Some of these events included the death of Tubman after over a quarter-century rule, the domination of the political landscape by the Tolbert brothers during the first half of the decade, the rise of progressive movements, the mayoral contest of 1978–1979, the rice riots of 1979, and the military takeover of 1980. The founding of the Movement for Justice in Africa (MOJA) in 1973 and of the Progressive Alliance of Liberia (PAL) two years later provided a platform for advocacy on issues of social justice, rule of law, and democratization in the case of the former and gave expression to latent aspiration for political choice through multiparty competitive elections, in the case of the latter (Sawyer 1987a, 1992; Taryor 1985). A third progressive movement of the "extraordinary seventies" was the Union of Liberian Associations in the Americas (ULAA), an umbrella group comprising Liberians mainly in the United States.

MOJA's core constituency consisted of students and workers, while its leadership consisted mainly of university lecturers. Its objective was to advance the empowerment of Liberians through processes of democratization and development. Because its preferences for self-reliant approaches to development, its emphasis on action research and praxis, and its struggle against repressive laws and leaders rang with left-leaning language, the movement was perceived under Cold War circumstances to be tainted with socialism. Scholars connected to MOJA were prominent among Liberian scholars who set the public agenda and the terms of public debate during the 1970s, identifying and defining issues having to do with the nature of poverty in Liberia, the role of ethnicity and culture in political life, and the trajectory of change, among other issues. MOJA provided the language of change and sought to develop the framework for democratization and development. Its university-based constituency was at the foundation of these activities. Its leadership was forced into exile by the Doe regime and many of its members sought asylum in other West African countries, the United States, and Europe. From their various sanctuaries, some elements of MOJA engaged in a flirtation with Libya. It was from elements of MOJA that Taylor adopted snippets of the language of people-driven change and the idea of seeking Libyan support. Although none of the senior members of MOJA joined Taylor, several of its junior members did, and they provided him the ideological language he used in maintaining Libyan support.[6]

PAL's preoccupation with electoral politics led it to build mass constituencies among the unemployed and underemployed. Mass mobilization campaigns were at the core of its political strategy. In a 1979 demonstration that ended in the rice riots, PAL displayed a formidable ability to rally the dispossessed. In the late 1970s, the movement became a political party, the Progressive People's Party (PPP), and in the mid-1980s, it became the United People's Party (UPP). Taylor drew from its mass mobilization strategy and recruited from among the ranks of its community and cell leaders. Its senior leadership had typically sought to forge governing coalitions with other groups. Many of its senior members were to become Taylor's associates.[7]

Although he was able to draw from MOJA and PAL, Taylor's roots among the social movements of the 1970s were planted in ULAA. As one of ULAA's early officials, Taylor established links to a network of Liberian organizations in the diaspora and through them to the U.S. political process. He made contacts that served him well, as was demonstrated in his ability to retain a former attorney general of the United States as his personal lawyer when he was arrested and jailed in Massachusetts, and his ability to command considerable support in the Black Caucus of the United States Congress even as he engaged in mass killings in Liberia. It was also through ULAA that he was able to establish links to Doe and his colleagues as the coup unfolded in 1980.[8] Through ULAA, he established his bona fides as an activist advocating democratic change.[9] Because Taylor was able to draw selectively on the symbols, rhetoric, orientation, and other resources of these movements without being committed to their principles or institutions, he was initially able to camouflage his ambition and organization within the political and ideological context of such social movements and by doing so was able to legitimize his quest for power as part of the larger movement for change in Liberia.

If Taylor's friendship with Quiwonkpa established his standing among the Gio and Mano youth among whom he recruited, his association with the social movements of the 1970s initially bestowed political legitimacy on his activities. There was yet another constituency into which Taylor tapped to broaden his appeal—that of the declining "Congo" establishment.[10] In private conversations with members of this group, he would present his movement as an initiative to restore Congo dignity and property rights, if not its political domination.[11] With this ploy, he was able to mobilize financial resources as well as utilize the connections of such families. But privately, Taylor seemed to harbor deep resentment of the upper class of Congo society, being an upriver boy who grew up in the shadows of the Monrovia elite.[12]

Thus, Taylor was able to establish superficial identity with and draw upon resources of a variety of groups that operated in a complex social situation without commitment to their basic value systems or group objectives. By intermingling these sources of legitimacy, Taylor was able to establish his autonomy from all sources of authority while pitting such sources against each other. This is how Taylor's entrepreneurial genius was deployed in an environment of state collapse and social distress.

■ Understanding the Nature and Reach of the Violence

For many observers, the viciousness and capriciousness of the killings have been difficult to explain. Some scholars have taken recourse in cultural explanations, finding inadequate the explanations that attribute such behavior to the breakdown of institutions.[13] None of the cultures to which such vicious killings are attributed have been known to permit such practices willy-nilly. In indigenous society, ritual killings under cultural institutions (for example, Poro, Gee) are hardly ever random and wanton. They are typically carried out authoritatively as sanctions within an institutional order. Condemnable and repugnant as such killings often are, they are carried out under codes of sanctions related to the maintenance of patterns of rule-ordered relationships and the attainment of certain community goals. It is when rules break down that individuals run amok; determination of what is permitted or prohibited is then contingent upon personal and contextual circumstances. Those who exploit the breakdown constitute their own "rules," sometimes drugging children and young people and using them as perpetrators of crimes outside all norms. The drive of personal ambition, facilitated by the availability of traumatized young people; the knowledge of modes of destructive behavior from an array of situations, cultures, and circumstances; and the opportunity provided by the collapse of order all combine to result in the humanitarian nightmare witnessed in Liberia and more monstrously in Sierra Leone.

To be understood, violence perpetrated by armed gangs must be distinguished from culture-based violence sanctioned by indigenous institutions. Factors in addition to culture must also be closely studied. In the case of the NPFL, critical explanatory factors can be found in the nature of its leadership, membership, and organizational pattern; the circumstance and environment within which it operated; and the dynamic of the terror it perpetrated. Charles Taylor was the sole and undisputed leader of the NPFL. He often boasted that he alone made decisions. His strategy of imposing terror, as observed by both those who broke away from his organization as well as his loyal functionaries, reflected remarkable entrepreneurship. He maintained a small group of fighters for his most covert operations.[14] Young fighters were encouraged to rival each other with more gruesome killings to demonstrate battle prowess and loyalty to him. As each horrific act earned recognition for its perpetrator, a new cycle would begin, setting ever higher thresholds of brutality as norms of war. Escalating terror without rules exposed victims as well as perpetrators: targets of terror became inclusive and perpetrators themselves became victims.[15] And this escalation of vicious killings drew from both local cultural modes and external influences, such as movies, legends, and the like.[16] It is in this perspective that we can explain both the escalation as well as the growing gruesomeness of the killings that attended the Liberian civil war.

Interestingly, while such criminal violence dominated the conflict process, authoritative culture-based interventions became an important element in the peacebuilding process. The authoritative use of Poro conflict resolution mechanisms was vital to the reduction of violence and the settlement of interethnic disputes where state-based conflict resolution mechanisms were either ineffective, as in the case of the Loma and Mandingo of Zorzor, or a source of conflict themselves, as in the case of the action of security officers in the Voinjama area (Sawyer, Wesseh, and Ajavon 2000).

While Taylor and the NPFL perfected the art of terror in the conflict, other armed groups contributed substantially. Several armed groups sprang up between 1990 and 1996—all were in response to the brutal onslaught of the NPFL and international acceptance of Taylor's claims to "effective occupation" of almost all of Liberia. All of these groups were largely ethnic based and led by individuals who ultimately found recourse in the methods of the NPFL. The behavior of some of their leaders was similar to Taylor's. Through the course of conflict, many of these groups underwent purges and splits.[17] All of them plundered and pillaged, committed some atrocities, and created deep wounds among ethnic communities (Sawyer, Wesseh, and Ajavon 2000). Two of Taylor's armed rivals, George Boley, leader of the Liberia Peace Council (LPC), and Alhaji Kromah, leader of the United Liberation Movement for Democracy in Liberia (ULIMO-K), also harbored presidential ambitions and became candidates in the elections of 1997. Thus, their ostensible claim of organizing violent responses in order to force Taylor to the ballot box seemed more infused with personal ambition than with patriotic altruism. Both men had to flee the country when Taylor was announced as the winner of the elections. Their prompt departure, along with the departure of other presidential contenders and anti-Taylor electoral campaigners, signified how the election of Taylor legitimized the victory of the biggest gun and the triumph of terror. Taylor was also to use his electoral victory as a license to plunder and pillage the country.

In the early years of the conflict, when armed groups sought to create terror in Monrovia, the interim government backed by the Economic Community of West African States (ECOWAS), organized a 500-strong gendarmerie force that worked in collaboration with the West African peacekeeping force, ECOMOG, to ensure the security of Monrovia. The Black Berets, as the force was called, was an effective partner in repulsing the forces of the NPFL during the latter's 1992 invasion of Monrovia code-named Operation Octopus.

Thus, to understand the character of the violence perpetrated by armed groups, one needs to understand that leaders of armed bands were prepared to draw from and use, in and out of context, an assortment of symbols, methods, and forms of violence—including those associated with indigenous culture, the occult, Western-style gangsters, and Rambo-like figures. The eclectic nature of the methods of violence reflected both the character of undisciplined armed groups that ravaged society when governing order broke down as well as the determination of the leaders of these groups to do whatever was possible in their quest to control territory and resources. To them, plunder, intimidation, and carnage were instruments of conquest to be used at will, and the conquest of large portions of territory and resources was an accomplishment to be surpassed only by total control of the entire country.

Becoming a Mano River Basin Area System of Conflict

Liberia became the epicenter of a conflict system that spawned in the Mano River basin area that includes Sierra Leone and the forest regions of Guinea and a beachhead linking this system of conflict to a new flashpoint in Côte d'Ivoire. In 1991, a little over a year after Taylor's armed group invaded Liberia from Côte d'Ivoire, columns of Taylor's men under the leadership of a Sierra Leonean, Foday Sankoh, invaded Sierra Leone. Disintegration and decay caused by governance failure constituted the combustible material for the violence and atrocities that made Sierra Leone such a tragedy (Bangura 2000). Using ideological slogans, rebel leader Sankoh was able to ride the crest of popular discontent in Sierra Leone and, under Taylor's supervision and with Qaddafi's support, took over larger portions of that country (Abdullah 1998). Unable to repel the rebels, the Sierra Leone government supplemented its forces by recruiting heavily from among Liberian refugees, especially from among Liberian soldiers who had sought refuge in that country. While fighting against the forces of Taylor and Sankoh in Sierra Leone, this group, which became the core of the ULIMO, opened a front against the NPFL in Liberia in August 1991.

Access to Sierra Leone's diamond resources ensured that the links between theaters of conflict in Liberia and Sierra Leone, and later Guinea, grew stronger. Economic transactions flourished as the armed groups and their networks of partners, clients, and supporters plundered and pillaged the resources of both Sierra Leone and Liberia. The fall of diamond-rich Kono in Sierra Leone to Sankoh's forces opened up new opportunities for both Sierra Leonean and Liberian fighters (Bangura 2000). Mineral-rich areas of Liberia and Sierra Leone attracted fighters from both countries. All the entrepreneurs of violence themselves saw the area as a single field of operation and at critical junctures recognized a single hierarchy of control. Taylor, for example, was acknowledged by Sankoh and Johnny Paul Koroma of Sierra Leone's Armed Forces Revolutionary Council (AFRC) as the leader of the collaborating armed groups. He mediated conflicts between the two men and served as third-party guarantor in the uneasy relationship between their groups (Global Witness 2003). After Sankoh's detention, his successor, Issa Cisse, continued a submissive relationship with Taylor (Global Witness 2002). Up to the moment of his departure into exile, Taylor maintained security units that comprised RUF and Liberian fighters who, under his orders, became a roving force in the basin area and in western Côte d'Ivoire.

Meanwhile, armed groups in Sierra Leone terrorized local people, often going beyond excesses seen in Liberia. For several years they committed some of the worst atrocities ever inflicted on humanity. Limbs of people, including children, were hacked off, and houses with people in them were boarded up and torched.

It was in the late 1990s that the southeastern forest region of Guinea became a theater of conflict when the rebel group, Liberia United for Reconciliation and Democracy (LURD) established staging points and rearguard bases in that area in their resistance to the witch hunting and continued violence perpetrated by Taylor's forces even after his election as president in 1997. Guinea itself had become prone to violent conflict due largely to the growing governance crisis. Pressured by international donors, President Lansana Conté, in 1991, dissolved his military junta government and embarked on a program of political and economic reforms. A new constitution was promulgated as part of the reform, but a few years later it was amended to remove presidential term limits. Conté routinely ignored Guinea's multiparty parliament and occasionally publicly ridiculed and intimidated its officials. Amid serious human rights abuses, Guinea's judiciary and civil society organizations were said to be both intimidated by and beholden to President Conté (*Economist* March 8, 2003; ICG 2003b). The flight of renegade soldiers into the forest region after an attempted coup in 1998 added to a sense of combustibility in the tri-country border region of the Mano basin area. These soldiers were said to have linked up with Charles Taylor and the RUF against LURD in the hope of gaining Taylor's support for their cause against the Guinean government.[18] Added to the movement of men and war matériel and the "conflict diamond" trade was the illicit trade in coffee, which went through Foya in Liberia, Koindu in Sierra Leone, and Guegekdou in Guinea. All of this made for a robust system of conflict in the three countries.

Although the conflict in Côte d'Ivoire was due largely to the fact that the Ivorian political elite, following the death of Félix Houphouët-Boigny in 1993, had been unable to successfully address the challenges of political decisionmaking in a multiethnic society, thereby pitting themselves against each other, the intervention of Liberian forces initially by Taylor had only served to exacerbate the conflict and link it to the wider system of conflict in Liberia, Sierra Leone, and the forest region of Guinea. Men, weapons, and illicit as well as legitimate trade moved through cross-border corridors that linked Guinea, Sierra Leone, Liberia, and Côte d'Ivoire in one extended system of conflict. Thus, in view of the fact that the conflict in Liberia had been transformed into a system of conflict that linked several countries in the subregion, addressing its multiple aspects through state-specific measures ignored the basic character of the conflict.

■ The International Context of Gangsterism in Liberia

If the breakdown of governance institutions in Liberia provided opportunities for armed gangs, could international and regional institutions have imposed constraints that would have reduced the prospects of such violence? Put differently, how could marauding gangs wreak so much havoc and commit such vicious atrocities in the face of multiple levels of order, including regional and international levels of order? The answer to this question requires situating Liberia and the West African subregion within the broader international order, especially with respect to the changing international security environment at the end of the Cold War, and examining the incentives this environment provided to those who plundered and killed thousands.

Effects of the Cold War on African societies combined with certain characteristics of the regional African order seemed to have provided an atmosphere within which gangster behavior could survive in the West African subregion. This is not to say that African peoples were without agency during the Cold War but to acknowledge that categories created by the Cold War deeply polarized many such societies and weakened their capacity to resist gangster violence.[19] Their efforts were frequently rendered futile or made exceedingly costly. In Liberia, for example, between 1980 and 1987—during the last days of the U.S. fight against Soviet communism, when, as Berkeley (2001) has revealed, Samuel Doe was in the pay of U.S. intelligence—the United States spared no effort to not only strengthen the military capabilities of Doe but also to stifle the growth of prodemocracy organizations. Interestingly, this was done largely through the forging of an ostensible nurturing relationship with such groups. The process of nurturing turned out to be a mechanism of control of such organizations. Instead of strengthening the democratic forces that were ostensibly being nurtured, the United States often encouraged their leaders to leave and granted them political asylum while backing Doe with military and economic support. Between 1980 and 1985, U.S. military assistance to Liberia was more than the combined total of all the previous years since 1946. Economic assistance also rose astronomically.[20]

To combat corruption, which was rife in the Doe government, the United States assigned "operational experts" to prop up Liberian government's financial management—this at a time when qualified and experienced Liberian financial managers and other professionals were forced to flee Doe's witch hunting and growing economic hardships.[21] Many of these professionals had gained ascendancy under the oligarchy as a result of criticisms of nepotism leveled against the True Whig Party (TWP) regime by those categorized as "socialists."

Intellectual discourse, contestation, and self-reliant development praxis carried a very high cost. Self-reliant community development initiatives except those supported by the government or select entities were prohibited. In the mid-1970s, a group of social scientists, some of whom were associated with the University of Liberia (myself included), formed an organization called Susukuu, Inc. to provide technical advice in self-reliant development strategies to rural communities. This initiative was labeled as "socialist." Individuals who promoted these strategies and communities that requested such assistance were often subjected to security surveillance and harassment. Leaders of government and many professionals employed in technical portfolios by the government were quick to impugn the motives of those who advocated or sought self-reliant strategies of development and questioned the viability of such projects.[22]

By the early 1980s, under the military, the socialist label was a virtual death sentence. The stifling of intellectual contestation and praxis made it easy to categorize intellectuals and activists and to label them as security risks. False contradictions were often created and major contradictions masked. Those who pressed critical inquiry and all those who simply shouted antigovernment slogans were branded as "socialists" and "communists" and were hunted. This deterred many from raising questions, choosing to remain silent in order to survive. Thus, the period of the Doe regime turned out to be the heyday of the unqualified and a time of prosperity for those who were manipulative and deferential.[23]

Chester Crocker (1999) has explained that U.S. fears regarding Liberia during the last days of the Cold War were not as much about Soviet influences as about Libyan–West African outreach. There is an irony in the fact that despite such claims, the United States abandoned the Doe regime as soon as the process of disintegration of the Soviet bloc began. In that climate, Taylor was able to present himself to the Americans as "an avowed capitalist" and to promote himself with the Libyans as a supporter of Libya's African revolution.[24] There is speculation as to why the United States did not intervene to prevent the carnage that overtook Liberia at the hands of armed groups. Some observers have claimed that U.S. involvement in the Persian Gulf demanded its single-minded attention; others maintained that despite his Libyan sponsorship, Taylor was not considered to be ideologically threatening to U.S. interests; still others contend that in view of Doe's falling out with the Americans, there was a desire to see him "stew." The main reason seems to lie in the absence of U.S. strategic interest at that time. As the Soviet bloc unraveled and Cold War–fueled conflicts in southern Africa seemed resolvable, Liberia's strategic role in U.S. security calculations in Africa diminished.[25]

One may further ask why, given that Libya was already considered a dangerous pariah state, the United States did not see fit, in the face of substantial intelligence reports, to raise international concern about an invasion of Liberia launched under Libyan sponsorship. Again, Cold War categorization drove perceptions here. U.S. policymakers on Liberia had already determined which Liberians were "dangerous" and which were not. By their estimation, Taylor was not; and if he could mobilize resources to teach Doe, the erstwhile agent of the United States, a lesson, the United States would be prepared to adopt a posture of indifference.[26] Had Taylor been a member of MOJA or been branded a socialist, the United States would not have stood by in benign complicity. A "revolutionary" who called himself "an avowed capitalist" and was able to gain the support of Ivorian president Houphouët-Boigny could not have been sufficiently dangerous to warrant the mounting of an initiative to stop him, the

United States must have figured. Viewing the crisis through both Cold War and colonial prisms, the other major actors in the international community perceived Liberia as an American problem. Lack of U.S. leadership in addressing the crisis signaled to them U.S. approval of its trajectory.[27]

Thus, it can be seen that Cold War imperatives left little room to accommodate among Liberians critical reflection and institution building that would promote resistance to internal repression; however, perhaps unwittingly, such imperatives provided space for chameleon-like and gangster-like behavior to grow stronger. The effects of Cold War interventions on Liberian leaders linger on today; their debilitating consequences are manifested in the deep suspicion and animosity that persist among key Liberian political actors who, as respected public entrepreneurs, should have worked together to resist repression and press an agenda for democratization and development. But the bad taste of past experiences continues to divide them. Ironically, many in the international community who bemoan division among such political leaders were among those who encouraged it at earlier junctures.

Against the backdrop of the divisive impact of the Cold War, the fight for the Liberian presidency has become an even more devastating struggle among political rivals. Capturing the presidency becomes the ultimate triumph, and its overwhelming powers become instruments for punishing foes and rewarding the faithful. In view of the all-inclusive powers of the Liberian presidency and the zero-sum approach to public affairs it sustains, former rivals may well be justified in having grave fears of the ascendancy of one another to the presidency. This is how mediocrity excels, corruption flourishes, and repression sets in. One can hardly make a more compelling case for reconstituting Liberia's political institutional arrangements differently.

■ Capitalizing on Predation in the West African Environment

With very little interest shown by the United States and the larger international community, intervention to stop the carnage in Liberia was left to the ECOWAS countries. As a regional economic cooperation organization, ECOWAS was unprepared for the tasks of peacekeeping and peacemaking that this challenge entailed. Moreover, divided by colonial heritage and subregional rivalries and by the involvement of some governments as hidden parties to the conflict, ECOWAS could hardly undertake a cohesive initiative. Even where consensus was reached, the organization could hardly mobilize the resources to mount an effective intervention. Only Nigeria commanded the level of resources required for such an undertaking. But the growing international isolation of Nigeria as a result of continuing military rule detracted even further from international support of the West African initiative.

Details of the ECOWAS peace initiative in Liberia have been well documented and need not be repeated here.[28] The point to be stressed in the present context is that for a decade, the Liberian conflict was ECOWAS' major preoccupation, as economic incentives and the involvement of several armed groups (some multinational in composition) supported by external actors had made for a very complex subregional situation. Disgruntled opponents of West African regimes could adopt opportunistic behaviors of regional scope, and wealth-seeking leaders could accrue benefits from cooperating with such individuals.[29] The internal character of West African regimes (problems of overcentralization, personal rule, and corruption) and the nature of their interaction (often characterized by personal friendships and bitter antagonisms) made for an ideal environment for complex intrigues and machinations. For example, President Houphouët-Boigny's strong dislike of Samuel Doe was well known; his privately expressed wish to see the subregion free of Doe remained an idle wish as long as Doe enjoyed U.S. support. Once Doe lost U.S. support, Houphouët-Boigny wasted no time in supporting Doe's overthrow. Suspicious of Houphouët-Boigny's intention, President Conté of Guinea was prepared to intervene unilaterally if necessary.

This was a conducive environment for Taylor. Changing his colors and becoming all things to all actors, he portrayed himself as an understudy to Ghana's Jerry Rawlings, as a son to Côte d'Ivoire's Houphouët-Boigny, as a Francophile to Togo's Eyadema, and as a potential business partner to Burkina Faso's Campaore. To Libya's Qaddafi, he had portrayed himself as an anti-Western revolutionary. Thus, he was able to receive initial support from such a diverse group of leaders, many of whom did not see eye to eye.[30] Once he got started, his access to natural resources provided the leverage he needed to deal with a wider range of actors.

The West African regional order, dominated by overcentralized, predatory regimes with leaders divided by colonial history, Cold War legacies, personal ambitions, and greed could not have provided a replacement security arrangement once the Cold War ended; instead it proved to be fertile ground for conflict, including cross-border conflicts waged by armed bands led by opportunistic leaders who could play on the fears, greed, and personal ambitions of individual leaders of states that were typically economic basket cases. In a sense, the West African region in the 1980s had become a veritable powder keg, and Liberia became its first explosion.

■ Armed Gangs and Global Economic Order

There is a growing body of scholarly work focusing on the economic motives, activities, and outcomes associated with internal wars and violent conflicts.[31] This literature analyzes an assortment of economic patterns involving economic incentives for starting and prolonging violent conflicts (Collier 2000, 2003); the nature of shadow states and what is called warlord politics (Reno 1995, 2000); and the integration of such economies within the global economy (Duffield 2000). Liberia presented a case that crystallized the global context within which a regime supported by armed bands provided the nexus where the underworld economy of illicit trade merged with legitimate international trade. At this nexus, economic transactions involving legitimate parties and rogue parties (both private entities and state parties) were often intertwined.

The economic role of the French government in the Liberian conflict clarified how state parties can become promoters of economic interests of unsavory private entities operating in collaboration with leaders who rely on armed bands to run the state. French policy toward Liberia throughout the Liberian conflict was formulated in the Elysée Palace and driven in large measure by French business interests, including those of associates of French foreign policy functionaries such as Jean-Christophe Mitterand, former African policy adviser to the president of France.[32] These foreign policy functionaries collaborating with French and Ivorian partners resident in Côte d'Ivoire—some of the latter having direct links to the household of Ivorian president Houphouët-Boigny—were involved in timber harvesting and mineral ventures with armed gang leaders of Liberia while advocating policies designed to ensure international acceptance of a prolonged state of balkanization of Liberia as an intermediate stage in the process of reaching a political settlement.[33]

Upon becoming president, Taylor continued to use armed bands as state security and to carry on both legal and illicit economic transactions, thereby using the Liberian state as an instrument for both criminal and legal purposes. The plunder of the natural resources of Liberia and Sierra Leone by Liberian armed gangs and their leaders became legendary and is well documented. It is estimated that between 1990 and 1994, more than $500 million was accrued annually by leaders of armed groups and their associates from exports of timber, rubber, diamonds, and other natural resources; Charles Taylor is reported to have gained $75 million annually (Caine 1999; Reno 2000). It is estimated that if the pace of indiscriminate logging allowed by Taylor had continued, just under half of Liberia's rainforest would have disappeared in five years (Global Witness 2001). In 1999, deals agreed between the president of Liberia (Charles Taylor) and the Oriental Timber Company, an Indonesian establishment with a notorious environmental record brokered by a shadowy Dutch businessman granted that company logging concession rights to close to half of Liberia's rain forest.[34] In 2000 and 2001, investigations by the Committee on Sanctions of the Security Council of the United Nations revealed that the president of Liberia was directly engaged in illicit economic activities. The reports uncovered links between the president of Liberia and an assortment of underworld figures of Ukrainian, Dutch, and Italian origins, among others, in gun-running and the smuggling of Sierra Leonean diamonds (UN Security Council 2001).

Those who did business with the Taylor regime included such diverse groups and individuals as DeBeers, Al-Qaida, and Christian fundamentalist evangelist Pat Robertson. All of these operated in the same market and under the same rules.[35] These developments seem to suggest that in the new post–Cold War order, the evolution of norms and institutions governing political behavior seems to be outpacing those governing economic behavior. While Pat Robertson and Al-Qaida operatives would scarcely be found doing political business in the same arena or under the same rules, they did undertake economic transactions under the same rules in Liberia. Efforts made to establish international judicial institutions to bring terrorists to justice seem to be outpacing those in favor of establishing similar international regimes to govern what are essentially economic crimes.

Monopolies dominated the economic strategies of the Liberian government under Taylor, and the personal stakes of the president and his circle of friends and advisers were indistinguishable from those of the state. Fuel and rice importation was controlled by monopolies run by Lebanese associates of Taylor.[36] As a measure to tighten monopolistic controls, the Taylor government proposed sweeping legislation designed to declare as "strategic commodities" all natural resources, including forest resources; agricultural and food products; and "unique and rare sculpture, artifacts, handiwork and hand craft of historical, cultural, social, spiritual and economic value to the Republic of Liberia." All such strategic commodities were to be "under the direct control of the president who was to have the sole authority to execute, negotiate and conclude all commercial contracts or agreements with any foreign or domestic investor."[37] Promulgation of this law was to be the final act completing the personalization of control of Liberia's resources by Taylor.

As the Taylor tenure shows, economic interactions from legitimate and underworld economies can be integrated through criminal regimes. The current global economic order permits this perversion to continue, enabling such regimes to maintain their international standing despite efforts to categorize them as pariahs. Except for the transcontinental regime against narcotics trafficking and the more recent efforts against terrorism, there is both a lack of will and a shortage of supranational institutional arrangements to address the array of illicit transactions flowing from what has been called shadow economies (Reno 2000). The United Nations' initiative to curtail trade in "blood diamonds" has risen out of the realization of the substantial contribution of such trade to the atrocities committed on innocent individuals in Sierra Leone. More recently, the role of illicit trade in the conflicts in Angola and the Democratic Republic of Congo has claimed international attention; however, as a factor in African conflicts, the range of illicit trade, which includes near slavery on West African cocoa, coffee, and rubber plantations to outright slavery in Mauritania, remains far more extensive and not fully addressed.[38] A strong international movement, such as those nongovernmental international movements that work for the promotion and protection of human rights, is needed to pressure for the establishment of appropriate international sanctions regimes against economic plunder and other illicit trade since the leading state actors in the international community are reluctant to take the lead in addressing this problem.

■ False Starts at Conflict Resolution

In 1990, proposals made by Liberian religious leaders were adapted by ECOWAS as the core of a peace plan for ending the conflict in Liberia. The plan called for the formation of an interim government composed of all armed groups, political parties, and leaders of civil society and headed by a civilian who would be ineligible to contest elections; disarmament and demobilization of all armed groups; and the holding of elections. The plan was accepted by civil society actors and all armed groups except the NPFL. Over three years, at least seven peace conferences were held and as many agreements and modifications of agreements were signed in efforts to bring the NPFL into a settlement. The NPFL would sign on to all subsequent agreements and promptly renege on them. Meanwhile, the peacekeeping force, ECOMOG, found itself caught up in a fight among multiple armed groups and incurring heavy casualties, while troop-contributing countries, wracked by internal problems and regime changes, tried to find a way out.

In 1993, the United Nations intervened as a partner of ECOWAS in the search for peace and put forward a new peace proposal calling for an interim government dominated by representatives of armed groups, the disarming of armed groups, and the holding of elections.[39] This agreement also failed to ensure peace, despite the fact that all parties signed on to it. Even when the leaders of armed groups themselves were the dominant actors in a power-sharing arrangement, peace remained elusive largely because Taylor, the leader of the largest armed group, sought special advantages. A modicum of peace was not attained until 1996, when, after a month-long violent outbreak and plunder of Monrovia by armed groups, a new peace agreement was signed by the leaders of these groups under threats of prosecution for war crimes of those who would breach it.

Yet the disarmament and demobilization program of 1996 was only partially successful. While more than 70 percent of the arms were said to have been retrieved, less than 60 percent of the fighters were actually demobilized (Sawyer and Wesseh 2000). Elections were held in an environment awash with arms and with armed groups whose structures of command and control remained reasonably intact. These elections were won by Charles Taylor. War-weary Liberians had seen in the elections the prospects for a trade-off, an exchange of liberty for peace. Unfortunately, as the Taylor government after elections embarked on a course of recrimination and exclusion rather than reconciliation and broad-based participation, there was no surprise when fighting flared up again within three years. LURD and later the Movement for Democracy in Liberia (MODEL) became the new armed challengers.

Flawed Starts

One of the most critical reasons why the peace agreements reached from 1990 to 1996 failed is that they lacked adequate provisions for monitoring compliance and imposing sanctions on violators. They were not backed by a third-party guarantee.[40] Leaders of armed groups were driven by a quest for power and by greed; the assumption that a power-sharing agreement unmonitored and without credible threats of sanctions would hold proved to be too optimistic. With leaders of an armed group holding territory and exploiting resources in fiefdoms, there was hardly any incentive for them to relinquish such control. The only potential incentive provided in the agreements was to be found in the prospect of winning elections and becoming president, and for all of them this path was strewn with uncertainties. The guarantees of a third party whose threats were credible would have served as sufficient disincentive against noncompliance.

A further shortcoming was that the peace agreements were more of a generic model and not sufficiently calibrated to meet Liberian circumstances. Their major provisions called for disarmament, demobilization, repatriation, and resettlement of the displaced and the holding of elections. None of the agreements saw the need for governance reform as foundational; thus, they embedded the assumption that electoral reform was the most important if not the sole governance reform needed. What seems to be ignored is the fact that elections are fought to the bitter end in Liberia because the unitary nature of power and its concentration in the hands of the president transforms political competition into a zero-sum game.[41] The holding of credible elections within such a governance arrangement is hardly the path to democratic governance and sustainable peace. Governance reform has been one of the missing links in Liberia's attempts to organize transitions from violent conflict to democratic peacebuilding (Sawyer 2004).

The Accra Peace Agreement of 2003

The forces of LURD seemed to have grown so strong by 2001 that they came to pose a significant threat to Taylor's regime despite his best effort. By early 2003, LURD and the newly organized MODEL moved closer to Monrovia attempting to put the city under siege. Undisciplined fighters from all sides plundered and pillaged local communities and left a trail of death and destruction. Liberian civil society organizations and their diasporic extensions mounted a major advocacy effort for the intervention of an international stabilization force and the initiation of a peace process. As a result of military pressure mounted by LURD and MODEL, diplomatic and political pressure of the international community, and the unsealing of the indictment by the Special Court in Sierra Leone, Taylor was forced into exile in Nigeria, paving the way for the holding of a peace conference in Accra in August 2003.

In early 2003, the Special Court of Sierra Leone issued a sealed indictment against Taylor for war-related crimes in that country. It was only in 2001 that the United Nations had declared the Liberian regime a threat to peace in the West African subregion. This declaration was not made as a result of the violence rained on the Liberian people by armed groups; instead, it came as a result of a United Nations investigation of atrocities committed by armed groups in Sierra Leone. It was only when the investigation linked Charles Taylor to atrocities committed by the RUF rebel group in Sierra Leone that the international community concluded that the Liberian regime had become a threat to peace in the subregion. The unsealing of the indictment in August 2003 added pressure for Taylor's ouster.

The peace agreement reached in Accra among armed groups, political parties and civil society organizations called for the establishment of an international stabilization force to disarm and demobilize all armed groups, the formation of a power-sharing transitional government, and the holding of elections. It also established several commissions on elections, governance reform, and government contracts and tenders. In early 2005, the transitional government seemed plagued by internal struggles for government jobs and the spoils of office. Leaders of political parties seemed poised for elections, each hoping to assume the overwhelming powers of the presidency and to give shape to the reconstruction process. The activities of all commissioners appointed seemed to be intended to effect marginal changes and not significant institutional changes.

Unfortunately, the Accra Agreement did not explicitly provide for a third-party guarantee, even though a special representative of the UN Secretary-General exercises oversight functions of the disarmament and demobilization process and, along with the representative of ECOWAS and an international contact group, serves as adviser to the transitional government. Fearing the collapse of the interim government, many of these advisers seem to prefer a rush to elections. Opposing this approach, many Liberians are now advocating holding a national conference to review the course of peace, to ensure accountable management of the transitional process, and to initiate essential governance reform prior to elections. Many Liberians, including myself, are calling for the holding of a national conference prior to elections so that an agenda for governance reform can be formulated as a national covenant to be appropriately implemented over time, such that the holding of elections is properly situated within the reform agenda. As of mid-2005 it is still not clear whether a national conference will be held prior to elections or how a precarious transitional process will be strengthened. One thing that is certain is that it will be very difficult to lay foundations for a sustainable system of democratic governance if appropriate postconflict peacebuilding programs are not carefully designed and implemented. I return to this question in Chapter 7; more germane here is the toll the conflict has taken on Liberian society.

■ Consequences of State Failure and Violence

The consequences of state failure and the toll on society are typically explained through the use of statistical indicators: numbers of fatalities, malnourished children, and unemployed heads of households; percentages of roadways, school buildings, and health care facilities in disrepair; and so on. Unfortunately, the pain, suffering, death, and destruction that wreck the lives of ordinary people and constitute the core of the human tragedy cannot always be fully captured in statistics about mortality rates and other indicators of survivability and quality of life, bleak as they may be. Complementing these with narratives about the people themselves can be useful for a deeper understanding of the true impact of state failure and violence on the lives of people. Even these, however, do not fully capture the long-term toll of such conflicts on a people: the scarring of culture and the staining of historical memory—all inflicting pain on succeeding generations.

Human Toll

Deaths. The most important consequence of state failure and the resultant violent conflicts can be seen in the toll they have taken on human beings, especially the magnitude of conflict-related deaths, injuries, and displacement. Though no scientific count has been taken, an estimated 200,000 people are said to have died, hundreds of thousands more have been wounded, and about 1.8 million have been displaced at peak periods, more than half of whom were internally displaced (see Appendix 2).[42] When considered against the background of Liberia's total population of 2.6 million at the outset of the conflict in 1989, these figures paint a picture of immense loss. Such a death toll represents more than 6 percent, while estimates of displaced at peak account for more than 50 percent of the population of Liberia. Human toll of such proportions can be staggering for any country.[43] The sad fact is that several other African countries have experienced losses of human lives of comparable magnitude. In the Democratic Republic of Congo, nearly 4 million people, or 6 percent of the population, died from war-related causes between 1998 and 2004 (see IRC 2004). Rwanda lost about 4 percent of its population to genocide and war-related causes between 1994 and 1999. Two million Sudanese, accounting for 6 percent of that country's population, have perished as a result of war since

1983; and, over the last decade, Angola has lost about 12 percent of its population to war-related causes.[44] Though estimates vary, it is generally agreed that more than 6 million people perished as a result of violent conflicts in Africa between 1983 and 2000 (CSIS 2000).

Displacement. A high level of displacement was also sustained in Liberia for several years. More than 40 percent of Liberia's population was internally and externally displaced from 1991 to 1997 (see Appendix 2). Hundreds of thousands of Liberians lived in refugee villages in Guinea, Sierra Leone, Ghana, and Nigeria and became the largest "migrant" groups in bordering towns in Côte d'Ivoire. Hundreds were dispersed in locations as far north as the Netherlands and as far south as Australia and South Africa. Those in refugee camps in neighboring countries were often harassed, intimidated, and accused of working against one armed group or another. At one time, young men in refugee camps in Guinea were said to have been forcibly recruited by armed bands and young women taken as "war wives." Refugee communities often lost their rations and harvested crops to intrusive armed gangs.

At the induction of Charles Taylor as president in 1997, hopes for an era of peace were high, and hundreds of thousands of Liberians returned home. But hopes began to fade as violence increased a year after the induction. By 2000, the steady return of Liberians home was halted; people fled their homes again as fighting intensified between armed militias of Taylor's government and LURD. By 2003, more than 400,000 people had been displaced; 280,000 of these were refugees in neighboring countries (Table 2.1). At the same time, Liberia became host to Ivorian refugees and continued to host Sierra Leonean refugees (Table 2.2).

With respect to the internally displaced, Liberia has been among Africa's worst cases of countries that "hosted" its own people as "refugees" (Global IDP 2001).[45] Others have included Angola (one out of four Angolans) and Sudan (one out of seven). In 2003, an estimated 25 million persons in the world were displaced within their own countries; of these, about 13 million were in Africa. (Global IDP 2004; see also Appendix 2).

Table 2.1   Liberian Refugees: Host Countries and Distribution, 2003

Host Country	Number (estimate)
Guinea	110,000
Sierra Leone	60,000
Côte d'Ivoire	50,000
Ghana	35,000
Other West African countries	25,000

Source: U.S. Committee for Refugees (www.refugees.org).

Table 2.2   Refugees in Liberia: Home Countries and Distribution, 2003

Home Country	Number (estimate)
Sierra Leone	40,000
Côte d'Ivoire	20,000
Other West African countries	5,000

Source: U.S. Committee for Refugees (www.refugees.org).

Astounding as are the statistical aggregates, a more gripping story of human tragedy is told as the figures are disaggregated and individual and group circumstances are revealed. Hidden in the aggregates is the story of hundreds of villages across Liberia that were plundered, pillaged, and burned down. No geographical region or political jurisdiction was spared. A chain of displacement and destitution linked people from all sections of the country and, as violent conflict also gripped Sierra Leone, extended the links to hundreds of villages and communities in that country as well. Throughout the decade of the 1990s, sections of the Mano River basin area of Liberia, Sierra Leone, and Guinea constituted veritable lands of destitution and misery. There are chilling accounts of forced travel, including perilous voyages at sea.[46] Again, and unfortunately so, this story is not unique to Liberia and the Mano River basin area. In the region of Central Africa and the Great Lakes, human displacement tells the story of disruptions of societies consisting of thousands of communities with linkages and spillovers that affect still thousands more. In Uganda in 2002, for example, internally displaced persons (IDPs) accounted for close to 3 percent of that country's population, with exponential impact on others. One-quarter of Uganda's forty-five districts (administrative jurisdictions) was in some form of upheaval. Armed bands operated in northern as well as western districts, and sporadic conflicts involving pastoralists were waged in eastern districts.[47]

When circumstances and duration of displacement are considered, a bleaker picture emerges. Loss of dignity and diminished hope associated with prolonged displacement can erode self-confidence and optimism—predispositions that are vital for self-reliance and self-organization.

Terror and trauma. The impact of extensive trauma associated with such crimes of war as rape, gruesome massacres, and brutal murders can hardly be fully assessed. It is estimated that a third of all displaced women and pubescent girls in Liberia were raped, and more than 50 percent of them by at least two attackers. Fifty percent of the crime of rape took place in the presence of helpless family members (cited in Cain 1999). The following story of rape and murder was recounted in *Africa Report* newsmagazine:

> A pregnant woman was walking toward Monrovia with her mother, father, husband and pregnant sister. The group was ambushed by armed rebels who publicly beheaded her husband, and then her father and mother, before subjecting her to multiple rapes. . . . The woman was forced to watch as her pregnant sister was raped, her stomach ripped open and her unborn baby thrown into a pit latrine. She was spared, made it to Monrovia, but for months refused to utter a word. She refused to eat, went to the toilet where she sat and lost the will to live. (da Costa 1994)

In 1996, John T. Richardson, Taylor's confidant and the military spokesman of the NPFL, was pleased to identify "progress" in the behavior of their fighters: "What the journalists have failed to point out is that this time, unlike previous fighting in Monrovia, the civilians have not really suffered. In the past, fighters would rip out people's intestines and use them to string up roadblocks, or cut off people's heads. This time there has been none of that."[48]

Stories of massacres at Tappita, Carter Camp, Senje, Lutheran Church, and Bakedu are yet to be recorded and appreciated. Mass killings, targeted killings akin to ethnic cleansing, and cannibalism were practices of warfare in Liberia. In 1994, the Catholic Justice and Peace Commission's fact-finding mission to Gbarnga, the stronghold of the NPFL, the largest armed group, reported:

> Cannibalism is another phenomenon attached to the bandits. The displaced . . . attested to seeing a bandit cut off a woman's breast, roasting and eating it, while leaving her to die of blood loss. . . . Cannibalism adds a whole new dimension to human rights abuses. The right to life is based on a persecutor's appetite, and there is fear of persecution based on one's fitness for consumption. (Catholic JPC 1994, 4)

Reports of cannibalism often surfaced during the Liberian bloodbath. Stephen Ellis (1999) reported the drinking of human blood in warfare by Taylor and his close associates. Though declining, cannibalism is occasionally heard of as a practice of cult members in certain ethnic communities of the West African rain forest. Such practices are said by their perpetrators to produce desired effect in warfare, as do the wearing of masks and the painting of the body, practices designed to invoke the assistance of ancestors and other spirits. Preoccupied with the search for the primitive, Ellis misses the significance of cannibalism as an instrument of warfare in Liberia in the context of this conflict. In the practice of cannibalism, gang leaders such as Taylor use cultural perversity as instruments of terror and destruction. This is the significant point that Ellis's analysis misses completely, but it is captured by Bill Berkeley (2001).

Toll on Life Chances

The human toll is also revealed by diminished physical well-being and survival prospects of Liberians generally. Relevant indicators tell an unpleasant story. Life expectancy in Liberia is only forty-seven years; 20 percent of children suffer moderate to severe stunting. Liberia has the fifth highest under-five mortality rate in the world. The maternal mortality rate, already as high as 560 per 100,000 before the conflict, stood at 901 per 100,000 in 1999. Associated with high mortality rates are problems of unsafe drinking water, poor sanitation, and other conditions that affect prospects of survival. Only 46 percent and 30 percent of Liberians have access to safe drinking water and sanitation, respectively. Displaced people living in uninhabitable buildings destroyed by violence—defecating in old newspapers and throwing the newspapers in the streets—had become a common occurrence in Monrovia throughout the 1990s.

Guinea and Sierra Leone, Liberia's neighbors in the Mano River basin area, are not faring much better with respect to the quality of life; neither is much of West Africa, for that matter. Five of the ten countries with the highest under-five mortality rates in the world are to be found in West Africa. All West African countries are among the third of the world's countries with the highest under-five mortality rates. And the annual rate of reduction is measly and disappointing.[49]

Resettlement can also be hazardous and rife with insecurity and can include rape and robbery. Trauma associated with returning to demolished homesteads, plundered communities, and loss of property acquired over one's lifetime has led to death and impairment. Many of the displaced have had to flee their communities several times in view of the intermittent but protracted nature of the war. In many areas, conflict raged off and on from the early months of 1990 until 2004. Villagers were forced to take refuge deep within the forest or trek long distances to safety in towns closer to Monrovia.

The HIV/AIDS pandemic is taking hold in Liberia, as throughout West Africa, and is limiting life chances. Although an AIDS surveillance mechanism was set up in 1987, monitoring was not effective and the spread of the disease was generally ignored. Only 326 cases of AIDS-related deaths had been reported by 2000. Reports in early 2005 suggested incidence of the virus among 10 to 12 percent of the adult population, with the percentage rising.[50]

Disintegration of Social Institutions

Linked to the enormous toll in human life and suffering is the disintegration of basic social institutions, especially those such as the family and other community-level institutions. Government failure and violent terror lead to the dispersal of people in ways that deeply affect families. During prolonged conflicts, tracing family members is one of the critical undertakings of international entities such as UNICEF and the Red Cross and Red Crescent societies. Although exact figures are not available, estimates have put missing individuals, mainly children, separated from families in the thousands. By 1999, close to 4,000 children could not be reunited with their families (SCF 1999). Thus, the roles of the family in nurturing, transferring values, and providing a safety net were seriously undermined.

The pervasiveness of poverty as a legacy of failed government and violent conflict also contributed to the declining capacity of the family. With 85 percent unemployment in late 2004, thousands of households could not afford the basic necessities of life. According to the Human Development Reports of 2000 and 2001, more than 80 percent of Liberians lived below the poverty line, and approximately 50 percent of these lived in absolute poverty (UNDP 2000, 2001). Parents often perceived themselves diminished by their inability to properly provide for their children. Many parents were at pain to ignore the fact that daughters who became breadwinners had in fact turned to prostitution.[51] Liberia has one of the highest rates of teen pregnancy in Africa (GOL 2000a). The status of parents as role models has long been under threat.[52]

Coupled with the family's declining capacity is the near collapse of the educational system. There is an acute shortage of schools and qualified teachers. In 2003, only 46 percent of primary and 35 percent of school-aged children were in school. When disaggregated, taking gender into account, only 32 percent of females and 52 percent of males of school age were attending school. Teacher quality and lack of basic facilities pose further challenges. In 2003, only 35 percent of all teachers in Liberia's public school system were certificated to teach. The prevalence of unqualified teachers poses further danger to an already ailing educational system. Textbooks, equipment, and supplies—and such basic facilities as working toilets—are scarcely found.[53] The urban bias of the distribution of schools is most glaring. More than 70 percent of schools are located in urban areas, most in Monrovia. In spite of the urban bias, schools, where available, have hardly been affordable. For example, with 70 percent of Monrovia's households earning less than the equivalent of U.S.$50 a month, basic physical needs such as food, shelter, and clothing can hardly be met (GOL 2000a).

The school system, like the family, can hardly muster the capacity to provide nurturing in wholesome values and training in needed skills. One of the most pronounced signals of the erosion of values was observed by some teachers in public schools who reported a growing preference among some young people to use force and artifice to cope with social problems rather than cooperation with others and achievement through merit and mastery. Children without guidance often tend to choose as models those who carry weapons rather than those who excel in education and cultivate productive skills.[54] Similarly, governing arrangements characterized by overcentralization, repression, and corruption are more likely to offer rewards on the basis of factors other than achievement through merit (Szeftel 2000). This is how a culture of violence and artifice can become entrenched.

Crisis of Youth

The Liberian experience has shown that where armed groups dominate, youth become not only important instruments in the use of force but leaders of government as well. The roles they play in the violent conflicts, including warring upon their elders, earn them access to power and resources. This generational shift in authority relations has exacerbated the decline of the family and the erosion of values, and undermined the foundations of the intergenerational cycle of learning. The generational shift, which is visible at all levels of authority relations in Liberia, has crystallized the crisis of youth and become one of the most menacing of the legacies of predation and violence.

Research done by the Center for Democratic Empowerment in 2000 showed that in several parts of Liberia, elders who traditionally held positions of authority in villages and townships had been refusing to serve as chiefs because of the uncontrolled and excessive powers exercised by young untrained armed men who had become state security officers. In some cases, elders of townships had sought out local boys who were ex-combatants and of similar temperament to serve as chiefs so as to provide protection from harassment and torture by their former colleagues who had become state security officers (Sawyer, Wesseh, and Ajavon 2000).[55] This is what Ibrahim Abdullah (1998) has aptly called the political rise of the "lumpen youth."

There is a growing body of literature on the impact of violent conflict on youth—more precisely, how participation in armed conflict affects their subsequent behavior. The notion of post-traumatic stress, for example, is validated by some researchers (Garbarino et al. 1991), contested by others (Boyden 1994), and held yet by others to be conditioned by circumstance (Bracken 1998). West (2000) has argued that commitment to the liberation struggle in Mozambique provided girls a steady rudder and a sense of empowerment leading to fulfillment of obligations considered constitutive of national service. Eric Gable's (2000) study of a youth "culture development club" in Guinea Bissau shows how youth can be a source of change by their use of traditional institutions as instruments of change. While there are many examples of the potential of youth to self-organize, I follow Gable in the view that in Africa today, the overall trend seems to support the notion of African youth in crisis. The decline of educational systems; high levels of youth unemployment as evidenced by the multitude of idle youth to be found in virtually all African cities; the HIV/AIDS pandemic that is taking a higher toll among women, children and youth; and the rise in youth criminality all attest to a crisis whose depth has not been fathomed and whose consequences pose a serious threat to Africa's capacity to develop and sustain a civilization. Having suffered a quarter century of violent conflicts and with 71 percent of its population under thirty, Liberia is tightly in the grips of this threat. Two generations of young people are now at risk. Unless due attention is given the plight of Liberian youth, Liberia's future will remain precarious.

Erosion of Sense of Shared Community

Government failure and violent conflict have their most destructive impact on society when they erode the sense of shared community. Alexis de Tocqueville (1969, 61) has argued that the township or village is the most basic form of human association, that "local institutions are to liberty what primary schools are to science." The existence of what Vincent Ostrom has called "shared understanding" is foundational to any group of people that can be called a community. This relates to the existence of a common sense of justice (fairness) and values of trust and reciprocity among them. If these seem to evolve naturally, as Tocqueville suggests, it is because local communities are typically characterized by cultural homogeneity with patterns of interaction girded by common history and norms. In the case of Africa, this is what Peter Ekeh (1975) described as the "primordial public," ethnic communities with a shared sense of obligations and rewards. However, in the matrix of communities that are constitutive of society, human beings must engage in patterns of interactions that extend beyond the communal, beyond the ethnic group.

Transcending the family and the larger kinship unit to other situations of collective action requires a broadened sense of "shared understanding." Henry Sumner Maine (1960) has argued that human institutions evolved progressively from the family to other institutions of collective choice. Patterns of human interactions correspondingly evolved from interactions underpinned by *status* within the institution of the family to interactions governed by rules of contract. He argues that this is how patterns of human interaction transcended the communal and established the autonomy of individual while still preserving social capital offered by family and culture. Tocqueville's conception of the establishment of constitutional orders rooted in the principle of covenanting bears relevance. The point to be made here is that Africa's challenge is to transcend the primacy of the communal public and elevate the "civic public"—to use Ekeh's second phrase. A legacy of government failures and violent conflicts in Liberia has seen a retreat into the communal and perhaps a hesitancy of individuals of various communal groups to establish trusting relationships across communal boundaries. It has seen the erosion of trust among neighbors and the pitting of friends and spouses from different ethnic and religious groups against each other in a variety of unproductive ways. In many multiethnic rural communities of southeastern and northwestern Liberia, conflict resolution mechanisms have broken down. Village councils that used to include broad-based ethnic representation have been delegitimized as trust among individuals of different ethnic groups has diminished.

Interethnic marriages have become strained and friendships have been broken. In Sinoe, for example, unarmed and demobilized ex-combatants of the Sapo and Kru ethnic groups who were schoolmates and members of the same social clubs before the war later stood at each other's throats or were forced to seek protection in ethnic enclaves of their kinsfolk because they were fearful of each other (Sawyer et al. 2000).

Armed bands began their violent acts in rural areas where they preyed upon villagers long before they reached the urban centers of Liberia. Hallmarks of pillage and plunder were more starkly visible in rural Liberia where villages were frequently razed. Youth and others, operating under command, committed enormous atrocities: killing and demeaning elders, forcibly taking teenage girls as "war wives," desecrating or destroying religious shrines, and leaving multiethnic communities shattered. Criminality and terror thrived longer in rural areas outside the glare of much publicity. Reestablishing or strengthening a shared community of understanding at village and township levels is a task of fundamental importance.

■ Gruesome Picture, Ray of Hope

At this point, the analysis of a scholar and the insights of an activist converge. As a scholar, I have exposed the nature and consequences of the destructive conflict and human tragedy that unfolded on Liberians; as an activist, I do see, out of this dismal picture, rays of hope. The gruesomeness of the Liberian situation cannot be denied, as the ruins are strewn across the land and the lives of the people. Liberia's path from overcentralization to gangster-style government has been very visible: A patrimonial order established at mid-nineteenth century reposed considerable powers in the presidency. By the turn of the twentieth century, state revenue increased as a result of the granting of property rights—first in rubber and later in iron ore— as concession rights to foreign establishments. As state revenues increased, the president became increasingly autonomous but unaccountable. Confronted with increased demands for inclusion, and with changed international circumstances in the later decades of the twentieth century, presidential autocracy collapsed in violence and gave way to a brutal dictatorship whose excesses accelerated the disintegration of the Liberian social order. This occurred at a time when significant change in the global order provided opportunities for the emergence of a gangster regime that inflicted terror on Liberian society and ignited violent conflict in the entire Mano River basin area.

Perceived to be presenting no threat to international peace, gangster rule gained international acquiescence and, with the support of the international community, was legalized through elections in which ordinary Liberians were constrained to surrender their struggle for freedom and democracy in exchange for a spate of peace. Such a trade-off brought neither peace nor unchallenged control by the government; instead, it created conditions of continued violence not only in Liberia but also in the wider Mano River basin area. These tragic developments are readily visible and well known.

With the expulsion of Taylor, the establishment of a transitional government, and the introduction of an international stabilization force to disarm all armed groups, the tide is expected to turn against plunder and carnage. Making this trend irreversible depends, in large measure, on how successful peace-building initiatives will be in creating a secure environment and appropriate foundations for longer-term governance, and on how Liberia's overcentralized and predatory governmental arrangements are henceforth reformed. These well-known challenges are discussed in subsequent chapters (mainly in Chapters 6 and 7).

What is little known and less visible to scholar-analysts are the initiatives of ordinary people. These may not make the international headlines as do the brutal atrocities. The prospects for renewal in Liberia do not lie in the ruins but in the capabilities of ordinary people. What makes the initiatives of ordinary people such powerful indicators of a hopeful future is that these initiatives are local and largely self-organized. Where scholars may experience a methodological blind spot and fail to see new possibilities for Liberia, others, like Methodist bishop Arthur Kulah (1999), have observed much ingenuity at work and proclaimed, "Liberia will rise again." This capacity for self-organization is the foundation upon which a new governing order can be built. I next turn to an examination of this ray of hope.

■ Notes

1. For a discussion of predatory regimes, see Evans (1992), Fatton (1992), and Lal (1984). For critical assessments of state failure and political violence in African countries, see Weiss (2000) and Nzongola-Ntalaja (1998) for the Democratic Republic of Congo (DRC); and Conteh-Morgan and Dixon-Fyle (1999) and Zack-Williams (1995) for Sierra Leone.

2. *Papay* is a Liberian expression used with reference to a father figure or in deference to any male.

3. Early in the conflict, Taylor had promised to fight Doe in what he called "a 12-round heavy weight bout." He anticipated a long grueling struggle against Doe but not against multiple factions and a peacekeeping force. He sought to take the country inch by inch.

4. In addition to Foday Sankoh of Sierra Leone, Kukoi Samba Sanyang of The Gambia was a senior official of Taylor's NPFL. Both men had previously sought to overthrow the government of their respective countries. For Sankoh, see Abdullah and Muana (1998); for Sanyang, see The Gambia (www.triwest.net/~cvfsc/countries/gambia.html), The Gambia (www.worldrover.com/history/gambia_the_history/html), and U.S. Department of State, Background Notes: The Gambia, July 1996 (http://dosfan.lib.uic.edu/ERC/bgnotes/af/gambia9607.html). Among other West Africans who joined Taylor's and Sankoh's forces was Gbago Zoumanigui of Guinea, who was also trained in Libya. See Fofana (1998).

5. Between 1991 and 1996, at least five armed bands were involved as warring parties in the conflict. Some of these are mentioned later.

6. Former MOJA members, such as Christian Herbert and Augustine Nyeswea and others influenced by MOJA, such as Lewis Brown and Tiah Farcarthy, provided Taylor's ideological language. Nyeswea and Farcarthy died in a motor accident in 1995. Herbert became Taylor's minister of labor, and Brown became special adviser and one of Taylor's closest aides.

7. Blamo Nelson, Taylor's director of cabinet, and Gabriel Matthews, director of public relations of the Oriental Timber Company, were senior members of the UPP who became associated with Taylor's government and interests. Matthews was the founding chairman of the UPP and Nelson an official of its executive council.

8. At the time of the coup in 1980, Taylor was in Monrovia as a member of a ULAA delegation sent to hold discussions with President Tolbert. Then married to a Gio woman, Taylor adopted Quinwonkpa as his sponsor and with the latter's support took control of the General Services Agency, the government's purchasing office.

9. Tom Woewiyu and Nyudueh Mornorkomana were among Taylor's associates who, like him, were senior officers of ULAA in the 1970s. Both became members of the Liberian legislature during Taylor's presidency. Woewiyu was a senator, and Mornorkomana was speaker of the house of representatives.

10. The term *Congo* originally referred exclusively to Liberians of settler background whose ancestry could be traced to recaptives who were resettled in Liberia upon their interception while being taken to American and European slave markets after the abolition of slavery. In more recent times, the term is used with reference to all individuals of settler background. See Karnga (1926); Jones (1962); Shick (1977); and Guannu (1983).

11. The son of a low-status Congo father and a Congo-assimilated mother of Gola parentage, Taylor grew up in the Congo settlements of Arthington and Millsburg.

12. Close associates of Taylor's often told stories of how some members of this group who had embraced Taylor were frequently kept waiting for hours to see him, even after he had invited them to meet with him only because he wanted to remind them that he was in charge.

13. Stephen Ellis (1999) is one such scholar; John C. Yoder (2003) is another.

14. These are the ones who would ensure mysterious disappearances or torturous murder of Taylor's targets. They consisted largely of illiterate or semiliterate youngsters who enjoyed special privileges from him. One such youngster was made a three-star general in the security service after Taylor's election in 1997 and was reported to have remarked during his wedding party: "I give thanks to President Taylor first and God second."

15. According to those who observed him operate, it was not unusual for Taylor to instruct a fighter or group of fighters to eliminate a target and then instruct still others to eliminate the eliminators. It was also not unusual for him to organize theatrics, such as bringing together a group of elders and later informing his victims that he had been bestowed with Poro authority, and then act in the name of such authority to execute those he wished. Similarly, while a rebel leader, he would organize investiture ceremonies and bestow bogus Liberian government decorations on rural elders whose compliance he needed and then turn mobs of young fighters on those elders who refused to comply with his demands.

16. Human capacity for creativity and entrepreneurship is boundless. There are hair-raising stories of how prison guards are able to devise disingenuous but nonetheless creative ways to inflict pain through torture. My own experiences and those of colleagues who were imprisoned in 1984 and 1985 are instructive.

17. By 1996, the larger groups included ULIMO-J, ULIMO-K, and the Liberian Peace Council. LURD and MODEL were organized in response to continuing violence and witch hunting perpetrated by Taylor's forces after his election as president in 1997.

18. Author's interview with informant in Conakry in 2000.

19. Although this discussion is specifically about U.S.-Liberian relations during the Cold War, the impact of Cold War alliances on African society as described here also has application to those African countries that were under Soviet influence—for example, Ethiopia under the Dergue.

20. From 1980 to 1985, Liberia received $63.3 million in military assistance. The total military assistance of all the previous years (1946–1979) was $9.3 million. Economic assistance jumped from $17.7 million in 1970 to $23.5 million in 1980, more than doubled in 1981 ($55.2 million), and more than tripled by 1985 ($75.5 million). See Dunn and Tarr (1988, 177).

21. By 1987, Doe had removed the forestry sector from the normal financial management system and established accounts over which he had direct personal control.

22. It is interesting that twenty years later, in the post–Cold War era, many of those who had previously perceived such initiatives as socialist undertakings became promoters of self-reliant community development projects themselves. Perhaps the ending of the Cold War has provided an opportunity for objective reflection on the part of Liberian professionals. Certainly, endorsement of community empowerment approaches to development by the Bretton Woods institutions and UNDP has helped some Liberian professionals see the value of such schemes. For discussion about Susukuu, see Kamara (1987); and Sawyer (1993a).

23. Taylor, who served as director of General Services, the government procurement entity, fell out with Doe after allegedly defrauding the government of $1 million in bogus purchases. He was going through deportation hearings in Boston when he broke jail. The chairman of Taylor's National Patriotic Party and close confidant fled the country after being accused of defrauding a reinsurance company of hundreds of thousands of dollars. Taylor's senior economic adviser and confidant was involved in numerous fraudulent schemes including complicity in defrauding an insurance company in a case after a hotel had been deliberately torched.

24. Arthur Abraham (2001) has called the quality of confidence artistry as exhibited by Foday Sankoh "chameleon-like."

25. For a discussion of Liberia's place in U.S. security strategy regarding conflicts in central and southern Africa, see Berkeley (2001).

26. This view is substantiated by recent reports that Taylor was in the pay of U.S. intelligence. Writing in the *New Republic,* Ryan Lizza stated he had learned from credible sources that at least from 1992 to 1995, Taylor reported regularly to the U.S. Defense Department intelligence service on his bimonthly trips to Libya (Lizza 2005, 10–11).

27. For example, this is why the pursuit of French business interests, as discussed in the next section, could have dominated France's significant involvement in the crisis.

28. There was such a rush of publications that most accounts are deeply flawed as a result of false information and the preconceptions and prejudices of their authors. Accounts worthy of close attention are Adebajo (2002); Anning (1994); and Jaye (2003).

29. Such was the case with Taylor and Burkinabe president Campaore. A similar relationship seemed to have been developing between Taylor and Laurent Kabila of the DRC before the latter's death.

30. For example, Houphouët-Boigny and Rawlings had long been at odds, as had Rawlings and Campaore. Houphouët-Boigny was no close friend of Qaddafi; more-

over, his close association with the French government with which Qaddafi was at odds made such collaboration with Qaddafi unusual.

31. See, for example, Berdal and Malone (2000); Cilliers and Mason (1999); and Rufin (1996).

32. Mitterrand has since been indicted by a French court for illicit business dealing elsewhere in Africa while serving as African policy adviser in the president's office. See Suzanne Daley, "Mitterrand's Son Free on Bail After 21 Days," *New York Times,* January 12, 2001, p. A11; and Paul Michaud, "Dodgy Arms Sales to Angola, *New African,* April, 2001, p. 16.

33. Author's interviews with Taylor's confidants and Ivorian sources, 1998 and 2000.

34. According to Global Witness, the deal included a $5 million "sweetener" to the president and the company's commitment to provide consignments of arms to the president. Liberia has been under a UN arms embargo since 1990. (See Global Witness, www.globalwitness.org, for a report entitled "The Usual Suspect," which provides an analysis of the role of logging companies in Liberia's conflict.

35. See *Washington Post,* December 29, 2002; "Pat Robertson's Letter to the Editor of the *Washington Post,*" www.patrobertson.com; and *New Republic,* November 19, 2001.

36. Two Lebanese traders controlled 90 percent of the rice imports, and one Lebanese establishment is licensed to import fuel. All of these operated in close association with a Lebanese partner of Taylor's called Talal el'Ndine. Prior to the civil war, el'Ndine, a storekeeper in the port city of Buchanan, was left to run a supermarket owned by his uncle, who fled as fighting forces advanced on Buchanan. El'Ndine was soon to become a business emissary of Taylor's.

37. See "An Act To Designate Certain Natural Resources, Minerals, Cultural and Historical Items As Strategic Commodities," 2000, proposed legislation (manuscript).

38. Neil Cooper (2001) is among scholars who are doing excellent research on this question.

39. See the Cotonou Agreement, July 1993.

40. See Hartzell (1999) for a discussion of the importance of a third-party guarantee to the stability of negotiated settlements of internal conflicts. See also Stedman (1991) and Walter (1999).

41. Adedeji (1999) has rightly argued that failure to "comprehend and master" African conflicts is a key reason for failure to properly address them.

42. See World Refugee Survey, 1991–2003 (published by the U.S. Committee for Refugees, www.refugees.org).

43. For example, a tragedy of this magnitude translates into 72 million deaths in China, 16 million in the United States, 7 million in Nigeria, and 3 million in the United Kingdom.

44. See IRC, 2004; CSIS 2000; and UN Population Division 2000.

45. IDP figures usually reflect those persons who are being cared for by humanitarian organizations and not those who take refuge deep within the forest and other ecological sanctuaries and have not been reached by such organizations. In Congo/Brazzaville, for example, hundreds of the estimated 7,100 IDPs were yet to be found and returned to their villages in mid-2000, more than a year after the fighting had ended (see ICRC News 2000).

46. See, for example, Nagbe (1996).

47. See UNOCHA, www.reliefweb.int (November, 2002).

48. See Howard W. French, "Ledger for Liberia's War: Profit(eering) and Loss, *New York Times.* April 30, 1996, A8.

49. According to UNICEF, from 1980 to 2000, the under-five mortality rate in West African countries averaged 186 per 1,000, with an annual average rate of reduction of 1.3 percent over the two decades. See UNICEF, 1980–2004.

50. See National Transitional Government of Liberia, UN/World Bank, *Joint Needs Assessment,* February 2004.

51. A young woman in her early twenties made the following comments: "I was my father's pride; he used to give me everything I wanted. Every time I take the bag of rice to him, I can see in his eyes that he is not happy but what to do? Even though he never asked me where I am getting the bag of rice from, I am sure he knows" (author's research note, 2000).

52. A professor at the University of Liberia told me of a disturbing conversation he had with his teenage son about role models. His son told him that there was no male figure in Liberia, including his dad, suitable as a role model. The teenager pointed to his dad's inability to adequately provide for the family despite his advanced degree and more than twenty years of employment at the university (author's research notes, 2000).

53. In 1999, a row broke out between petty traders and students in Gbarnga. Students from a school close to the market grounds had taken the makeshift stalls of the petty traders to be used as desks in their classrooms (author's research notes, 1999).

54. Author's interviews with public school teachers in Monrovia, 2000.

55. The case of an elder from a town in Zorzor district, Lofa County, is quite revealing. He explained: "Everybody knows that I am supposed to be the town chief. My great grandfather founded the town, my grandfather was chief and my father was the last chief before the war. When we came back from the refugee camp in Guinea, all the people wanted me to be the chief. But I don't want to be chief. One night the ATU [antiterrorist unit, one of Taylor's security units] commander from Voinjama came to our town. One old man was in charge of the town at that time. It was raining; the CO [commanding officer] told his men to drag the old man from the house because the old man was not outside waiting for him. He put his boots on the old man's head. All the people in the town woke up and ran into the bush. I am too old for that kind of treatment. That is why I do not want to become chief. We choose one young boy to be chief because he is a former fighter. This time when the CO comes in the night we can hear them cursing each other. All the women and children can run in the bush" (author's notes, 2000).

CHAPTER 3

Foundations for a New Order

HERNANDO DE SOTO (2000) HAS REMINDED US THAT POOR PEOPLE ARE POOR NOT because they lack resources or assets but because the assets they have are not always transformed into productive capital and utilized at the optimum. Assessing the assets (not only needs) of individuals and communities is an indispensable first order of business in reconstruction initiatives if individuals and communities are expected to sustain those initiatives. Understanding how individual entrepreneurship and social capital entrenched in associational life are utilized is of critical importance in assessing individual and societal capacity for self-reliant development. Understanding how people craft institutions of collective action provides clues as to their possibilities for self-governance (E. Ostrom 1990) and constitutes the proper point of departure in considerations of how, confronted with the circumstance of state failure and violent conflicts, political order can be reconstituted with reduced prospects for predation and collapse.

The discussion of the violent legacy of government predation, repression, and governance failure in Liberia (Chapter 2) presents a picture of a society of deep wounds, abject poverty, and growing hopelessness. While there is much pain and poverty, Liberians are not without hope. They tap deeply into their human resources and mobilize social capital to cope with their circumstances. Individual ingenuity and social organization have blended to ensure survival. Despite state failure and extensive violence, many Liberians have employed wholesome and ingenious entrepreneurship to cope; many communities have taken recourse in their own social organization to provide education for their children, health care services, and security protection. This capacity for entrepreneurship and community self-organization constitutes the foundation of self-reliant development and of a potentially self-governed political order.

This chapter focuses on the potential for self-organization as revealed in associational life in Liberian society. It assesses the prospects for a new begin-

57

ning by deepening an understanding and appreciation of how individuals and communities have coped amid grave difficulty and to what extent their social organization and coping mechanisms constitute building blocks or foundations for self-governing political ordering. Not all social organizations and coping mechanisms are constructive and worthy of consideration as building blocks, yet it is important to understand them if they are to be discouraged or their harmful effects overcome. Transcending autocracy and avoiding state collapse require a new approach to the constitution of order in Liberia. Such an approach must involve the crafting of governance institutions from the bottom up, and this is why assessing the resources among ordinary people "on the ground" is fundamentally important.

Michael Bratton (1989) has argued that one of the gaps in our understanding of African political processes is the lack of a deep understanding of the impact of voluntary associations and other such entities of associational life on governance processes at all levels. How have Liberians been coping in the face of state collapse and all its consequences? What residual institutions have sustained them? What potential do these offer for rebuilding? These questions constitute the major concern of this chapter. Unfortunately, such questions are hardly ever asked when donor-driven reconstruction programs are formulated and implemented. In such situations, emphasis is typically slanted toward the assessment of *needs,* especially as seen through prepackaged profiles. There is little effort to assess the potential, capabilities, and strengths of local people so that these become seed capital. The needs assessment survey published jointly by the National Transitional Government of Liberia (NTGL), the UN, and the World Bank reflects this shortcoming. The document is disappointingly quiet on the critical question of what Liberians themselves possess, even in their state of misery. What skills, institutions, and other resources do they bring to their processes of recovery?[1]

In addressing questions related to the potential and capabilities for recovery, I begin with an examination of governance strategies employed by local communities confronted with the imposition of armed rule. I then discuss how, through their local mechanisms, such communities have been addressing problems of interethnic conflicts. Some of the networks and organizations that are part of associational life in urban and rural Liberia are discussed largely to show how people and communities have coped with the circumstance of state collapse and violent predation. This chapter provides a glimpse of self-organizing institutions of Liberian society and their potential as building blocks for the constitution of a self-governing political order.

■ Local Institutions and Local Governance

The question of how authority relations at township and community levels have been affected by state collapse and sustained destructive conflict in Liberia is yet to be fully investigated. Although there are brief analyses of the impact of military violence and government-sponsored or government-allowed banditry on rural communities, the question of how, in the face of the collapse of the central state, individuals and communities organize survival strategies to cope with security predicaments has not yet become the central concern of scholarly research on contemporary Liberia. Warren d'Azevedo's (1969–1971) seminal work provides an excellent analysis of Gola strategies in response to the penetration of the Liberian state in the nineteenth and early twentieth centuries; others, such as Svend Holsoe (1971, 1974), have provided similar analyses with respect to other political communities vis-à-vis the creation of the Liberian state and the imposition of its authority on indigenous communities. However, since the military takeover of 1980, there have not been many studies investigating how local communities have responded to increasing state-sponsored violence and state collapse.[2]

Domination of local communities by the central state has been a defining feature and most enduring characteristic of autocracy in Liberia as is the case elsewhere in Africa (Wunsch and Olowu 1995). Control by the presidency over the process of selecting chiefs and local leaders and their manipulation by that office is a strategy of domination and predation inherent in the nature of autocratic rule in Liberia (Liebenow 1969; Dunn and Tarr 1988; Sawyer 1993b, 1995). Since the founding of the Liberian state, state-sponsored violence has always been one of the instruments that ensured such control. However, during the years of military rule, such violence became the main instrument of control.[3] Local officials were routinely harassed, violently intimidated, and capriciously hired and dismissed. Such practices intensified when the civil war broke out in 1989. What institutional strategies did local communities adopt to cope with state collapse and its attendant violence?

It is important to remember that every town and village in Liberia was not only affected by violence but also ruled by an armed commander or an individual associated with an armed group. This pattern did not change throughout the period of Charles Taylor's presidency (1997–2003). Young ex-combatants and their associates constituted the largest number of village and township heads.[4] Although responses of villagers and townspeople to their new rulers varied, in almost every case, local communities typically sought recourse in traditional institutions in order to cope with this new situation. Examples from northwestern and southeastern Liberia reveal two forms of community response to domination by this new breed of armed rulers.

Poro Authority and Armed Rule at the Village Level

In many parts of northern and northwestern Liberia, villagers deepened their resilience and adapted to the rule of their new armed leaders through Poro solidarity. Poro has been the foundation pan-ethnic social institution embracing the collective social and historical experiences of most Mel- and Mande-speaking groups in Liberia, Sierra Leone, and Guinea. It is considered to be of a deeper order of legitimacy than any group of secular rulers and commands a wider pool of resources than those available to any single ethnic community. It has been the protector of values and provided a source of sanctions that transcended the prerogatives of secular authority. It has exercised authority that is considered "sacred and secret." With deep roots in vast sections of the rain forest, Poro institutions have been embedded in social organization from the domain of the village to higher levels of authority. With hierarchical and gerontocratic principles central to its operations, Poro was a source of stability in the rain forest prior to the spread of Islam or the establishment of European colonial control (Little 1966). Despite commitment to these principles, Poro organization has seemed flexible when necessary and has provided scope to accommodate opportunistic behavior in adapting to change (d'Azevedo 1962).[5]

While it is true that the new armed leaders were obeyed and accommodated, efforts were made in many cases to co-opt them. In several towns in Lofa County, Poro authority is said to have constituted a parallel but unobtrusive authority structure that supported some initiatives of the new armed leaders where considered appropriate, but artfully and quietly organized resistance where necessary and feasible to protect the interest of local people. In some towns in the districts of lower Bong County, for example, local people clothed their "armed chiefs" with the traditional chieftain authority and constituted advisory councils in accordance with traditional practices.[6] These councils sought to constrain the actions of armed fighter-chiefs. Historically, the dynamic of co-optation between central government and Poro has worked both ways: Liberian government officials have often co-opted Poro symbols and Poro authority has often adapted opportunistic behavior vis-à-vis the government. More widely understood is how the president and his senior officials have over the years attempted to influence Poro authority.[7] What is now becoming evident is how in recent times, Poro authority and local communities have also adopted strategies of manipulation and accommodation to ensure their survival.[8] Thus, by co-opting the new leaders, Poro authorities of villages and towns sought to restrain the actions and behaviors of armed men who operated with hardly any supervision and whose loyalty was only to a leader in Monrovia.

Community Retreat and the Formation of Auxiliary Forces

In southeastern parts of Liberia, some communities tended to respond to the imposition of the rule of armed bands by retreating from their towns and villages to smaller hamlets located deeper in the rain forest. In the southeast, villages and towns are typically smaller than those found elsewhere in Liberia.

Seeking sanctuary in the forest has been a security strategy used by all forest communities; however, since violence erupted more frequently in the southeast between 1990 and 1998, southeasterners were on the run more frequently and constrained to abandon their towns and villages for longer periods of time.[9] In other parts of Liberia, villagers who were forced to flee their communities and seek sanctuary in the forest usually returned to their homes as soon as fighting ended or remained there for long intervals between fights. By contrast, in southeastern Liberia, villages remained sparsely populated years after fighting ceased. There are two reasons for this situation: First, the isolation of the southeast from other parts of the country and the small size of towns provided ideal settings for armed rulers to operate with greater levels of impunity. Second, there is an absence of strong panethnic institutions capable of imposing sanctions across clan and ethnic groups.

Thus, unrestrained by local sanctions and well connected to the leadership in Monrovia, the armed rulers in the southeast operated with impunity against local people who lived in sparsely populated villages scattered over the landscape and separated from one another by long distances. In some parts of the southeast, roads remained impassable up to the end of the conflict in 2003–2004; towns that once bustled with trade remained deserted, and local people were forced to develop stronger relationships with communities in Côte d'Ivoire. Kwee is a social institution that exists across many clans and in many ethnic groups of southeastern Liberia. However, unlike Poro, its authority is circumscribed and its scope of operation is limited. There is no panethnic authority with jurisdiction over most of southeastern Liberia comparable to the Poro in northern and northwestern Liberia.

Where communities did not or could not retreat into the forest, a common strategy used widely in the southeast and sparingly in the northwest was the mobilization of local men in age-set units for the defense of local communities. These units operated in association with the occupying armed group. Local elders negotiated with the occupying armed group to have such local militia units accepted as part of the occupying armed group. In this way, local communities were often tentatively spared the ravages of armed bands. However, violence always flared up when another armed group sought to dislodge an occupying band. Suspicions ran high between local forces and occupying groups, and arrangements of cooperation often broke down.

In some urban centers in the southeast, rival groups of local elites developed competitive strategies to co-opt or win the favor of their new local rulers. Using connections in their ethnic communities in Monrovia, rival groups sought to enhance their local standing vis-à-vis the new local authority. These rivalries were debilitating to local communities and left both local elites and their communities powerless and more vulnerable in the face of repressive armed rulers. This powerlessness was substantially manifested in their approach to conflict resolution, a subject to which I turn after briefly discussing how urban dwellers struggled to cope with challenges of insecurity at the hands of armed young men.

Urban Dwellers' Response to Armed Insecurity

People of urban communities faced a difficult challenge where there was no recourse when members of state security forces behaved like criminal gangs. Local people were constrained to develop a range of survival strategies. A common strategy was to observe a self-imposed curfew so that by dusk people hurried home and stayed indoors. Neighborhood watches had also become a typical community response against burglary and related crimes, but such arrangements often proved inadequate against well-armed gangs associated with state security units. Faced with such situations, urban families took to reinforcing doors and windows of homes and organizing makeshift alarms to alert each other when under assault. In certain urban ethnic enclave communities, such as New Kru Town in Monrovia, such alarms typically brought out scores of screaming people armed with machetes and other weapons. Seeking out interlocutors and paying protection fees were strategies also tried, often unsuccessfully, to deter armed gangs.

While it is true that not all forms or uses of social capital are productive, what we see are patterns of responses to security threats rooted largely in the nature of indigenous social organization extant in each area. Poro, as the foundation of social organization and authority relations in northwestern Liberian and transboundary communities in Sierra Leone and Guinea, provided an institutional framework for responding to the onslaught of the new armed rulers. Even though community responses might have differed tactically, Poro hierarchies remained the dominant actors in providing institutional responses to armed assault in many communities of northern and northwestern Liberia. A different pattern obtained in southeastern Liberia, where communities are mainly acephalous. Communities formed smaller clusters of families and sought refuge deep within the rain forest or sought the intervention of kinfolk who lived in Monrovia. The mobilization of local forces as auxiliaries to armed bands proved effective in some situations. In all cases, local people found recourse in indigenous and local institutions to cope with their security dilemma.

◼ Local Institutions and Conflict Resolution

Poro Authority and Interethnic Conflict Resolution in Northwestern Liberia

Poro authority has also been a force for ending violence and managing and resolving interethnic conflicts. The case of violent clashes between Mandingo and Loma communities in Zorzor district, Lofa County is illustrative and deserves discussion. Mandingo and Loma have lived together in the same villages and towns in the area of Zorzor district on the border of Guinea since before the founding of Liberia (Anderson 1971). Most towns in the area are predominantly Loma; a few, such as Bakedu, are predominantly Mandingo. Both local communities are part of larger ethnic communities that extend into Guinea. Mandingo are largely Muslims while Loma are Christians, Muslims, and adherents to forms of indigenous worship. Poro is an important institution in Loma society but not in Mandingo; nonetheless, Mandingo have always demonstrated respect for Poro authority. The two ethnic communities have been closely linked through intermarriage (more often Loma women to Mandingo men), shared myths, and a common history. In their shared mythology, the Loma are recognized as uncles of the Mandingo. The "uncle-nephew" bond imposes duties and privileges. The Loma have the duty to protect the Mandingo and ensure their well-being, and, in turn, the Mandingo have a duty to respect Loma institutions and support Loma undertakings. These bonds were said to have been sealed by rituals involving joint sacrifices and ancestral oaths committing the two communities to a permanent relationship of peace, friendship, and cooperation, free of deceit, hypocrisy, and treachery (Sawyer, Wesseh, and Ajavon 2000).

Joint mechanisms of conflict resolution that have evolved between the two communities, typically at the village or town level, include arrangements by which elders of the various *quarters* constitute a court, with decisions sanctioned by the chief and council and enforcement ultimately backed by Poro authority (Loma) or by quranic authority (Mandingo). Since the consolidation of the Liberian state, state-based conflict resolution processes have intervened and imposed a higher level of authority through the interior bureaucracy (district commissioner, county superintendent, and the office of the minister of internal affairs) and a judiciary (courts of justices of the peace, magistrates, and circuit judges).

In recent times, Mandingo, strained by war, have accused the Loma of not only abandoning the commitment to protect them but also of joining the onslaught against them. They accused Loma youth of torching mosques and demeaning Mandingo elders. The Loma, in turn, labeled the Mandingo's retaliatory strikes as ethnic targeting and accused the Mandingo of desecrating Loma Poro groves. They accused Mandingo youth of defacing Loma Poro objects and absconding into Guinea with them. Both sides accused each other of breaking the age-old covenant that had bonded them. Early in the conflict, Mandingo were first forced to flee into Guinea; later, Loma were forced to flee the retaliatory attacks of the Mandingo. Both communities have been seething with bitterness and suspicion against each other.

Reconciliation between the two groups has become one of the most important postconflict challenges. Government's mediation initiatives were superficial, confined largely to mass meetings presided over by central government functionaries and targeted more to winning the support of both communities than to bridging the divide between them. Moreover, actions of central government's security operatives also tended to exacerbate the problem (Sawyer, Wesseh, and Ajavon 2000). Nongovernmental organizations (NGOs) serving as facilitators were better able to get both sides to begin a dialogue.[10] As dialogue progressed, Poro leaders from Loma communities in Guinea were said to have been indispensable in initiating a process of recovenanting. Pan-Poro solidarity provided a context for security and a framework for problem solving among the Loma. Loma Poro objects were retrieved through Pan-Poro channels that involved the intervention of Guinean Loma communities with their Mandingo compatriots. Appropriate rites of restoration were performed and, with due respect accorded by the Mandingo, the basis for reconciliation was established. The Mandingo received assistance from Loma communities in the construction or renovation of mosques and both communities were subsequently engaged in establishing joint mechanisms for early warning and for dispute settlement.

Such mechanisms functioned with the endorsement of both Poro and quranic authority.[11] As a result of the impact of such local conflict resolution processes, continued violent conflicts in the region between central government forces and dissident groups have not further strained the relations between Loma and Mandingo, as was the case earlier in the conflict.[12] Thus, the Poro seems to have partially provided a nested arrangement for local mechanisms of conflict resolution as the Taylor government itself became more deeply involved as a party to armed conflict.

Property Rights and Conflict Resolution in Northern Liberia

Postwar conflict resolution among the Mano, Gio, and Mandingo of Nimba County in northern Liberia has taken a different course from that seen among the Loma and Mandingo of Zorzor district, Lofa County. Unlike their ethnic kinfolk of the northwest, the Mandingo of northern Liberia are relative newcomers to the area of Nimba County. Most were traders from Guinea who settled in Mano and Gio country and married local women. While many Gio embraced Islam, the Mano remained a Poro community.[13] Mainly agriculturists, Mano and Gio reached an accommodation with Mandingo traders for whom landownership was not a critical concern once use rights were granted.[14] With such rights, Mandingo traders exploited streams, creeks, and riverbeds prospecting for alluvial gold and diamonds. They also dominated land transport and the housing market in northern Liberia.

As a minority group perceived as "strangers," the Mandingo always felt vulnerable in Nimba, despite intermarriage and years of good relations with other groups. They ultimately relied on the central state for their protection and, as a result, were often viewed as allies of the settler oligarchy and later, when Doe took over, as allies of the Krahn. After the 1980 coup, growing enmity between the Mano and Gio on the one hand and the Krahn on the other held serious consequences for the Mandingo, especially those from Nimba County. Relations between them and the Mano/Gio ruptured during the war. Mano and Gio constituted the largest group within the dominant rebel group during the violent conflict, and Krahn and Mandingo became their prime targets. Most Mandingo of Nimba fled to Monrovia or neighboring Guinea.

Property rights in land have become the critical issue in postconflict relations between the two groups. Many Mano and Gio communities were said to have revoked land use rights granted Mandingo, while the Mandingo demanded the restoration of property rights that had been granted by the national government through licenses and mining claims. Up to 2000, community-based approaches to the settlement of land disputes had had some success. Mandingo elders and Mano and Gio ethnic leaders agreed that all lands that had been sold or otherwise given to Mandingo in urban areas were to return to Mandingo ownership. With respect to the settlement of mining claims, by 2000, Mano and Gio leaders working through the county branch office of the Ministry of Lands, Mines, and Energy seemed to have been able to establish a "rolling registration" scheme such that Mandingo claims were considered on a case-by-case basis. The Ministry of Lands, Mines, and Energy granted tacit approval to such an arrangement, and up to the end of hostilities, most Mandingo leaders seemed prepared to live with it as a tentative solution.

Consanguineous ties have been critical in the process of interethnic conflict resolution among the Mano/Gio and Mandingo of Nimba. Individuals of mixed ethnic backgrounds, especially men whose fathers are Mandingo and mothers Mano or Gio, have been able to shuttle between communities, and this has helped promote sympathetic understanding on both sides. In addition to the role played by ethnic elders as solvers of ethnic-based problems, younger and more educated individuals from both communities resident in Monrovia have also played significant roles in conflict resolution. In some cases, their ability to hold discussions in Monrovia away from the emotionally charged environment of the home county, in some cases, accelerated the process of conflict resolution.

"External Elite" as Conflict Resolution Catalysts in Southeastern Liberia

In southeastern Liberia, reconciliation among ethnic groups proceeded differently. Organized on principles associated with acephalous societies, there is hardly a single indigenous institution whose legitimacy cuts across all ethnic communities. Kru and Sarpo elite living in Monrovia have been the prime initiators of reconciliation activities between the two groups, and local people seem to have relied on the lead and advice of their educated sons in Monrovia. Kru and Sarpo development organizations located in Monrovia have been active not only in mobilizing resources to assist reconstruction of Kru and Sarpo communities in the southeast, but also in organizing interethnic discussions about matters that divide their kinfolk in the towns and villages of Sinoe and other parts of the southeast (Sawyer et al. 2000).

Such an externally-driven approach to conflict resolution has not been without noticeable consequences. First, until the ending of violence, generally in 2003, rifts between communities in the southeast did not seem to be healing as fast as they appeared to be in northern and northwestern Liberia— among the Loma and Mandingo, for example. Second, these processes of reconciliation, based as they are in Monrovia and not within local communities, were more easily manipulated by Charles Taylor up to his downfall and expulsion. Rival Monrovia-based elites could hardly avoid the temptation of turning to the Ministry of Internal Affairs for some form of intervention. Third, solutions evolved from such government-tempered reconciliation processes seemed designed more to redress perceived ethnic-based imbalances in appointments to county-jurisdiction positions in the government than to heal wounds between people who have committed egregious breaches against each other. As a result, when differences among such elites about job placements proved irreconcilable, demands for the creation of new political jurisdictions, such as new statutory districts or townships, have been heightened.[15]

The case of ethnic conflict between the Krahn and Grebo, also of the southeast, was even more illuminating with respect to the creation of new political jurisdictions as a strategy for the resolution of ethnic-based conflict. The military takeover of 1980 catapulted the Krahn to national as well as local leadership in their southeastern home county of Grand Gedeh, which they shared with the Grebo. Until that time, individuals from the Grebo ethnic group held most of the key positions in local government and professional areas due largely to their superior educational achievements.[16] During Doe's rule, Krahn and Grebo elders and elites were unable to arrive at a common understanding of their differences and an approach to resolving those differences; hence, at the outbreak of the conflict, Grebo youth massively supported Charles Taylor's forces, and this was attributed in part to their desire to end Krahn domination and control of their jointly shared home county. Since ending such control meant redressing imbalances in appointments to local government positions, the role of the president became critically important in resolving this conflict. Grebo leaders used their newfound influence with Charles Taylor to press for the creation of a new county by carving out the Grebo section of Grand Gedeh County. The creation of Grebo-dominated River Gee County has ended the competition for central government–allocated positions, which has been a major bone of contention between Grebo and Krahn elites over the years.

Deeply affected by state collapse and violent disruptions, local communities found recourse for conflict resolution in their own indigenous conflict resolution mechanisms where such institutions were available and appropriate. Operating unobtrusively, Poro authority has interacted with quranic authority to provide a basis for coexistence and gradual cooperation between the Loma and Mandingo of northwestern Liberia during times of violence. A more eclectic approach to conflict resolution seemed to have been taking place in Nimba in northern Liberia between the Mano/Gio on one hand and the Mandingo on the other. Personal predispositions and consanguineous relationships at the town level seem to be a critical factor in conflict resolution in that area. In southeastern Liberia, among the Kru and Sarpo, the role of elites of the two ethnic communities resident in Monrovia seemed pronounced; where reconciliation has proved to be more difficult due to lack of appropriate institutions, as is also the case between the Grebo and Krahn, rival local elites have opted for the creation of new political jurisdictions to provide opportunities for both. Thus, both the existence of viable community-based conflict resolution mechanisms and the availability of opportunities to create new institutions for inclusion, such as new jurisdictions, have been critical to the resolution of conflict among local communities.

What we have seen here are communities with enormous adaptive capacities deploying a variety of adaptations in the use of indigenous institutions or creating new ones where deemed necessary. Far from the perception of institutional rigidity, we have ample evidence of remarkable flexibility and adaptation, ranging from Poro adaptations in the northwest to the creation of new governance institutions (jurisdictions) in the southeast—all with a view to problem solving.

◼ Collective Action and Associational Life

Claude Ake (1996) has correctly noted that, although extensive in its reach, the state's penetration of African society has been rather weak and more extractive in nature than catalytic in the area of community development. Society's resilience can be observed in the nature and quality of associational life, which in some cases has made survival possible in spite of state predation and collapse. By associational life, I refer to the full array of collective action situations organized by individuals and communities in pursuit of a full range of desired outcomes. These include formal and informal groups, networks, and associations established on the basis of a variety of boundary rules for collective action for the provision, production, and use of collective goods (E. Ostrom 1990, 1992).[17] Also considered here are market-based activities derived and operated as a result of individual and group initiatives rather than by the state.[18] The crucial point here is to consider nonstate institutional arrangements, rooted in the initiatives of local people, that have been the source of their resilience to predation and violence.[19] Illustrative listings of these organizations and networks are given in Appendix 3. Many of these organizations and networks have external linkages with members who live outside Liberia. A brief discussion of creative activities of a select number of these collective action units illustrates how local people provided both collective and individual goods during a period of violent conflicts.

Clan-Based Institutions of Collective Action

The most enduring form of collective action that ensured community survival despite violent conflicts was undertaken by networks and organizations whose membership is based on clan-related identity. These are genuinely self-reliant and demand-driven groups. Typically, they are referred to as "development" associations. Many of them have several voluntary associations nested within them. Organizations such as the development associations of Bopolu in Gbarpolu, Palipo in River Gee, and Dugbe River Union in Sinoe counties are well known for their multiple roles as safety nets, for their conflict resolution mechanisms, and for the social and physical infrastructure development activities they undertake independent of the state—and often in spite of state predation. In northern Liberia, among the Mano and Gio, the accomplishments of clan-based organizations have been indispensable to the survival of local communities. Seletorwaa, the development association of the Mehnsonnoh clan, and the development association of the Zao, for example, have been extraordinary in their development initiatives. They have built schools, clinics, and roads and have organized scholarship schemes to assist promising young men and women to go to college. Seletorwaa was founded in the early 1980s by members of the Mehnsonnoh clan resident in Monrovia. It was a response to the military takeover and its consequences on Nimba County. Among the numerous projects it has undertaken over the years is a clinic it built in Guotowin and several scholarships it gave young people of the clan to pursue studies at technical schools and institutions of higher learning in Liberia. Selezoway, the Yarwin-Mehnsonnoh district development association of which Seletorwaa is a member, has, over the years, transformed the district by building roads, market sheds, community halls, and other public facilities.[20] Women's clubs within the development association have catered to the needs of the sick and disabled and have often organized for increased production of food to ensure food security. Male members of the clan have been responsible for maintaining roads within the clan.

As self-reliant entities, clan development associations are largely supported by the resources of their individual and constituent community members, through labor quotas and through taxation of individual production. The role of clan members in Monrovia and abroad is critical in resource mobilization. Many such organizations receive regular contributions from members now resident in the United States. More recently, members of Seletowaa in the United States have been providing equipment and supplies for elementary schools in the clan. Members of various Nimba County clan-based associations living in the United States have organized a countywide organization, the United Nimba Citizens Council of North America, and are engaged in substantial initiatives designed to rehabilitate and equip schools and clinics in Nimba County.[21] Clan-based development associations are often able to tap into external resources mobilized through intergovernmental entities such as those of the country offices of organizations of the United Nations system, the European Union, and international and local nongovernmental organizations.

International entities, such as the country office of the United Nations Children's Fund (UNICEF) and the Lutheran World Service/World Federation (LWS/WF), by offering useful assistance in the capacity building of clan-based organizations, have contributed to the sustainability of clan-based undertakings. The provision of agricultural tools to farm families in the southeast (Maryland and Grand Kru), assistance in the establishment of seed multiplication facilities in Bomi and Nimba, and the provision of extension services to farming groups in several communities—all through the institutions of clan-based organization—have enabled local communities to improve survival prospects and enhance sustainability in the face of continuously difficult circumstances.[22]

Clan-based organizations become more prominent as communities become marginalized or repressed by central state authority. The case of Nimba is well known. Self-help became the strategy for development during the 1980s when, as a result of Mano/Gio targeting by the Doe regime, the people of Nimba found recourse in their local institutions. Amid intermittent violence, Mano and Gio communities of Nimba County were rehabilitating clinics, schools, and roads even in remote parts of the county. Communities in the southeastern counties of Sinoe, Maryland, Grand Gedeh, and River Gee, for example, were left stranded as their forest resources were consigned through concession agreements to government-designated logging companies that have had no legal obligations to such communities. Some communities have tried to negotiate with such logging companies for access to forest resources. Needless to say, such negotiations are weighted heavily against local communities. Deprived of access to their forest resources, all such communities have been left to their own devices to survive, and clan-based organizations have been a critical survival resource.

Community-Based Organizations

The dominant manifestation of associational life in urban and periurban areas is community-based organizations (CBOs). These are constituted largely on the basis of a variety of overlapping boundary rules, ranging from those based on ethnic and communal identity, to those based on spatial and geographic location (uptown/downtown, right bank/left bank, north/south), to those based on a sense of common social history (e.g., a Togolese descendants organization). Like clan-based organizations in rural Liberia, they have been the fulcrum of development in urban and some periurban communities. In Monrovia, for example, the Slipway Community Association and the Soniwein Development Association have been known for initiatives in building latrines and repairing roadways. In upriver communities, community-based organizations have had an extensive track record in building and maintaining community centers and roadways.[23]

Outside Monrovia, community-based organizations have been active in undertaking roadwork and sanitation projects; in constructing irrigation canals, market sheds, schools, and bridges; and in sinking community wells in various parts of Liberia. Most of these initiatives were typically supported by intergovernmental organizations (IGOs) and NGOs. World Vision, Catholic Relief Services (CRS), the International Rescue Committee, Action Aid, Save the Children Fund UK (SCF-UK), and LWS/WF are among the more prominent cooperation partners of community-based organizations.

Community-based organizations are distinct from government-established local jurisdictions, and relations between the two are not always cordial. Leaders of township government are typically appointed by and responsible to the minister of internal affairs; their recruitment is largely on the basis of partisan affiliation or other political or familial connections. Leaders of community-based organizations are typically public entrepreneurs given to taking initiatives in community matters. Most are civic-minded individuals not necessarily driven by partisan politics. The initiation of collective action and the exercise of control over local resources can become sources of conflict between community-based organizations and local government authorities, often to the disadvantage of local communities.[24]

Despite state predation, community-based organizations have contributed to community survival and need to be seen as significant local capabilities for the reconstitution of governance order in Liberia. Because they are typically driven by community demands and rely on the support of their membership, they can be self-sustaining. Demand for clean and safe drinking water, latrines, passable roadways, and community meeting facilities can provide a sufficiently strong incentive to motivate social entrepreneurs within the community to initiate steps leading to collective action.

■ Religious-Based Institutions

Religious-based institutions in Liberia have played a critical role in strengthening people's capacity to cope in a war-torn society. By providing solace and meeting spiritual needs, churches and mosques have enabled thousands to maintain a sense of sanity if not serenity and a psychological capacity to cope with the tragedies and perversities that were all around them. Religious-based organizations have been the prime providers of trauma counseling;[25] and they constitute the driving force for reconciliation and healing. They have also been credible advocates for the protection of human rights. The Justice and Peace Commission, established by the Roman Catholic Church, has become the foremost human rights advocate in Liberia. The Interfaith Council, a body organized by leaders of the Liberian Council of Churches and the National Muslim Council has, during peacemaking negotiations, been at the forefront of efforts to secure the type of peace that promotes justice and human rights and facilitates democratization.[26] The Interfaith Council is considered the conscience of Liberian society; it is the only entity that was not cowed by the Taylor regime, despite Taylor's effort to smear the name of its leaders and to sow discord among religious leaders.[27]

In addition to undertakings having to do with social healing and the promotion of human rights, religious-based organizations such as churches are the largest providers of educational and health care services in postconflict Liberia. Churches and other religious organizations operate 60 percent of all educational facilities. The Roman Catholic Church alone operates 30 percent of all educational facilities.[28] All institutions of higher learning except the University of Liberia are run by religious bodies, and despite difficult circumstances, religious bodies have established several new postsecondary institutions since the outbreak of violent conflict.[29] Although many of these institutions are of questionable quality, the fact that under circumstances of massive breakdown initiatives are taken by entities other than government is amply demonstrative of local self-organization. Such self-organizing initiatives are even more remarkable when taken by ordinary individuals, as I discuss in a subsequent section. At the level of technical and vocational education, religious-based institutions and international nongovernmental organizations (INGOs) provide more than 70 percent of available facilities.[30]

With respect to health facilities, initiatives of religious-based entities are just as overwhelmingly significant. The Catholic Church runs the medical facility that serves as a referral and teaching hospital in Monrovia The government-run medical center and teaching hospital has suffered total neglect for years. The Catholic Church has also established community clinics in several communities in Monrovia and a number of health posts in rural areas. It runs the only continuous professional nursing training program available and has taken the lead in providing education on HIV/AIDS prevention.

The Lutheran and Methodist churches have also established rural health facilities in key towns and communities in large sections of rural Liberia.[31] To the extent that there are government-run health facilities, they have been supported substantially with resources from IGOs and INGOs; but even with such support, they are faltering.[32]

■   Economic Organizations

Even while conflict raged, there was an assortment of organizations for collective action designed to enhance economic entrepreneurial opportunities for
their members, despite failed macroeconomic institutions and an erosion of
credibility of governmental institutions and of trust generally. Notable among
these were rotational receiving arrangements called *susu* clubs, microcredit
schemes, retailers and wholesalers networks, and transport organizations. The
food retailers' networks and the Wheelbarrow Association are interesting
examples of ingenuity and hard work under difficult circumstances. Food
retailers' networks connect women who purchase local food items wholesale
from farmers (who are mostly women) with women who are retailers. The
correlation between ethnic identity and items bought and sold is very high.[33]
These markets operate at a high level of trust that protects the reputation of
sellers and buyers, ensures quality, and reduces the prospects of a "lemons
market."[34] At great peril to themselves and accused by all sides of being
informants, these women operated throughout the war. Despite injury and
abuse, they worked not only to make food available to communities but also
to protect their menfolk and children from conscription by armed groups and
certain death. One such group, the Sinoe Women's Development Association,
also served as a force for reconciliation. While engaged in the wholesale and
retail sale of food items, members of this group were always busy promoting
dialogue across ethnic divides. They were fast becoming a significant local
focal point of reconciliation between Sarpo and Kru communities in the
southeast (Sawyer et al. 2000).

The Wheelbarrow Association was much celebrated. Fuel shortages and
commandeering of motorized vehicles by armed bands created a demand for
wheelbarrows as a means of transportation, especially for the sick and disabled and for food and household items. Wheelbarrow operators covered
great distances taking items such as charcoal, vegetables, and other produce
from sources of production to market stalls in the cities and from such stalls
to local homes. The Wheelbarrow Association required high standards of discipline of its members, and through a system of certification and monitoring
and the imposition of sanctions, among other measures, it was able to ensure
a commendably high level of performance by its members, despite conditions
of intermittent violence and high levels of criminality in the society at large.

Microcredit schemes among both urban and rural women constitute
another area of collective action that survived state predation. Many of these
schemes can boast of repayment or collection rates as high as 90–95 percent,
indicating a high degree of peer pressure to fulfill obligations and the existence
of strictly observed sanctions regimes among their members. From time to
time, Charles Taylor's government threatened to take over these schemes. Far

from causing diminished commitment to obligations, these threats surprisingly increased solidarity among members, especially in southeastern Liberia.[35]

In addition to these economic entities of collective action, there are numerous stories of successful entrepreneurial initiatives undertaken by ordinary people in both urban and rural areas. These suggest that amid the rubble of violent conflict, there exists substantial potential for the development of a strong and highly motivated community of business entrepreneurs composed of townspeople and villagers—plain ordinary people.

■ Entrepreneurial Spirit in Service to Self-Governance

Stephan Kuhnert (2001) has argued that entrepreneurship is the link between environmental context and institutional order creation. The ability to identify or create opportunities is the essence of human entrepreneurship. This quality is most highly valued in situations that test human fortitude. It is indispensable for escaping the temptation of seeking recourse in letting others determine one's possibilities. Conflict situations tend to bring out the best and the worst of human potential. People are capable of committing heinous crimes as well as displaying amazing valor and generosity. The spirit of entrepreneurship is amply manifested in Liberia as people struggle to cope with their circumstances. It was too often used by some for harmful purposes. Happily, such entrepreneurship has also been demonstrated in producing public goods as well as in advancing wholesome private endeavors. Two examples of wholesome individual endeavors are indicative.

Economic Entrepreneurs

The family enterprise. There is the case of a displaced family whose home was destroyed during the war. The father was a junior-level civil servant who, like others, had not been paid for months. The family moved into makeshift housing on the outskirts of Monrovia near an out-of-town car park.[36] Humanitarian organizations occasionally provided the family rations of bulgur wheat and soybeans. As the conflict continued, the father sought to find ways to earn a living. His children could not attend school because he could not afford to buy food, let alone pay daily transport costs. He observed that the vehicles that came from out of town were usually covered with dust and mud; so with water from a nearby stream, he began a carwash business. Very soon, demand for his services grew and long queues developed. People waiting in the queue needed to eat, and with earnings from the carwash business, his wife opened a cookshop, selling bread and lunchtime dishes. Soon, additional labor was needed because the part-time help of their two children, who were now attending school, was inadequate. The cookshop was expanded and two additional people employed. Thus, a set of profitable family enterprises had been launched providing much-needed services and employment.

The boutique proprietor. There is the story of the young woman who had just completed a bachelor's degree in business administration at the University of Liberia when Monrovia was invaded by armed groups. Under normal circumstances, she would have sought employment in government or in a private business entity. With such opportunities foreclosed due to widespread violence that left people to their own devices, this young woman graduate, far from relying on humanitarian relief, waded in shallow streams and set traps in swamps to gather crabs and related food items. After making several sales, she was able to establish a rolling credit arrangement with a cold storage business to buy frozen chicken parts in bulk and sell them retail. After accumulating close to U.S.$300, she traveled to Nigeria, riding in the back of a truck, to buy an assortment of clothing and related items to launch a clothing business. She initially developed a clientele among Liberian employees of IGOs and INGOs. In three years she had established a clothing boutique.

There are numerous stories of economic entrepreneurship from every part of Liberia. They involve people whose initiatives enhanced survival prospects and led to the establishment of thriving business entities that produced benefits that rippled throughout the society. Conditions of questionable security and uncertainty and the existence of excessive tax regimes that consist of formal and informal levies did have a debilitating impact on local economic entrepreneurship; nonetheless, people continued in their entrepreneurial pursuits. Earnings from local enterprises, combined with remittances sent by relatives abroad— especially those resident in the United States—constituted major sources of livelihood for a significant segment of Liberians.

Social Entrepreneurs

Entrepreneurship has not been restricted to the economic sphere. Development of human capital has involved considerable individual initiative. In the area of education, schools run by private individuals constitute a considerable proportion of the total number of available schools. Many of them meet the highest standards. While West African examination scores of students from public schools have been consistently dropping, those of students from certain private schools have remained relatively high.[37] What is interesting is that most private schools are no better equipped than public schools; nonetheless, standards are higher because school resources are used more efficiently and effectively, discipline is enforced, and committed proprietors, teachers, students, and parents operate in the spirit of community. Together they organize projects for the support of such schools, including mobilizing financial and other resources to pay teachers' salaries.

Diana Davis School project. The case of Diana Davis School is impressive. Beginning as a two-classroom school for first- and second-graders of a poor neighborhood in Monrovia, Davis now operates a junior high school with high standards. Her first undertaking was to reinforce with parents a perspective of education as the key to a better life and to stress to parents that their own human resources were the most essential requirement for the education of their children. Through parent-teacher meetings, ideas and strategies were developed and a variety of projects undertaken for the support of the school. Bake sales, school garden projects, and drama productions ensured seed money. Others from the larger society chipped in.[38] Despite intermittent violence, the school grew over a period of six years into an elementary school and provided a solid foundation for scores of children each year. In the mid-1990s, students from Diana Davis School performed above the Liberian average on the West African examinations. Jimmy Jolocon High School is another example of a successful educational program organized by purely private initiative.

The Albert Porte library project. The initiative of an underemployed librarian and her husband is also noteworthy. They launched a project to establish a reading room for children. Through careful selection, they put together a collection of books, including books discarded during the conflict, on themes having to do with self-respect, tolerance, peace, justice, and trust—themes that resonate through the writings of Albert Porte.[39] Today many schools are using the reading room as a general education resource as well as a resource for peace education.

There are numerous such accounts of entrepreneurial initiatives taken under extremely difficult circumstances: accounts of scores of individual entrepreneurs who ran courses in computer skills development, architectural drafting, bookkeeping, office practices, and many other fields, despite the climate of fear and uncertainty and the conditions of poverty imposed by violent conflict.

■ Local Nongovernmental Organizations

Local nongovernmental organizations constitute another form of collective action designed to respond to the circumstances of state failure and predation. Over the years, especially since 1990, local NGOs have proliferated in Liberia. They range from short-term groups formed as special tools to address specific emergency situations to professional bodies of long standing.[40] Many of them have overlapping memberships and objectives. The proliferation of NGOs that are independent of the government is a product and manifestation of the struggle to widen civic space; it is indicative of initiatives to expand the public realm, despite efforts of the state to control them. The public policy advocacy role and cross-cutting interests of large numbers of local NGOs situate them immediately within the national political process, and that is why they seem to have the potential for deepening an emergent process of liberal democracy.

A major shortcoming of most local NGOs, however, is that many are wholly dependent on international donor support; consequently, they are donor-driven in their agenda and have a life span determined by external funding sources. Moreover, it is not infrequent that donor interest and local needs diverge. A classic example has to do with approaches to reconciliation. Donors seemed more willing to support superficial projects in reconciliation characterized by radio jingles and sound bites than to invest in long-term solutions that could emerge from research and policies that provide new approaches to social ordering and opportunities to transform conflict. Preference for short-term , quick-fix approaches have often encouraged the creation of local NGOs specifically to "get funding." Donors, in turn, are gratified by "progress" made by such local NGOs, as reported in the number of jingles played on the radio, for example. Considered closely, such arrangements look very much like a scam pulled on both the targeted population, which is promised a quick fix, and on taxpayers of the donor country, whose money may not have been effectively or efficiently used.

Donor-driven NGOs were also more easily manipulated by Charles Taylor's government. Threats to withdraw legal registration or to create or fund rival organizations were well-known strategies used by government to manipulate and control such organizations. Many local NGOs faced the dilemma of a trade-off between maintaining a sense of integrity and being pressured out of business by government. Ensuring donor funding and keeping in the good books of the government require such skillful navigation that some NGOs spend much more time on these than on pursuing the objectives for which they were established.

With the supply of donor funds, the proliferation of local NGOs can provide a false sense of enduring social organization and create a falsely competitive situation among NGOs. The challenge of sustainability and relevance faced by local NGOs requires that they deepen their links within Liberian society in order to become an organic part of problem-solving capabilities and let the demand for their services drive their actions and open opportunities to mobilize resources internally. By deepening their roots within society they will also develop stronger horizontal ties among themselves. Stronger internal networks can only strengthen capacity for sustainability.

■   International Nongovernmental Organizations

International NGOs are very much a part of the landscape of social organizations and coping mechanisms in postconflict Liberia. Like local NGOs, INGOs cover a broad spectrum of objectives and engage in a full range of activities. Some, such as Christian Aid and the Sudan Interior Mission, are pursuing a mission of spiritual and physical healing; others, such as World Vision, are devoting their efforts to the rehabilitation of agricultural and social infrastructures; and still others, such as the Carter Center, are pursuing issues of human rights and democratization. Many, especially those concerned with child rights, are engaged in a variety of mutually complementary activities.[41]

The significant role played by INGOs in socioeconomic and political construction raises the question of sustainability of initiatives. This question becomes more pertinent where INGOs are themselves involved in hands-on implementation. Quite often, well-funded INGOs involved in activities that are essential to local growth and development over long periods may reduce opportunities for the building of local capacity for sustainable performance, especially when such INGOs do not assist in the building of local capacity. This has become clearly evident in the areas of health care.

The case of Médecins Sans Frontières (MSF) is illustrative. Initially involved in emergency health care delivery during the violent conflict, MSF operated in collaboration with Liberian physicians and other medical professionals. Later, as Liberian physicians were forced to leave the practice of medicine or seek opportunities to practice elsewhere as a result of local circumstances, MSF continued to run hospitals and clinics, ignoring the fact that Liberian physicians who are experts in local medical problems and have always worked under conditions of hardship were constrained to leave due to lack of minimal employment opportunities.[42] What is even more interesting is the fact that MSF drew a substantial portion of the support for its Liberia operation from the African Caribbean Pacific (ACP) agreements of the Lomé Convention, an agreement that pegged economic assistance to trade, including the maintaining of quotas on the export of primary products.[43]

The operation of the Carter Center also presents a similarly interesting situation. Buttressed by the international reputation of former U.S. president Jimmy Carter, the center has been involved in reconciliation activities in Liberia since 1990, shortly after the outbreak of violence. Though well intentioned, for many years its approach typically emphasized reconciliation over justice, cooperation with government over curtailment of repression, and participation in elections over establishing the basis for democratic governance.[44]

For all intents and purposes, INGOs are, indeed, participants in the system of governance that affects local societies. They constitute a set of external actors who together with internal actors make decisions about local affairs. The decisions they make do have far-reaching consequences for local communities, but INGOs often operate without the obligation of accountability to those communities. Their typical pattern of reporting to their boards and funding sources illuminates this point. Such reports are replete with frequency-of-intervention aggregates, targets expressed in numbers, accomplishments defined in percentages, and time lines defined in quarters. Reports of the views, perceptions, and life stories of local people are hardly featured in these reports. Questions of empowerment of people are addressed simply in terms of numbers of meetings held with target communities and individuals and assurances given them about their "ownership" of projects.[45] Not all INGOs operate in this manner, but the trend is rather pervasive.

The need to have international nongovernmental organizations assist local communities in coping with their circumstances is critical, and many INGOs are indeed helping. However, meeting that need sustainably requires approaches geared toward ultimately enabling local communities to take charge of their own processes. This is best done through capacity-building undertakings. Approaches that involve skill development, use of local knowledge, appropriate technology, and the formation of partnerships with local NGOs and other associations of collective action are imperative if such initiatives are to be sustained.

■ The Liberian Diaspora Communities

Liberian communities abroad are a significant part of the capital available for reconstituting order in Liberia. Liberians in the United States, for example, are in many cases more highly trained and proportionately wealthier than their compatriots elsewhere in the Liberian diaspora. Although exact figures are not available, they are known to remit hundreds of thousands of dollars monthly in cash and kind to relatives and causes in Liberia. Almost all community-related organizations extant in Liberia have branch extensions or affiliated networks in the United States. There are scores of township, clan, district, and county organizations; alumni associations; professional groups; and religious bodies organized to advance the welfare of their members in the United States and to support parent or related communities in Liberia.

The Union of Liberian Associations in the Americas has seventeen chapters around the United States, some of which provided humanitarian support for Liberians at home during the violent conflict. County associations, such as the Grand Gedeh Associations in the Americas and the National Association of Bong County Citizens, are known to be supplying educational materials, medical supplies, and other welfare relief to counterpart or parent organizations in Liberia. Alumni associations, such as the Cape Palmas High School Alumni Association in the United States, are involved in renovating school buildings, paying teachers' salaries, and sending books and educational supplies to their alma maters. An organization of Liberian physicians in the United States currently has a membership of more than 125 physicians and is currently planning to restore the standards of the medical school of the University of Liberia.

Smaller communities of Liberians in Europe and less prosperous groups in other West African countries also make transfers. Many of the Liberian communities found in West African countries, including those categorized as refugee groups, have developed amazing capabilities over the last fifteen years. One of the more vibrant of such communities is the Liberian community at Buduburam, Ghana. With the support of the Media Foundation of West Africa, it publishes a bimonthly newsletter called *Exile News,* and undertakes several community development initiatives, including HIV/AIDS screening and the provision of water and electricity through arrangements with the appropriate Ghanaian utilities authorities.

■ Resources for Survival and Building Blocks for the Future

Institutional analysts argue that institutions or rules facilitate the use of assets to provide benefits to individuals and communities over time; they have identified four types of capital: human capital, which includes the talents and skills of individuals and the knowledge generated by such human resources; social capital, which includes the norms, institutions, and networks within society that facilitate collective action; physical capital, which consists of the physical infrastructure (farms, roads, dams, factories) constructed by human beings; and natural capital, which comprises the endowments of the ecology. These forms of capital constitute the capabilities available for governance and development in any society. This chapter has provided glimpses of the indomitable human spirit and creative artisanship of the Liberian people—examples from their reservoir of human and social capital. If postconflict reconstruction initiatives are to yield outcomes that can be sustained, they must be founded upon the capabilities—the capital stock—already extant among Liberians. This stock includes the wisdom of elders and the skills of fishermen, schoolteachers, basket weavers, medical doctors, blacksmiths, herbalists, and engineers—all alike. It encompasses the sum total of knowledge and skills acquired by the people of the society over time.

As stated several times in this chapter, there can be "good" use of human capital as well as "bad" use of human capital. The skills of the burglar, the pickpocket, and the "black money" boy—or the marksmanship of a child soldier—may have helped them survive fifteen years of conflict, but these are not uses of human capital that should be encouraged in reconstruction. Similarly, not all networks and organizations that constitute social capital can be considered suitable for or promotive of productive collective action. Armed gangs or prostitution rings may be characterized by strong relationships of trust and display exceptional internal cohesion, but their activities can be harmful to society. Such forms of social capital should not be tapped.

What is important is that the Liberian reconstruction process be perceived essentially as one designed with emphasis on helping Liberians develop and utilize their talents and skills for wholesome and productive purposes, such that as individuals they become not only providers of their own livelihoods and drivers of their own future, but also contributors to the development of their communities and transmitters of values, knowledge, and skills to suc-ceeding generations. It is further important, in this respect, that extant stock of social capital in Liberian society be assessed and used where appropriate as what Anirudh Krishna (2002) calls "bonding" capital to strengthen cohesion within communities; as "bridging" capital to establish or strengthen coopera-tion among or between people of different communities; and as "linking" cap-ital to nest communities within even larger communities. In this way, Liberi-ans will be able to fully appreciate the need for ethnic-based institutions, such as clan-based organizations, and the support they provide their members; the importance of interreligious organizations, panethnic associations, alumni associations, and professional bodies—all of which serve to bring individuals of different communal groups into collective action and to build bridges among various communities; and the role of county-based or national-level organizations that help all of them develop a sense of nationhood. This is how democratic political orders build foundations rooted in society and construct governance institutions from the bottom up. And this is why a new constitu-tional paradigm is needed for Liberia if Liberia is to depart from the top-down system of government and if its people are to truly become the governors of their own system of governance.

■ Notes

1. See *Liberia: Joint Needs Assessment,* National Transitional Government of Liberia, United Nations/World Bank, February 2004.
2. Sawyer (1987a) provides a passing glance at the impact of military rule on rural life.
3. The period of military rule in Liberia began with the military takeover of 1980. Although in 1986, the military leader Samuel Doe was elected in rigged elections, the pattern of postelections rule did not differ substantially from the preceding five years. Threat and use of military force, decrees, and strongman arbitrariness were as much the dominant features of postelections rule as they were earlier. Thus, except where otherwise stated, the entire period of control by Doe (1980–1989) is referred to as the period of military rule.
4. Domination of villages and towns by military men was a feature of the military takeover of 1980. What was different in the conflict that began in 1989 and ended in 2003 is that the new armed local leaders were not largely members of the officially organized state military force. As ex-combatants of a rebel force, all owed loyalty to Charles Taylor but were not always systematically organized in a publicly known com-mand structure.
5. It is not known when Poro began; however, its activities have been noted since the sixteenth century (d'Azevedo 1962).
6. Author's interview with informant.
7. We must remember that both Doe and Taylor imposed themselves on the Poro as its highest authority.

8. D'Azevedo (1969–1971) saw the offer of Gola girls as wives to settler-leaders and government officials as elements of Gola strategy for accommodation with the Liberian state.

9. With violence breaking out between LURD and the Taylor government in 1998, this pattern was changed.

10. The Center for Democratic Empowerment, the Catholic Peace and Justice Commission, and the Lutheran World Federation are among the nongovernmental organizations that have played facilitation roles.

11. There is no sense of *sharia* legal application in these matters. Mandingo Islamic clerics operate in conjunction with Mandingo elders, many of whom are of mixed parentage.

12. The use of indigenous institutions as mechanisms for conflict resolution is an important strategy currently employed in Rwanda. The Gacaca is an indigenous institution considered legitimate by both Hutu and Tutsi for the settlement of disputes. It is now playing a role in resolving certain conflicts connected with the genocide of 1994. See Neuffer (2000); and *New York Times,* October 7, 2001.

13. Chief Tuazama of the Gio town of Bahn is said to have been a convert to Islam and to have given many Gio girls in marriage to Mandingo men.

14. To the Mano and Gio and to all other ethnic groups in Liberia, ownership of land is inalienable. Most land is communal property charged to the custody of the elders of the community, who serve as "owners of the land." Use rights can be granted but ownership can only be attained through community sale. See Sawyer (1992), especially Chapter 10.

15. The creation of the statutory district of Tarjaurzon out of Juarzon is a more recent example.

16. Grebo communities extend from the Atlantic coast into the interior; as such they were among the first ethnic groups to have access to schools first established along the coast by missionaries and, later, by the Liberian state. Located entirely inland, the Krahn lived largely in hunting and gathering communities well into the early decades of the twentieth century. See Schroder and Seibel (1974).

17. Boundary rules are membership rules that determine who has rights and who is excluded. Elinor Ostrom and her colleagues have demonstrated that an extraordinarily large number of collective action situations are possible in view of the correspondingly large number of membership rules that can be generated. See Elinor Ostrom (2005, especially Chapter 6).

18. Discussion about associational life in Africa frequently becomes central to the debate about what constitutes civil society in Africa. That debate largely centers on the potential of civil society to advance democracy in Africa. See Barkan, McNulty, and Ayeni (1991); Harbeson, Rothchild, and Chazan (1994); Hutchful (1997); Kastir (1998); and Orvis (2001). Although critical, this debate is not my central concern in this chapter. My focus here is on how individuals and communities organize themselves for collective action to meet the variety of dilemmas they confront in the circumstance of state predation, collapse, and violence. That some of these collective action arrangements are "undemocratic" or potentially so is not of immediate relevance to this discussion.

19. In a technical sense, this discussion revolves around the boundary rules and provision of goods by groups. It is more a snapshot of the landscape than an analysis of specific collective action situations. Even in sketching the landscape, it falls short of a substantial discussion about the sustainability of collective action situations identified. However, the fact that groups discussed have survived state collapse and violent

conflicts and continue to operate with observable success seems indicative of their potential sustainability.

20. Interviews with members of Seletorwaa.

21. The amalgamated initiatives of clan-based organizations that sustain interclan development projects must not be confused with such countywide development associations that are organized by the central state through the Ministry of Internal Affairs. The former are the result of local initiatives; the latter are top-down government-driven structures that seem to become very active on special occasions, such as a pending visit of the president. A Ministry of Internal Affairs local officer, called the assistant superintendent for development, coordinates the county development association. The district development council is its basic unit of operation. The minister of internal affairs ultimately directs its activities on behalf of the president.

22. See Lutheran World Federation 1999. Not all international cooperation entities are prepared to work through already-existing local institutions such as clan-based organizations. Some prefer to create new entities. Such strategy has a way of creating a dependency relationship. Sustainability in the absence of donor funding becomes impossible. This issue is further discussed later.

23. Upriver communities are settler-established communities located along the banks of Liberia's major rivers. Most of these communities are within twenty miles of the major coastal cities of Liberia.

24. A typical example is the conflict between the commissioner of the township of Brewerville, located on the outskirts of Monrovia, and the Lower Brewerville Community Association. Affected by a shortage of water since the only community well is located several miles away from the Lower Brewerville area, members of this organization decided to sink a well within their area and therefore sought technical assistance from UNICEF. The commissioner of the township ordered the termination of the project as soon as it got under way, claiming that the association had no authority to sink a well in the township. She threatened to disband the organization if work continued on the well project. The prospects of unfavorable publicity in view of Brewerville's location within the orbit of greater Monrovia and pressure exerted through the Ministry of Internal Affairs led the commissioner to back down. Had this incident occurred in a community far from Monrovia, the commissioner could have terminated the well-digging project. Author's notes, and conversations with the deputy minister of internal affairs and members of the Lower Brewerville Community Association.

25. The Roman Catholic, Lutheran, United Methodist, and African Methodist Episcopal Zion denominations have been the foremost providers of postconflict trauma counseling. Zion Academy, a junior college operated by the AME Zion church, was the first school not only to provide trauma counseling to its students but also to organize a training of trainers course in postconflict trauma counseling.

26. The Interfaith Council, formerly known as the Inter-Faith Reconciliation Committee, was organized in 1990 as war loomed over Liberia and both the Doe government and its armed opponents seemed poised to torch the society. This group organized initial peace talks in 1990, and the peace proposals ultimately adopted as the original ECOWAS peace plan were first put forward by them.

27. Its leaders, the Catholic archbishop of Monrovia and the secretary-general of the National Muslim Council, are individuals of high reputation and integrity. Supported by an expanding domestic congregation and the Roman Catholic Church worldwide, the archbishop of Monrovia is by far the most influential Liberian today. The secretary-general of the National Muslim Council enjoys the support of the largest number of Muslins in Liberia and considerable international support. Even in the heat of Taylor's repression, most Liberians heeded pronouncements of the Interfaith Coun-

cil against repressive acts of the government. Playing on Christian fundamentalist sentiments, Taylor tried to cultivate a rival organization called the Christian Community, a group of largely Pentecostal preachers who promote precepts of religious intolerance. He also tried to create a rival organization of Muslims, led by an individual called Alhaji Taylor.

28. See Ministry of Education, Republic of Liberia, Annual Reports, 2001.

29. These include a new university established by the United Methodist Church. The African Methodist Episcopal Church and the African Methodist Episcopal Zion Church have both created postsecondary institutions.

30. The Catholic Don Bosco Center is noted for teaching its students not only high-level craftsmanship but also skills in finding employment or creating opportunities for self-employment. The Opportunity Industrial Center of Reverend Leon Sullivan operates in a similar manner.

31. From Phebe Medical Center, which is operated mainly by the Lutheran Church near Gbarnga, a network of rural health posts has been established to serve inhabitants of central Liberia.

32. The case of Francis J. Grant Memorial Hospital of Sinoe is illustrative. Owned by the state, this facility was, in 2000, jointly supported by the government of Liberia and an international nongovernmental organization called Children Aid Direct (CAD). The government's failure to pay salaries of health workers caused hospital staff to draw from a revolving fund established by CAD to provide drugs and supplies, thus exacerbating shortages of drugs and supplies and undermining hospital services. Health workers took recourse in organizing private health services with the drugs and equipment provided to this government-owned facility. Needless to say, the hospital has not been able to provide essential health services. See Sawyer et al. (2000).

33. For example, Loma women sell and buy vegetables, Grebo women coconuts, and Kru women fish.

34. For an understanding of the concept of "lemons market," see Akerlof (1970); as applied to peasant organizations, see Popkin (1988).

35. Author's interviews with leaders of microcredit associations (2000).

36. A car park is a terminal for buses and taxis that run out-of-town service.

37. See West African Examination Council Senior High School Results, 1999–2001, Ministry of Education, Monrovia.

38. Until 2000, I served as a member of a committee of the school board charged with resource mobilization.

39. Albert Porte was a distinguished schoolteacher and publicist whose critique of Liberian political processes spanned a period of fifty years—from the mid-1920s, when he wrote against corruption in government and excessive presidential authority, to the mid-1980s, when he criticized the military dictatorship and advocated the search for a new constitutional order. The proprietor is Porte's daughter-in-law.

40. An example of the former is a group called Special Emergency Life Food (SELF), organized during the course of war to assist in the short-term distribution of relief food; the Liberian Women's Initiative is an example of a local NGO with the long-term goal of women's empowerment.

41. SCF, for example, is involved in the rehabilitation of school facilities, of clinics, and, where pertinent, of roads to facilitate access to clinics and schools.

42. In 2000, there were fewer than fifty Liberian physicians working in government-run health delivery—a fraction of the number of Liberian physicians who now live on the eastern seaboard of the United States.

43. See European Union: African, Caribbean Pacific Economic Cooperation Agreements, otherwise known as Lomé I–V.

44. In 1992, at the suggestion of Taylor, the Carter Center persuaded ECOWAS to remove defensive weapons situated on the periphery of Monrovia. Shortly after the removal of the weapons, Taylor's NPFL launched "operation Octopus," a three-prong assault on Monrovia. Several thousand people perished. In mid-1997, the Carter Center encouraged political parties to participate in an electoral process that was stacked against them and subsequently to accept the results of the elections. Later, it pressured for the establishment of a human rights commission apparently to ameliorate the situation. The commission created by the government never actually functioned. Discouraged by the lack of progress in democratization, the Carter Center closed its office in Monrovia in 2000. Returning in 2003 at the height of Taylor's repression and violent conflicts in northwestern Liberia, the center's initial interest was in exploring the possibilities for holding elections.

45. There seems to be a standard format designed to provide for boards of directors' and donor entities' snapshots of local situations. A review of the quarterly or annual report of INGOs operating in Liberia, such as the International Foundation for Education and Self-Help (IFESH) and World Vision, reveals this pattern.

CHAPTER 4

Rethinking Governance

I F THE RAY OF HOPE IS TO BE CAPITALIZED UPON, A NEW CONCEPTION OF GOVER-
nance is needed. Like in other African countries, Liberia's failed political
order was founded on a theory of unitary sovereignty. This theory is unable
to support the constitution of a system of democratic governance.

In making the case for a new way of conceptualizing governance, I turn
first to the theory of unitary sovereignty and the unitary state as found in Africa
generally and Liberia in particular. I argue that adaptations in authority relations that have been attempted through decentralization and good governance
projects have failed to yield patterns of democratic governance in Liberia
mainly because Liberia has a highly centralized constitutional order, which is
underpinned by a theory of unitary sovereignty. Decentralization and good
governance programs, when attempted, did not lead to democratic governance.

With the prevailing tendency in the reconstitution of order in postconflict
situations in Africa being to refix the central state, efforts to "quick-fix Liberia,"
as Patrick Seyon (1998) calls it, has involved reassembling the state bureaucracy and the military and holding presidential and legislative elections in the
shortest possible time. Participatory opportunities offered to ordinary citizens in
these circumstances hardly extend beyond the periodic vote for leaders of the
central state, who are then expected to shape the "capable state" by implementing "good governance" programs. The fact that over the last quarter-century
such quick fixes have repeatedly failed in Liberia gives reason for deeper reflection and a search for alternative institutional arrangements. As discourse about
an alternative form of governance has usually taken place at the time of elections, concerns about who wins the presidency have tended to overshadow the
importance of constitutional reform and institutional design. Consequently,
campaign promises of candidates have led to high expectations among ordinary
people and obscured the impact of structural flaws that contribute to the failure

of the government to create conditions for democratic governance and self-reliant development. Repeated failure leads to cynicism and frustration and even violent outbursts. Thus rests the case for examining the limitations of the model of government used in Liberia, and for emphasizing placing constitutional reform at the core of postconflict reconstitution of governance and elections as one of several important reform measures.

■ Theories of Sovereignty and the Trajectory of African Governance

Theories of sovereignty have always helped scholars understand how institutions of governance are organized and how authority relations are structured in society. In complex societies, human beings engage in an array of rule-ordered relationships characterized by hierarchies as well as horizontal relationships and mixes of numerous kinds. Within any given context, the challenge is to fashion rule-ordered relationships that ensure peace and provide opportunities for self-actualization while ensuring standards of equity and justice.

Unitary Sovereignty and the Centralized State in Liberia and Elsewhere in Africa

As shown in Chapter 1, power in Liberia has been concentrated in the central government and reposed in the president. This arrangement is not unfamiliar to scholars. Thomas Hobbes's theory of unitary sovereignty helps us understand such situations where there exists a single source of authority. Vincent Ostrom (1995) has stressed that a fundamental problem ensues when sovereign authority consists of a monopoly of power: it cannot be held accountable to the law that it applies to others.

Liberia is not alone in its pattern of unitary sovereignty. Authority relations as structured in the colonial and postcolonial states of Africa have typically reflected the underpinnings of Hobbesian sovereignty. The French, for example, organized a highly centralized form of colonial administration that penetrated deep into African societies to ensure control and facilitate extraction. In Guinea, French administrators appointed village *manga* (headmen) and supervised them directly (Derman 1973); they also frequently presided over customary courts of appeal (Mamdani 1996) and appointed individuals without standing, even houseboys, as chiefs. This overcentralized system of administration was directed from Paris and referred to as the "overseas department" of the French government. Its chief preoccupation was to secure labor and ensure French monopoly of trade (Suret-Canale 1964).

Even with its system of "indirect rule," British colonial arrangement did not allow much autonomy. Chiefdoms and independent villages that were autonomous during precolonial times were frequently amalgamated and given ethnic classification and paramount chieftainships under leaders who were responsible to the British colonial governors, whose most important responsibility was the protection of British trade monopolies (Abraham 1978). Despite variations in style and structure, colonial rule in Africa was overcentralized in organization and unaccountable to the African peoples who were ruled.[1]

The structure of authority in the postcolonial state was not significantly altered at independence. Kathryn Firmin-Sellers (1999) has argued that even before independence was formally declared, what she calls the "processes of constitutional creation"—patterns of negotiation during the process of decolonization—were designed to produce a Hobbesian model of sovereign authority. She has shown how in Ghana (then the Gold Coast), British colonial actors and various clusters of African protagonists manipulated negotiating processes, seeking preferences that would yield exclusive control to one group of political elites over others in postindependence governance. The same strategies of aggregation of preferences obtained in the decolonization processes in francophone Africa. Even where negotiations broke down as in the case of Franco-Guinea negotiations in 1958, abrupt and hostile disengagement by the French created the conditions for total control by the Democratic Party of Guinea (PDG) (Yansane 1980).

With such beginnings, it is no surprise that after independence, African political elites built upon principles and practices that promoted exclusion even as they pronounced policies said to be intended to attain unity and development. Strategies frequently articulated to enhance "unity" and attain "development" typically encouraged recourse to the colonial legacy of command and control (Young 1994; Ake 1996). Centralized presidential (Selassie 1974) and neopatrimonial (Bratton 1994) orders became the dominant governance arrangements.

Although Liberia had a different colonial history, its process of state building in the postindependence period also yielded patterns of exclusion and hierarchical command and control. The creation of new political jurisdictions in the mid-1960s (as discussed in Chapter 1) did not curtail the powers of appointment of the president. Instead of appointing heads of provinces, the president now appointed heads of counties and the full array of county officials. Increased membership of the single-party legislature did not diminish the influence of the president over that body or authority relations within it.

At the regional scale, the formation of the Organization of African Unity in the early 1960s as well as Cold War rivalries of that period served to buttress the central state and reinforce presidential authority within African states. Principles of territorial integrity and noninterference were widely accepted regional norms that boosted solidarity among African leaders generally, even though enmity did exist between certain leaders (Naldi 1999; Thompson 1970). Cold War imperatives contextualized Hobbesian authority within the framework of one ideological *ism* or another. In Guinea, for example, Sékou Touré established a brand of personal rule under the banner of "African socialism" with a leaning toward the

"Eastern" bloc. In Sierra Leone, a chieftaincy brand of clientelism was established by the Magais with favorable disposition toward the British. In Côte
d'Ivoire, undisguised neocolonial control was evident. In most other West
African countries, struggles for control of the state continued among military
and civilian elites that maneuvered between and enjoyed the sponsorship of one
global power bloc or the other.

The exercise of sovereign authority in Liberia was not immune to these
postindependence developments and the dynamics generated by the Cold War
in Africa.[2] Campaigns for African "unity" and "development," as they played
themselves out within the context of the Cold War, created both internal and
external pressures to which Liberian authorities were constrained to respond.
For example, the structures of "native administration" patterned precisely on
colonial models required adjustments in the face of rising expectations from the
grassroots, sentiments of "African nationalism," and struggles for self-determination around Africa (Fahnbulleh 1985; Dunn 1979). The pervasive presence
and economic domination of multinational corporations also transformed the
nature of presidential authority by reducing dependence on hut taxes, fines, and
other forms of direct exactions from local communities and by increasing
reliance on corporate taxes, royalties, and export levies as the sources of governmental support. Yet presidential control over labor policies and practices and
over economic opportunities linked to the plantation and iron ore economies
became even more critical and required adjustments.[3] For a quarter-century
after World War II, presidential sovereignty bore the imprimatur of Tubman, as
Liberia remained nested within the U.S. ambit of global polarity.

Despite their calls for unity and the pursuit of development, Africa's centralized states failed to deliver either development or democracy. Much has
been written about their failure and need not be reviewed here.[4] Suffice it to
say that as the promise of development receded by the mid-1970s as the Cold
War waged on, the legitimacy of the centralized state was called into question.
As African societies relied more and more on alternative institutions to meet
basic needs, African states struggled to remain relevant and to exert control. In
some places, resistance to predation invited repression. Structural adjustment
programs (SAPs) were a set of responses fashioned by the Bretton Woods institutions to meet the economic challenges posed by growing crises of economic
governance in the late 1970s and early 1980s. While SAPs were meant to instill
economic discipline, decentralization was introduced as the most appropriate
governance framework to ensure improved access to goods and services and to
the prerogatives of governance at subnational jurisdictions.

■   Decentralization as Governance Strategy
     in the Context of the Unitary State

As institutional adaptations within the unitary state, decentralization strategies
were designed when the notion of meeting "basic needs" through "poverty

reduction" programs became the core objective of development initiatives. Dennis Rondinelli and others associated with the World Bank provided a basic definition of decentralization as the transfer of authority and resources to local and regional arenas. They also developed a classificatory scheme that distinguished three types of decentralization: *deconcentration*, the transfer of decisionmaking to subnational arenas without the transfer of control over resources or the prerogatives of accountability; *delegation*, the transfer of authority and control over resources but the retention of the prerogatives of accountability at the center; and *devolution*, full transfer of authority, resources, and accountability.[5] *Privatization* is sometimes seen as the fourth type of decentralization, in which authority, resources, and accountability interact in patterns directed by market forces.[6]

More recently, decentralization has been emphasized as a component of the good governance agenda and is seen as a strategy to enhance efficiency, participation of citizens, and responsiveness of government to citizens (Agrawal and Ribot 1999). Some studies have also noted the positive impact of decentralization on the reduction of corruption (Fisman and Gatti 2002) and as a strategy for postconflict peacebuilding (Seely 2001).[7]

Most analysts seem to agree that deconcentration is the form of decentralization most often experienced in Africa and that this is due mainly to the reluctance of centralized regimes to share control over resources with autonomous subnational institutions. Overcentralized regimes when pressed to decentralize are more likely to establish regional and local agencies of central authority than to devolve authority and resources to local or regional scales. Legal mandates and charters promulgated for the implementation of decentralization schemes in African countries hardly ever attain the goal of devolution. At best, local institutions of governance may be granted limited authority in resource generation and control, which often proves inadequate to accomplish the tasks prescribed in their mandates. For example, Uganda's much-acclaimed decentralization experiment presents a situation of local actors functioning with inadequate resources within a national political system that is guided by the influence of a strong national political leader (Livingstone and Charlton 2001).

In other cases, such as in Ghana, decentralization initiatives have not yet succeeded in breaking the hold of central bureaucracy and powerful central government–appointed district executives on regional decisionmaking processes (Ayee 1997). Observers tell us that even in Botswana, with its contemporary history of credible elections and open public realm, the decentralization program has not effectively devolved authority to local regimes (Olowu and Wunsch 2004). Lack of political will and viable strategies and the resistance of entrenched bureaucracies are among the factors most widely seen to impede decentralization (Smoke 2003). James Wunsch (2001) has identified four dimensions of decentralization that have not been carried out successfully in Africa as a result of central governments' reluctance to relinquish control.

These are planning and capital investment, budgeting and fiscal management, personnel systems and management, and finance and revenue.

■ The Liberian Experience with Decentralization

In Liberia, advocacy for decentralization is as old as the founding of the Liberian state. At the constitutional convention held in 1847 to proclaim the Liberian state, a major faction opposed the establishment of a unitary state dominated by a central government established in Monrovia (see Chapter 1). Led by the Reverend John Seys of Bassa, that faction also opposed the retention of property rights by the ACS (see Huberich 1947, vol. 2; Sawyer 1992). The domination of the central government over Liberia's governance processes and of the president over central government has been a recurrent concern throughout Liberian history. Calls for institutional reform have come from various quarters and are often driven by divergent motivations. Historically, leaders of upriver settler communities and coastal counties have always wanted greater local autonomy and Monrovia's acknowledgment of their subproprietary control, especially when they were isolated from Monrovia. Indigenous political communities such as the Grebo, Kru, and Vai also sought political parity as municipalities and townships, and their leaders sought to exercise leadership prerogatives similar to those exercised by local county officials.[8]

In the nineteenth century, revenue-sharing schemes between central government and county administrations evolved perforce as a result of transportation and communications difficulties and were codified into law.[9] However, the material conditions that influenced patterns of interaction that characterized subproprietary control in nineteenth-century Liberia began to change increasingly in favor of stronger central government control and excessive presidential prerogatives as the interior bureaucracy was established and strengthened in the early decades of the twentieth century.[10] As already stated, royalties and other receipts from Firestone and other foreign firms with whom resource extraction agreements were concluded as of the mid-1920s reduced central government's dependence on hut taxes to support its activities. By the mid-1940s, the resource base provided by natural resource concession agreements consolidated the concentration of centralized authority in the hands of the president. Gus Liebenow (1969) has shown how the erosion of the authority of the chairman of the TWP and the ascendancy of the role of the Standard Bearer of the TWP reduced the role of the party as a counterbalance to presidential authority within Liberia's de facto single-party system. Presidential exclusive control over government expenditure after legislative approval of the budget, among other factors, rendered perfunctory the legislative oversight of presidential authority in financial matters (see also Sawyer 1992). The exercise of presidential patronage reached its apogee under Tubman with the introduction of a public relations office system that distributed presidential largesse and encouraged sycophancy and fueled repression through the establishment of a network of presidential security informants, as mentioned in Chapter 1.

The need for institutional reforms to improve the distribution of the benefits of growth and to spawn development has been stressed in successive technical studies and by blue ribbon commissions since the 1950s.[11] Reform measures promulgated to achieve these more frequently led to increased presidential authority than to the dispersal of that authority to other centers. In the early 1960s, for example, the Special Commission on Government Operations (SCOGO) was established as one of the significant postwar attempts to fashion a strategy for institutional reforms of the public economy (Bettis and Imig 1969). Strategies adopted by this initiative and all others subsequently were driven by the prescriptions of the Reform tradition that dominated the field of public administration during the 1950s and 1960s.[12] For example, the centralization of government purchasing and of revenue collection was among the institutional changes promoted by SCOGO. Needless to say, such institutional reforms did more to strengthen presidential authority than to foster a diffusion of authority. The centralization of government disbursements under the warrant system ensured exclusive presidential control over the timing, magnitude, and nature of the disbursement of public funds, thereby giving the president near exclusive control over setting national priorities, despite constitutional provisions that require legislative oversight of financial transactions.

During the 1960s, as reforms designed to strengthen the management of public economy ended up strengthening the prerogatives of the president, a number of political reforms were also under way. As mentioned earlier, the creation by the central government of new political subdivisions with the status of counties, territories, statutory districts, and townships greatly expanded the administrative machinery of the government, especially of the executive. The politics of creating new political subdivisions and appointing local officials weighed heavily in favor of increased presidential authority and undermined the objective of rationalization and effectiveness, which management reforms were meant to promote in the first place. Creating statutory districts and townships and redrawing boundaries of chieftaincies and districts were most frequently guided by political considerations, such as the need to consolidate clientele relationships and create sinecures for the loyal. Thus, up to the end of the 1960s, efforts toward decentralization remained unimpressive and ineffective.

Tolbert's Decentralization Initiative

Institutional reforms designed to achieve decentralization developed more seriously after the death of Tubman in 1971 and the ending of the vast system of patronage that formed the foundation of his twenty-seven-year patrimonial presidency. A wave of rising expectations overtook Liberians following the death of Tubman. The upsurge of claims to property rights generally had to be addressed through institutional reforms.[13] Tubman's death after all those years of both benevolent and brutal control foretold the birth of a new era and the urgent need for a paradigmatic shift in governance approach. The need for a paradigmatic shift in the constitutional order became evident as calls for the election of county superintendents were made more frequently as of the early 1970s.[14]

Changing internal circumstances were also attenuated by external factors. Because the oil crisis and falling commodity prices left Liberia with high expenditures and lower export earnings, new economic strategies were needed. Regional and international pressures emanating from the struggle against Portuguese colonialism, rising anticolonial violence in southern Africa, the quest for a unified African position on the Arab-Israeli conflict, and the dynamics of Cold War competition, among other factors, required of the Liberian government new African-centered responses. The magnitude of the changes demanded by these internal and external developments far exceeded anything that could be achieved by refashioning the style of the presidency or dismantling the patronage system that supported it. Nothing short of a transformation of the constitutional order seemed appropriate. It was within this context that Tolbert sought to advance a decentralization initiative.

Between 1972 and 1978, Tolbert attempted to enhance decentralization by increasing local participation in development programs, by effectively coordinating government entities involved in developmental activities, and by integrating disparate development projects at the county level. He created in each county a position of assistant superintendent to be in charge of development activities and elevated the role of the superintendent in county development activities. Until this time, the superintendent was essentially the political vicegerent of the president. National ministries were engaged directly from Monrovia in the construction of roads, schools, and clinics and other developmental projects, and hardly any linkages existed among such projects. Through these changes, the role of superintendents and district commissioners as agents of development was accentuated.

Changes made incrementally toward decentralization when Tolbert became president in 1971 were assessed in 1978 when the Rural Development Task Force was established. The main reason the task force was established was to provide a coherent framework and trajectory for rural-based development, going beyond the ad hoc manner in which such programs had been undertaken over the previous seven years. By March 1979, the task force had developed a framework and plan of action that sought to fashion a more systemized and effective approach to decentralization. The new decentralization plan called for the establishment of subnational development councils as arenas of decisionmaking on development initiatives. This change, however, was not immediately accompanied by fiscal decentralization or the decentralization of decisionmaking regarding access to other resources. Transfer of fiscal and other resources was supposed to take place at later stages in the decentralization program. Equipment and supplies as well as financial controls remained centralized at government ministries in Monrovia as local outposts of national ministries were instructed and staffed to provide technical assistance to county and district development councils.[15] Despite increased staffing, local offices of national ministries were not provided with corresponding resources to provide the services required at subnational jurisdictions. They had to rely on support from Monrovia, so they did not even turn out to be effective depots in the process of deconcentration. For example, actors operating at the county level had to travel to Monrovia to process vouchers in order to access budgeted funds.[16]

The plan also failed to provide opportunities for horizontal integration so that two or more counties could cooperate on common development initiatives. Only national ministries were allowed such collaboration, but within a single county. The plan claimed to be a bottom-up approach to development, but it seemed oblivious to the importance of local knowledge and the role of indigenous expertise. Discussions about training, information flows, and problem solving generally proceeded with reference to imparting knowledge downward to district, chieftaincy, and village jurisdictions by multisector technical teams from the national government or external organizations. This orientation suggests that local people have nothing to offer by way of expertise in matters concerning their own development.

Notwithstanding its shortcomings, Tolbert's decentralization scheme as crafted by the Rural Development Task Force stimulated a national discussion that would have likely triggered a shift away from the governance pattern of overcentralization and concentration of authority in the hands of the president. Its potential contribution lay in the fact that it would have encouraged pressure, ultimately leading to devolution. However, this potential was also the most important obstacle to its full implementation. In a constitutional order dominated by hierarchies and supported by a national political culture that sustains such stratification, even strategies of deconcentration can be perceived as threatening to entrenched interests. President Tolbert was confronted with a challenge when he began putting the plan into effect. Unfortunately, he did not issue the final executive order authorizing fiscal decentralization as was expected on February 1, 1980. Apparently, caught among conflicting pressures, he could not muster the will to do so. Sadder still was his assassination in the military takeover of April 12, 1980.

The Limits of Deconcentration

Liberia's plan for decentralization, like others in Africa, could have hardly advanced beyond deconcentration without significant transformation of the constitutional order. The unitary state recognizes a single center of authority. Both Tubman's death and the exhortation of his successor, Tolbert, to the Liberian people to work toward "total involvement for higher heights" and to strive to move "from mat to mattress" heightened expectation of democratic change; however, the magnitude of the change required could not be reached within the framework of Tolbert's decentralization scheme.

At best, Tolbert hoped his plan would have led to more efficient performance of public economies and progressively greater participation of local people in managing the delivery of local public services. He pursued an impressive program of constructing rural roads, market sheds, and health posts; however, far from appeasing citizens, these development projects increased local people's quest to truly become meaningful participants in governing their own affairs. In the agricultural communities of Lofa, for example, coffee and cocoa farmers grew increasingly disgruntled with the intermediary role of government marketing boards and strove to explore the prospects of direct access to international markets. Local communities in Nimba and Lofa organized themselves to extend feeder road networks to outlying villages and sought access to community forest resources that had been ceded to private entities through concession agreements issued by the government. While government was reluctant to implement plans for fiscal decentralization and to fully implement a strategy of deconcentration, local communities were already engaged in the generation of resources through self-reliant initiatives. Even county superintendents appointed by the president protested attempts to redraw county boundaries by fiat.[17] A new pattern of government with multiple sites of authority was needed. The governance reform that was to potentially unfold in a cascading manner, beginning with Tolbert's program of deconcentration would have required the establishment of multiple sites of authority and would therefore have been a departure from a system based on a principle of presidential sovereignty.

As the government vacillated with programs of decentralization, self-organization of this period took on forms of horizontal linkages. Emergent linkages were more visible in the relationship between certain groups in the society, such as between the Federation of Liberian Youth (FLY) and rural communities in Bong County, and between Susukuu and rural communities of Grand Gedeh County.[18] Increased self-organization triggered by the new climate that prevailed after Tubman's death directly and quickly impacted governance processes and created an environment conducive to enlightened contestation. The sudden proliferation of independent newspapers and the availability of radio as a medium for the exchange of ideas supported this new environment. Within months after Tubman's death at least three independent news organs appeared on the newsstand; by 1978, no fewer than five appeared daily.

The TWP itself, the de facto single party, struggled under internal pressure to make the higher echelon of its leadership more inclusive, as many others in the larger society were already forging ahead with initiatives to organize opposition parties.[19] Unfortunately, by this time, conflicts generated by these contradictions could not be resolved through courts that were controlled by the president and the TWP—or by other conflict resolution mechanisms created by an oligarchy now under threat. Any informed observer would have concluded by the time of the overthrow of the TWP government in 1980 that Liberia's governing paradigm had been stretched to the limits of its capabilities and that neither government repression nor the decentralization program the government sought to put in place would provide a solution.

■ Going Beyond Decentralization

It is important to note that decentralization does not automatically create opportunities for citizens to participate in running their own affairs. Power devolved to subnational jurisdictions could very well be appropriated by local bosses. Even where elected by local constituencies, local leaders could hold themselves accountable to national leaders or to sources other than local people.[20] There are numerous cases in Africa where local elites exclude certain groups from participation in community development activities or deny or limit their access to the outcomes of those initiatives (Osmani 2001). There are cases where traditional chiefs cease being accountable to their people and no longer exercise authority in their interest or on their behalf. African history has its share of local chiefs who were despots (Lonsdale 1986). Insensitivity to the rights and interests of women and ethnic and religious minorities, or even their exclusion, is a common occurrence in many local government arrangements (Blair 2000; Peters 1994).[21]

Thus, while attaining devolution is a step forward, it is insufficient. That is why Osmani's (2001) notion of democratic devolution and Jesse Ribot's (2003) ideas on democratic decentralization have placed added emphasis on the importance of anchoring local governance in the broad-based participation of all categories of local people, both as individuals and as participants in the variety of organizations that define associational life in their communities.[22] It is critical that the participation of individuals and groups be substantive and significant enough not only to demand accountability of leaders, but also to endow ordinary local people with appropriate capabilities and opportunities to serve as local governors. This means that ordinary people must be actors at the constitutional level of decisionmaking; they must be participants in the making of rules (about how rules that govern their affairs are made) and who get to make such rules. Such local political processes must also reflect the vibrancy that is typically characteristic of associational life of local communities. The discourse that attends interactions in their rotating credit (*susu*) clubs, women's organizations, age-set associations, and others must find expression in the local political process and thereby lend vitality to the local public realm. All of these activities—not simply the act of voting in elections—define the democratic character of local governance.

Democratic devolution attained in local governance carries no implications of atomization or isolation. Local communities are never self-sufficient. Human beings aggregate in communities of various types and sizes to meet their needs. A primary school could be established and run by a single village, but several villages may be required to establish a high school. It may further require the efforts of an entire province or perhaps two or more provinces to establish and run a university or a referral hospital. This is why democratic devolution cannot be seen as the ultimate in democratic governance.

The crafting of institutions linking communities vertically and horizontally is indispensable to the functioning of human beings in complex societies. Thus, patterns of democratic local governance must exist as both discrete entities as well as integral parts of configurations of patterns of governance of various levels.[23] This is how decentralization can be transcended and polycentric institutions for self-governance attained. Can polycentric institutions of self-governance be crafted for Liberia? Before addressing this question in the next two chapters, I discuss the good governance framework, which is the second adaptation made to the centralized state in Africa generally and in Liberia particularly in efforts to constitute democratic governments upon a theory of unitary sovereignty.

■ The Good Governance Agenda as a Post–Cold War African Governance Framework

The exercise of unfettered presidential authority was not always a prescription inscribed in the written laws of African countries, although this was the case in some countries that were declared one-party states or states whose leaders were declared presidents-for-life (Zolberg 1966; Jackson and Rosberg 1982). Authority relations that were absolutist in character were more often defined by rules-in-use and not always by stipulations of written documents called constitutions.[24] In many cases, Lockean principles of government by consent of the governed and majoritarianism were enshrined in written constitutions of African countries (Locke 1952). Also enshrined in some African constitutions, such as that of Liberia, were principles of separation of powers as articulated by Montesquieu ([1748] 1966). Whatever the case, in the context of the Cold War, these principles were not always considered critical to African governance, surely not by external actors for whom the fight for or against communism was of the highest priority. Authoritarian and repressive African governments frequently received external support against the demands of local populations for democratic participation. Popular uprisings were frequently labeled as proimperialist or procommunist, depending on the ideological lenses through which they were seen. This was to change significantly after the fall of the Soviet Union and before the fight against terrorism took on such high visibility after the September 11, 2001, attack on the World Trade Center in New York.

While it is much too early to determine the future directions of the global antiterrorist campaign and their possible impact on the course of African governance, one can say that since the ending of the Cold War, African governance frameworks have been influenced largely by principles of liberal democracy promoted by the Bretton Woods institutions. Using these principles, the Bretton Woods institutions have taken the lead in developing what is called the *good governance* agenda for African countries and have promoted that agenda as a conditionality for development assistance.

With emphasis on governance and not solely on government, the good governance agenda marks a departure from previous times when only governments were considered relevant actors in running the affairs of African countries. Good governance seeks to bring civil society and the private sector into partnership with government. It anticipates a vibrant civil society and a viable private sector as copartners in what should be a tripartite partnership.[25] Considered within the context of the larger international community, a context characterized by globalization, a larger partnership is conceived that involves an array of external actors, including individual foreign governments, IGOs, INGOs, and multinational corporations.

As a political governance arrangement, the good governance framework is meant to provide the political and administrative enabling environment and institutional support for market-driven economic development. It is meant to produce the "capable state," one that is responsive to relevant elements of the society—"embedded autonomy," as Peter Evans (1992) calls it, ensuring effective and efficient macroeconomic institutional management, a competent and credible legal system, a streamlined and efficient public service system, and so on, all operating with transparency and accountability. Specific outcomes sought by the good governance agenda include the attainment of constitutionalism; political pluralism; the protection of human rights generally and the rights of women and children particularly; decentralization; transparency and accountability in governance; and the strengthening of civil society and the private sector.

Constitutionalism is the term used with reference to the entrenchment in governance processes, habits, and practices having to do with a commitment to rule of law, to the spirit and letter of written constitutions, and to the institutions of governance those constitutions prescribe. Constitutionalism attempts to depersonalize power. Subsumed under this rubric are concerns that include commitment to principles and practices of due process of law; support for and acceptance of the establishment of independent legislatures and judiciaries; and stipulation of and faithfulness to the observance of term limits—especially for the office of president. Political pluralism underscores the need for departure from the de facto single-party systems of the postindependence era and establishment of competitive multiparty political arrangements. It emphasizes the role of elections in choosing political leadership and thus the need for the establishment of electoral bodies that are autonomous, properly funded, and capable of conducting credible and competitive elections.

Respect for human rights and respect for the rights of women and children are among the commitments African governance processes are also expected to uphold as part of the good governance agenda. Africa's agenda for human rights and the rights of women and children is grounded in provisions of international and African regional conventions and is driven by influences emanating largely from the international community through a network of governmental organizations, NGOs, and IGOs that operate on all scales at all levels of governance.[26] Considerations of transparency and accountability have to do with the openness of public processes and the accountability of public actors to constituencies of individuals and communities. These considerations are more frequently raised with respect to processes of public policy decisionmaking and implementation, especially within the area of economic and financial affairs, with a view to curtailing corruption and rent-seeking.[27]

The Promise of Good Governance

The good governance agenda has presented African regimes and peoples with new opportunities. In some African countries, it provides a much-appreciated relief to prodemocracy activists, opposition political leaders, and others who have been struggling to expand and preserve civic space at the national scale. It has been able to ease, if not resolve, some of Africa's governance dilemmas if in no other way than by serving notice on Africa's dictators that they are not likely to find allies in the global order and that they must negotiate with their compatriots new forms of governance accommodation. Thus, the agenda has resulted in the elevation of elections, sovereign national conferences, and coalition arrangements as standard features of African governance. Removal of external props that supported regimes such as Mobutu's in Zaire (now the Democratic Republic of Congo), Doe's in Liberia, and Siad Barre's in Somalia led to their unraveling in violence that, in some cases, set wider areas ablaze.

The proliferation of civil society organizations is a direct product of the good governance agenda. Initiatives to promote human rights, freedom of the press, judicial independence, and many other governance concerns are indicative of the vibrancy, new hope, and sense of efficacy infused into African governance processes by efforts to implement good governance programs. However, as discussed earlier, unless deep roots are planted by civil society organizations in African societies, their vibrancy could prove ephemeral.

At African regional and subregional scales, efforts to establish judicial regimes to address human rights and criminal offenses seem to be taking on greater urgency. Sentiments against military takeovers, which are becoming pervasive, are being crystallized in resolutions, and concrete steps are being made to build or strengthen capacities for peacekeeping and conflict resolution.[28] For the first time since its founding in 1963, the OAU, in 1990, sponsored an all-Africa conference of civil society organizations and popular movements to review African governance situations and to consider ways to improve the participation of African peoples in African governance arrangements (UNECA 1990). Although more recently the mechanism of peer review established by the New Partnership for African Development (NEPAD) falls short of making leaders accountable to the people on whose behalf they speak, there is some movement toward greater accountability at the African regional scale. All of these are good governance's responses to post–Cold War global transformations and the new governance challenges they presented in Africa.

Limitations of the Good Governance Agenda in Postconflict Situations

Frequently, and unfortunately, good governance programs are presented as a solution to the broad range of Africa's governance dilemmas. When applied as cure-all, good governance programs can overstep the limits of their capabilities. Classic examples can be found in the attempts to implement the good governance agenda in countries whose social fabric has been deeply torn by war and violent conflicts. In Rwanda, for example, a major aspect of the good governance package designed for implementation four years after the genocide of 1994 was the holding of elections. Not only was this prescription insensitive to the deep-seated ethnic rifts that has denied Rwandans any sense of shared community as a single body politic, it also ignored the turbulent regional environment that surrounded Rwanda and of which Rwanda has been an integral part.[29]

The case of Liberia is equally demonstrative of the limitations, if not the futility, of the standardized good governance program when applied in inappropriate circumstances. Liberia's good governance program began with an emphasis on elections as an exit from war and the beginning of a process of democratization. Elections were held in 1997 in an environment of fear and deep suspicion, where armed men continued to roam the countryside and where the leader of the largest fighting group maintained considerable military influence even in the presence of a regional peacekeeping force. All efforts by civil society organizations and most political parties to secure a postponement of elections until a more conducive atmosphere could be created were rejected by regional and international sponsors of the Liberian peace process. Elections saw the installation of a repressive regime. Subsequent to elections, the United Nations and other sponsors of a good governance agenda for Liberia attempted to implement initiatives designed for building state institutional capacity, as if the fundamental postelection problem in Liberia stemmed from a lack of state capacity. No one was surprised when the program failed and closed down.

The Challenges of Good Governance

Good governance programs have sparked or exacerbated political struggles in other parts of Africa where there have not been violent conflicts of the magnitude of those in Liberia or Rwanda. In some African countries, debates about term limits, for example, have degenerated into serious conflicts that have deepened divisions and sown or nourished seeds of potential violence.[30] Electoral reforms proceed haltingly as executives struggle to dominate electoral systems in many African countries.[31] In countries such as Nigeria, the very concept of constitutionalism is under threat as legislators and the executive become deadlocked in power struggles that defy mediation and criminality resulting from years of military misrule put ordinary people at risk. There is also the threat to stable governance posed by the misuse of majoritarian principles as a weapon against large oppositions that represent significant portions of the population.[32] These are only some of the dilemmas that the good governance program is challenged to address.

With all its shortcomings, the good governance program is obtaining substantial success in some African countries. Mali, Senegal, and Ghana are among the most visible success stories. From the establishment of processes of reconciliation and peacebuilding to the formation of a multiparty political system and the holding of two presidential elections, Mali has apparently progressed beyond ethnic-based political conflicts and military rule and can be said to be in the process of consolidating a system of liberal democracy through the good governance approach. Multiparty political processes are under way, and values of political consensus building are taking root. At the national level, Senegal has had a long experience with building political consensus for multiparty governance. Along with Ghana, it represents one of Africa's rare cases where the ruling party has been defeated in multiparty elections, and one of a very few cases in Africa where an incumbent president was defeated and relinquished office without a substantial struggle.

Thus, good governance can be considered an important step forward if seen as a strategy designed to move Africa beyond the circumstance of personal rule and single-party dictatorships, which has been the dominant pattern of governance from independence to the ending of the Cold War. However, if the nurturing of civil society is one of good governance's most important contributions to democratic governance in Africa, then the evolving role of civil society in establishing and sustaining governance institutions must be one of its most important preoccupations. The record shows that in many African countries, civil society's existence is precarious, its engagement with government entails more feuds and acrimonious struggles than partner-like collaboration, and its survival hinges more on the availability of external life support than on nourishing roots deeply planted in local society.[33] African governments are only grudgingly accepting civil society's limited participation in political decisionmaking processes. And even this grudging acceptance is often induced by pressure from external donors. In some cases, local NGOs have been emboldened by external actors and have seized the opportunity to demand such partnership participation.[34]

Deepening Governance Experience

Considered fully, the good governance agenda is an effort to move African countries beyond autocracy and authoritarianism to political liberalism. The movement from autocracy to liberalism is significant, because it begins to put African peoples in the governance picture by extending political and civil rights to larger constituencies, employing electoral systems to select leaders, and establishing a system of laws independent of the wishes and prerogatives of leaders. Yet, even at their best, political formations with sovereignty modeled on such Lockean principles present a circumstance of continued struggle to ensure that sovereign authority does not revert to absolutism. Constitutionalism, where crystallized in the separation of powers, especially where legislatures and courts are independent and credible, can serve to limit presidential excesses in the exercise of executive authority; however, Robert Michels ([1911] 1966) has reminded us that even elites with opposing or conflicting objectives can, through constant interaction, forge strong solidarity. Success of this arrangement requires constant struggle and perpetual vigilance of citizens. Vincent Ostrom (1995, 236) is reserved about the promise of this arrangement when he asserts that "the separation of powers tradition offers only the prospect that the struggle to maintain human freedom in the context of political order can continue as an unending struggle." Vigilance manifested in seasonal demands for accountability through periodic elections is insufficient. Efforts to maintain a stable process of elite circulation do frequently yield elite collusion or gridlock. Such efforts do not always unlock the potential of ordinary people to govern themselves, thereby fulfilling the promise of democratic governance. As René Lemarchand (1992) has correctly argued, terminating authoritarianism is a far cry from establishing democracy.

If efforts to attain democratic governance are to be deepened through good governance, it should be remembered that struggles for engagement with government are not without implications and consequences for power relationships. Those who exercise prerogatives of power are not likely to share such prerogatives only because they are called upon by external donors to establish governing partnerships with civil society. This is why calling on governments to work in partnership with civil society in a single center of authority offers less profound possibilities for democratic transformation than reconstituting order such that multiple sites of authority are established at multiple levels of governance. At the very least, civil society organizations, seeking partnership in governance with government under the good governance approach, will have to deepen their roots in local communities if they expect to stand up as effective partners in governance at the level of the central state. Failing to do so, they tend to become largely economistic, as is typically the case with professional associations and interest groups; escapist, as is the case of cultist associations; or broadly civic, as is the case of prodemocracy and human rights organizations.[35]

By establishing overlapping linkages and aggregated forms of collective action rooted in cooperation among communities of citizens, civil society organizations can draw from and be sustained by the immense capital stock available to aggregates of local communities even when the support such organizations receive from external sources would have long since been terminated. In this way they can truly claim ownership as genuine actors in processes of governance and development. Amartya Sen (1999) reminds us that entitlements are rights we derive from our participation in development and not as gifts from benefactors be they government or others. The challenge that faces civil society organizations that struggle for engagement with governmental hierarchies through good governance programs is to appropriately ground themselves in society and press the governance agenda beyond what is essential to attaining good governance to that which is essential to attaining self-governance. This transformation requires a different configuration of governance institutions and a different theory of sovereignty.

■ The Case for Constitutional Change in Postconflict Liberia

To say that patterns of unitary government practiced in Liberia over the years have now failed and are no longer appropriate to meet citizens' demands for meaningful participation beyond the election of the leadership of the central state is quiet obvious and has been at least since the 1970s. As already discussed, in the late 1970s, the TWP government's program of decentralization was essentially a plan for deconcentration that turned out to be too little too late. Even that limited program of deconcentration was overtaken by the coup d'état of 1980.

After purging his opponents from both the military and the political process, Doe, as of 1984, sought to reinvent himself into the mold of Tubman. The story of how he manipulated the constitution-making process, which was at the core of the transition from military to constitutional rule, demonstrates how Liberia missed a good opportunity to lay foundations for establishing a system of democratic governance and is worth highlighting.

The 1986 Constitution: A Missed Opportunity

The constitution-making process following the military takeover of 1980 provided a good opportunity to carefully analyze Liberia's governance dilemmas and to fashion appropriate constitutional reforms. The commission appointed to draft the new constitution viewed its assignment as an opportunity to set in motion a process of constitutional choice and not only as a technical task of preparing a legal document.[36] For two years the commission circulated versions of the suspended constitution to various public audiences, raised critical issues for their consideration, and facilitated informed debates in a variety of forums, ranging from village palaver huts and townhalls to university auditoriums and radio talk shows. Written submissions were received from a spectrum of organizations. Although the draft produced by the commission after such broad discourse did not provide as adequate a basis for local participation in governance as the people had insisted during the debates, many of its provisions that curtailed presidential authority and called for greater presidential accountability and broader participation by local people were deleted by the constitutional advisory assembly that was set up to review the commission's draft.

An inspection of key differences between the draft prepared by the constitution commission and the revised constitution approved by the assembly (Table 4.1) shows that an opportunity for making strides toward democratic governance was indeed missed. For example, the constitution commission's draft provided for the election of a "committee of county leaders," whose responsibility would have been to select a panel of candidates from which the president would have appointed the county superintendent and would have, twice a year, reviewed the performance of the superintendent, reported its assessment to the president, and published that assessment within ninety days. The "committee of county leaders" was to consist of one member elected from each of the county's legislative districts and the paramount chief, also elected from each chieftaincy jurisdiction. While this arrangement did not provide adequately for local governance, it did strive to give local people greater voice in the selection and oversight of their superintendent. This provision was wholly deleted from the revised draft, and the president was bestowed with the unrestrained authority to appoint and dismiss superintendents at his pleasure.

Two other examples are also illustrative: The draft constitution provided for the establishment of a number of independent bodies, including a judicial service commission, a public service commission, and the office of the auditor general. Provisions were included to ensure that those appointed to these commissions would be individuals of integrity and high qualification and that their tenure and remuneration would be protected, thus ensuring their inde-

Table 4.1 Key Differences Between Constitution as Drafted by Constitution Commission and as Revised by Advisory Assembly

Issue	As Drafted by Commission	As Revised by Assembly
Appointment of judges by president	From list submitted by Judicial Service Commission	Proposal eliminated
Appointment of super-intendents by president	From list submitted by proposed Committee of County Leaders	Proposal eliminated
Creation of Committee of County Leaders	To include paramount chiefs of county and one member elected from each legislative district in county	Proposal eliminated
Responsibilities of Committee of County Leaders	Recommend to president candidates for appointment as superintendent; assess performance of county officials, submit report to president and publish report; recommend dismissal of superintendent	Proposal eliminated
Appointment of military officers by president	As of rank of colonel or equivalent	As of rank of lieutenant or equivalent
Tenure of president	Four years; eligible for second term of four years; provision entrenched, not subject to amendment	Six years; eligible for second term of six years; entrenchment eliminated
Death of president-elect	Incumbent holds on; new elections held in 60 days	VP-elect accedes to presidency commencing a term of office
Declaration of assets	Senior officials of government to declare assets before taking office	Proposal eliminated
Creation of Judicial Service Commission	Majority of members recommended by Bar Association; commission to recommend candidates for judicial appointment and monitor performance of judicial officials	Proposal eliminated
Creation of Ombudsman Commission	Three-person commission to investigate public complaints, including administrative acts of arbitrariness except where matter is before judiciary	Proposal eliminated
Creation of Public Service Commission	Five-person commission to supervise an open and merit-based system of public services	Proposal eliminated (civil service continues to operate under presidential control)
Auditor general	Tenure to be protected; legislature to exercise oversight of office	Proposal eliminated (auditor general works under presidential oversight)

pendence. The responsibilities of the judicial service commission, for example, included setting standards for recruitment to the judiciary and monitoring compliance to those standards. The auditor general's office was to be independent of the president, operate with legislative oversight, and perform services authorized by both the executive and the legislature. In the assembly's review, provisions establishing these commissions were deleted or altered so that the need for the legislature to establish some of them was only acknowledged. Thus, despite years of questionable judicial performance and seething corruption in government, efforts to improve the situation through constitutional reform were thwarted.

Promulgation of the reforms proposed by the constitution commission would have opened the door for further reforms, especially with respect to presidential appointments and control over public expenditures, two areas in which executive latitude is hardly limited. For example, the executive exercises sole control over expenditure after the budget has received legislative approval through what often amounts to a perfunctory process of scrutiny. Decisions regarding dispensing allotments and making budgetary transfers across government agencies are solely the prerogatives of the executive and are legally handled without legislative oversight; consequently, they have become a source of enormous powers assigned to the president and his subordinates. Questions of fiscal equivalency and revenue sharing raised by local people during the constitutional debates would have gained currency in an ongoing debate if the incremental steps proposed toward greater accountability and democratization in the draft constitution had not been compromised by the constitutional advisory assembly.

It is clear that choices made by those in the constitutional advisory assembly who reviewed and revised the draft constitution at that time were not influenced by the openly expressed views of the Liberian people but instead by other considerations. As it turned out, many members of the assembly subsequently joined the political party organized to promote the presidential candidacy of Samuel Doe and became officials in the elected government headed by Doe, who heavily rigged the 1985 elections. Sensing defeat in view of the high voter turnout, Doe disbanded the elections commission and appointed a fifty-person vote-counting group that declared him the winner of the presidential poll. Senior U.S. government officials encouraged opposition leaders to accept the results of the elections, claiming that since the vote-counting group had declared Doe the winner by 51 percent of the votes, the elections reflected substantial progress in Liberia's democratization process and represented a significant departure from standard African electoral practices where leaders typically claim winning as many as 99 percent of the votes.

The revised constitution reestablished presidential autocracy, the rigged elections confirmed the transformation of a military strongman into an autocratic president, and cooperating members of the constitutional advisory assembly became officials of government and beneficiaries of Doe's autocratic regime. For the majority of Liberians who had hoped that the constitution-making exercise would have provided an opportunity to reform Liberia's governing institutional arrangements, a referendum held on the revised constitution offered no acceptable alternative to their adoption of the flawed document. It offered a choice between adopting a constitution that confirmed the overlordship of the president on the one hand, and prolonging the tenure of a repressive military government on the other. For most Liberians, this choice was as painful as it was unfair.

False Start with Good Governance

The failed constitutional reform exercise of the 1980s and the legalization of autocratic rule through elections in 1985 contributed in no small measure to a deeper crisis of governance and the collapse of the state in 1989. The peace settlement of 1996 could have benefited from reflections on these experiences and those of earlier periods in Liberia's political history. Those involved in the peace process could have sought to examine how the system of unitary sovereignty had become so perverse. The rush to elections foreclosed opportunities for such reflections, and once again elections provided the legal framework for installing an autocratic leader. Thus, like Doe a decade earlier, Charles Taylor showed how in a system based on unitary sovereignty, presidential prerogatives placed in the wrong hands can be exploited, legislatures co-opted and humiliated, and judiciaries rendered resolutely impotent regardless of the assistance and prodding from external sources. The most glaring lessons from these two experiences is that a good governance program for Liberia that does not focus on the nature of the governance paradigm itself can be a false start with tragic consequences.

It is true that individual stewardship and personal comportment in office are very important, but even more important in the long run are the institutional arrangements—the rules that pattern authority relationships. The creation of an electoral system for choosing leaders is an important governance reform measure; however, its impact can be short-lived if deeper systemic flaws persist. A president who has the sole authority to appoint prison wardens, sheriffs, district commissioners, county attorneys, superintendents, the minister of justice, and judges of courts, including the Supreme Court, is legally entrusted with all-inclusive prerogatives to shape the rule of law and the course of justice in society. This is too much power for any person, no matter how humble, compassionate and knowledgeable that person may be. A president who has the sole authority to determine disbursements of public funds through a warrant prepared by his assistant and passed unchecked by any other independent authority is empowered to exercise exclusive control over the public purse, notwithstanding the legislature's authority to review and approve the national budget. The centralization of control over the natural resources of a country and the exercise of that control through governance mechanisms that are ultimately responsible only to the president provides leeway for the manipulation and use of those resources for whatever purposes.

Some have argued that presidential domination does occur because the other branches of government have been weak. This is partially true. For most of Liberia's existence, there has been a single party–dominated legislature. But with a reservoir of powers assigned to the presidency, how could presidential machinations not overwhelm the competitive multiparty system upon which legislative independence depends? How could members of the legislature not act strategically in their own interests in such situations? A sense of mutuality of interest and bond of solidarity is likely to develop over time, and this is likely to deeply affect the quality of representation that a legislature provides. Alternatively, legislators who are not prepared to dance to the tune played by the president will at best find themselves isolated, unable to deliver, and therefore wholly irrelevant; or at worst, they could find themselves impeached, expelled, and branded as subversives. What check can exist on a president who has available the entire governmental infrastructure as a patronage machine?

Citizens who may act only as seasonal voters also cannot constitute a significant check on presidential powers. Establishing autonomous sites of decisionmaking powers where citizens can act in matters that affect them turns out to be the most critical aspect of democratic governance. Citizens' participation in town, city, and county councils and on boards that make decisions about schools, health care delivery, security, and the vast array of public goods is at the core of a system of democratic governance and the foundation of democratic peace.

Liberia may possibly present an extreme case of presidential sovereignty in an overcentralized governmental system, but it is not unique. Several other African countries have similar patterns of government. Many are struggling to institute good governance reforms. However, the general experience is that only those who seek to institute reforms that establish sites of power at multiple levels of governance are likely to establish processes of democratic governance (Olowu and Wunsch 2004). What African countries need is a fundamental shift away from a system of unitary government so that there can be several centers of authority underpinned by a system of shared sovereignty in which ordinary people acting as empowered citizens can *meaningfully participate* in an array of governance institutions at local, provincial, national, and even regional scales where necessary. Chapter 7 explores in practical terms the possibilities of establishing such a polycentric system of governance in Liberia.

▦ Notes

1. Although historians have differed regarding the nuances of colonialism's impact on Africa, there is broad agreement as to its dominant nature, organizational structures, and relationship with African societies as described here. See, for example, Boahen (1964, 1987); Suret-Canale (1964); Crowder (1968); Rodney (1973); Ki-Zerbo (1978); and Fieldhouse (1999).

2. By postindependence, I refer to the period immediately following the wave of African independence that began in the mid-1950s and continued through the 1960s; this is the early part of the longer period referred to as the postcolonial era that extends from the late 1950s to the ending of the Cold War at the close of the decade of the 1980s.

3. See Sawyer (1992, chap.10); van der Kraaij (1983); and Clower et al. (1966).

4. See, for example, Wunsch and Olowu (1995); Zartman (1995); and Schwab (2001).

5. See Cheema and Rondinelli (1983); Rondinelli, Nellis, and Cheema (1984); and Rondinelli, McCullough, and Johnson (1989).

6. See Cohen and Peterson (1999); Barkan (1998); and Rondinelli, McCullough, and Johnson (1989).

7. Although Seely (2001, 505) was concerned with the use of decentralization as a political strategy for what she called "co-optation, legitimization and consolidation," her analysis really shows how, faced with Tuareg insurgency, the Malian government deployed decentralization as an instrument of peacebuilding.

8. The upsurge of Grebo ethnonationalism, for example, has been well documented. See Martin (1968).

9. See Revenue Acts of 1869 and 1875 in Republic of Liberia, *Acts of the National Legislature.*

10. These developments are fully discussed in Sawyer (1992); see Chapters 7–11.

11. Even before the 1950s, the League of Nations Commission of Inquiry, established in 1930, had recommended the substantial government reform.

12. The Reform tradition sought to rationalize and improve efficiency in public administration through processes of consolidation and amalgamation. For an incisive critical analysis of this tradition, see Vincent Ostrom (1974).

13. Liebenow (1987) has referred to the upsurge of claims during the period of the 1970s as "the gathering storm."

14. Abeodu B. Jones and Edward B. Kesselly were among Liberian intellectuals making such calls.

15. See Rural Development Task Force, *Plan of Action for Operationalizing the Strategies and Tactical Measures for Rural Development in Liberia,* RDTG/DOC/7, Monrovia, April 1979.

16. According to the task force, some government agencies, such as the ministries of finance and of planning and economic development and the bureau of the budget, were most resistant to any form of decentralization. See, *Plan of Action,* cited in the preceding note.

17. See Clapham (1976) for an account of one such protest.

18. The collaboration among young professionals, traders of the marketing association, and students in support of my candidacy for mayor of Monrovia in 1978–1979 was illustrative of such horizontally linked self-organization for enhanced political participation.

19. Again, my own experience is illustrative. In 1977–1978, I was offered the position of superintendent of Sinoe County or the post of ambassador to newly independent Mozambique.

20. Ribot (1999) has documented several such cases in Senegal and elsewhere in Africa.

21. Examples of strongmen and autocrats who rule local communities can also be found elsewhere in the world (Fox and Aranda 1996).

22. Emphasis here is on civic engagement in which horizontal patterns of association are not only prevalent but dominant. As Putnam (1993) has observed, associational life dominated by vertical patterns of association is more likely to breed relations of subjects to masters. Horizontal associations are more likely to encourage reciprocity and mutual trust and respect, factors essential to democratic participation.

23. These issues are central to the establishment of multiple-level governing institutions and are discussed in greater detail in the next chapter.

24. Elinor Ostrom (1990) and her colleagues, in formulating the Institutional Analysis and Development framework, have rightly differentiated "rules-in-use" from "rules-on-the-books," distinguishing the actual rules that drive patterns of interaction from those that are supposed to be upheld and specified in written documents. This and related analytic distinctions are further discussed in the next chapter.

25. Civil society is used with reference to the array of organizations of collective action that are not directly a part of the government or profit-making entities associated with the private sector. These range from religious-based bodies to professional organizations such as teachers associations. Debate about the definition of civil society and its role in governance is vigorous and ongoing. See, for example, Howell and Pearce (2001).

26. Since the Universal Declaration of Human Rights, a number of other international conventions on rights have been declared. These include the International Covenant on Civil and Political Rights, and the International Covenant on Economic, Social and Cultural Rights. For Africa, there is also the Declaration on the Right to Development, adopted by the General Assembly of the United Nations in 1986. Related African instruments include the African Charter on Human and Peoples Rights. International conventions on women's rights include the Convention on the Elimination of All Forms of Discrimination Against Women (CEDAW), and the Beijing Declaration and Platform. The most widely known international convention designed for the protection of the rights of children is the Convention on the Rights of the Child (CRC) adopted by the General Assembly in 1989.

27. See, for example, UNDP's Program of Accountability and Transparency (PACT), www.sdnp.undp.org, and the World Bank's Financial Management, Transparency and Accountability Project (FMTAP), www.worldbank.org.

28. See, for example, the website of the AU (formerly OAU), www.africa-union .org for documents such as the Grand Bay Declaration and Plan of Action, adopted in 1999, *The OAU Mechanism of Conflict Prevention, Management and Resolution: An Assessment,* the Algiers Declaration of 1997, and numerous resolutions and protocols designed to establish an African criminal court and implement provisions of the African Charter on Human and People's Rights, which called for the establishment of an African human rights court.

29. Four years after elections were originally scheduled under a UNDP-sponsored good governance program, Rwanda continued to struggle with deep-seated ethnic-based political strife, as was reflected in increasing rather than decreasing ethnic appropriation of Rwanda's national political processes. This was evident in the dismissal, detention, and controversial trial of President Bizimungu and others and the assumption of the office of president by Vice President Kagame. Scores of thousands of people allegedly connected with the 1994 genocide remain imprisoned. Heavily disputed elections were eventually held as reconciliation continues to be a most difficult challenge within the framework of current governance arrangements.

30. From about 2003, several African countries have either experienced crisis or been brought to the brink of crisis as a result of the imposition of presidential term limits. In Guinea, as a result of a government-sponsored referendum, the provisions of the written constitution that limited presidential tenure were altered, allowing President Conté to contest elections for additional terms. He was declared winner of allegedly heavily rigged elections, and disgruntlement among opposition parties and civil society was met with strong-arm, often violent, measures by the government. In January 2005, the government announced an assassination attempt on President Conté's life and seemed fixed on linking this development to opposition parties. Reports circulating in April and May linked Charles Taylor to an alleged plot to kill the Guinea leader. After encountering parliamentary defeat and strong opposition from within his party, President Muluzi of Malawi reluctantly agreed to step down after his second term; however, in a fit of anger, he imposed a handpicked successor on his party and the electorate. As soon as the new president sought to exercise some independence, he was forced out of the party by Muluzi. In Togo, after more than thirty years in office, President Eyadema engaged in all sorts of subterfuges to prolong his hold on power. When he died in office in February, the Togolese military, Eyadema's most loyal support base, quickly inducted his son into the presidency in violation of the Togolese constitution. International pressure forced the holding of elections, which were heavily rigged in favor of Eyadema's son, Faure Gnassinghe. In Zambia, legal measures taken against former president Chiluba, who lost out in a bid to extend his term of office beyond the constitutional limits, seemed to be motivated as much by his misdeeds as by his opponents' desire for recrimination. In Kenya, President Moi attempted to handpick his successor after being forced out of office by Kenyan opposition parties and the international community insisting that he respect constitutionally imposed term limits.

31. Prominent cases more recently are those of The Gambia and Côte d'Ivoire in West Africa, Uganda in East Africa, and Zimbabwe in southern Africa. In some countries, such as Guinea, bodies that conduct elections are integral parts of ministries of government or indirectly responsible to senior government officials. Even where such bodies are removed from government, they rely on government for their support, which might well be provided with conditions.

32. Signs of such practice are said to be creeping up in Sierra Leone and Mozambique, and they are quite evident in Zimbabwe, to give a few examples.

33. It is important to clarify that while it is true that civil society encompasses a broad spectrum of organizations of collective action of various sizes and interests, those associated with the rise of political liberalism and are struggling to become partners in governance are the focus of this discussion. They are typically urban based and broadly prodemocracy in orientation and goals. They include groups involved in human rights advocacy and education, electoral reforms, and an array of interests ranging from environmental concerns to the rights of the disabled. While they may have provincial and local units, their visibility is more pronounced in capital cities, where the dynamics of power relationships ultimately assume finality. For insightful discussions on the role of civil society in African politics, see Orvis (2001); Ndegwa (1996); Bratton (1994); and Gyimah-Boadi (1996). Lewis (1998) has provided an analysis of the conceptual categories of civil society as used in contemporary discourse in an attempt to put an end to the confusing uses of the concept.

34. Zimbabwe and Liberia under Taylor were among the extreme cases where assistance from most IGOs and many bilateral partners was channeled through NGOs, thus causing tension and creating a circumstance of grave suspicion on the part of the government. Such a stance by external actors emboldened the National Constitutional

Assembly in Zimbabwe, a cluster of prodemocracy civil society organizations in Zimbabwe, to stand up against the government of President Mugabe. In Liberia, such support for social programs through INGOs exposed the rapacious nature of the Taylor regime.

35. In the last several years, these patterns have been readily visible in Guinea, Liberia, and Sierra Leone. Civil society movements are so fearful of being branded "political" or "antigovernment" by the government that they often engage in self-censorship that compromises their mission and reduces their effectiveness. The Civil Society Movement of Liberia under Taylor is a case in point. In Guinea, civil society movements are typically sponsored by the government or are constrained to walk a tightrope.

36. The National Constitution Commission (NCC or Con-Com, as the commission was called) was appointed by the Provisional Ruling Council (PRC) and consisted of twenty-five persons drawn from an array of professions. They included eminent jurists, scholars, experienced public administrators, business entrepreneurs, and others. The selection of these individuals reflected regional balance, as members were drawn from every county. I, then an associate professor of political science and dean of the college of arts and sciences of the University of Liberia, was chosen to chair the commission.

CHAPTER 5

Framework for
Democratic Self-Governance

IN THE LIBERIAN EXPERIENCE, OVERCENTRALIZED POWER BASED ON A THEORY OF UNI-tary sovereignty has significantly contributed to the predation, repression, and governance failure that has resulted in violent breakdown. How then can Liberians reconstitute order differently? In this chapter, I conceptualize an approach to reconstituting political order in Liberia using the language of institutional analysis as it relates to constitutional choice. I argue that the challenge of effectively moving African peoples in constitutional processes is fundamental to the creation of democratic governing orders in Africa, and that there is need for an appropriate theoretical framework for thinking about how such processes of constitutional choice are to be designed and how appropriate institutions of governance are to be crafted.

I therefore discuss here the relevant issues and offer some guideposts that are critical in organizing a framework for constitutional choice and an institutional design for democratic governance as an alternative to the overcentralized, unitary state in Liberia. I begin with a discussion of the place of African peoples, particularly Liberians, in the processes of constitution making. I then identify and discuss critical issues that need to be understood in the crafting of institutions in Africa—especially Liberia—that can support democratic governance arrangements. I conclude the chapter with a summary discussion of guideposts for constructing an appropriate bottom-up or democratic self-governing order for Liberia.

■ Bringing African Peoples into Processes of Constitution Making and Constitutional Reform

The challenge of constitutional choice calls upon the people of a society to arrive at a theory of governance suitable to their own circumstances and to establish appropriate governance institutions based on that theory. As previously stated, this is a task that requires open, informed, and enlightened deliberations with careful exercise of choice. Successful processes of constitutional choice rely upon a deep understanding of how existing patterns came about and how they are relevant to changing circumstances. New orders emerge from or are constructed upon older orders. Knowledge of and sensitivity to contemporary values, rituals, and other practices that constitute the uniqueness of a society are essential for successful processes of transformation. Thus, meeting the challenge of constitutional choice requires considerable pooling of knowledge and critical analysis among people themselves in discourses about their collective dilemmas, aspirations, and goals; their conflicts and potential conflicts; and their capacity to transform them.

In Africa, constitutional discourse is typically confined to elite circles. If democratic institutions are to be created as a product of such discourse, the base of participation needs to be broadened to include ordinary people from all sectors of African society. To be meaningful, the discourse must lead to a deep diagnostic assessment of the physical and material endowments of African societies, the human and social capital of those societies, a sound understanding of the fundamental principles that underpin modes of governance extant in Africa, and the external factors that affect governance processes in Africa. This type of diagnostic assessment should yield a deeper understanding of Africa's governance challenges and make it possible to craft appropriate institutions of governance through processes in which the peoples of African societies become central and as such the providers of solutions to their dilemmas and challenges and masters of their own destiny.

Considered in this light, establishing appropriate processes of constitutional choice for Africa requires that villagers and dwellers of urban and peri-urban areas are brought into the discourse about governance. Such issues as justice, freedom, rule of law, equity, property rights, water resources, education, and health become the subject of informed and enlightened discussion by ordinary people in village, town, and district halls; among women's groups, minority groups, young people, and the elderly; at colleges and universities; and, indeed, in national parliaments, by specialized commissions and constitutional assemblies. Too often such discourse is carried on among officials of the central state, constitution commissioners, and consulting experts from the international community. As stated in Chapter 3, citizens must be assisted in developing the capabilities for enlightened participation in such discourse if democratic governance is to take root and be sustained in Africa.

The Place of Constitutional Choice in Constitutional Reform in Liberia

The main puzzles in Liberian political discourses have been about how to bring presidential powers under control and how to curtail corruption in the conduct of governmental affairs. These remain the dominant concerns in contemporary debates. However, debates about how to handle excessive presidential powers more frequently tend to focus on the search for ways to establish effective checks on the president by strengthening the legislature and the judiciary rather than by actually reducing the powers of the president, important as are the former. Led by political practitioners and other public entrepreneurs, these debates have not always generated new ideas as to how to ensure effective legislative oversight and judicial independence and competent performance, let alone address the widespread demands of ordinary Liberians of both urban and rural areas for voice in the institutions of governance. The demands of those ordinary people to participate in choosing their county and district leaders, for example, have persisted for decades but were more widely articulated during the constitutional discourse of the early 1980s. Contemporary calls by women's groups and others for greater inclusion in political decisionmaking in postconflict Liberia reinforce these demands. Even contemporary discourse among political parties and the elections commission about the type of electoral system that is appropriate for the immediate postconflict period is essentially about what should be the match between constituencies and elected representatives and to what extent representatives should be directly accountable to citizens. These debates call into question the capacity of the extant constitutional arrangement to offer greater participatory opportunities to broader sectors of citizens and point to the need for an inclusive process of constitutional choice to consider appropriate constitutional reforms.

Similarly, debates about corruption have viewed the question more narrowly as an accounting problem requiring more efficient public sector management achievable through public sector reform.[1] These debates have not addressed the links between corruption and participation, the fact that greater participation of citizens in decisionmaking as coproducers of public goods reduces information asymmetries and enhances transparency and accountability. A system of democratic governance is important in the struggle to curtail corruption. This is why constitutional reforms bear vitally on the fight against corruption.

The challenge of constitutional choice for the creation of a democratic system of governance in Liberia imposes a special responsibility on Liberian intellectuals to deepen their understanding of Liberian reality by applying sharpened tools of analysis in new and creative ways so that they can become the catalysts of enlightened discourse in the open public realm and in processes of constitutional choice.

The 1981 constitution-drafting process demonstrated how people of various communities in Liberia can engage in productive discourse on critical issues of governance; but it also showed how a process of constitutional choice can be stifled or ignored from the top. A process designed in anticipation of the ascendancy of certain political preferences or as an urgent precondition for holding already-scheduled elections is likely to be unduly influenced by factors other than the sober reflections and considered choices of diverse communities of Liberians. It is important that discourse about constitutional reform in Liberia not be linked to, or limited by, an urgent drive for elections but rather that the nature and timing of elections become an outgrowth of the process of constitutional choice and institutional design.

The constitutional choices to be made by Liberians, like those made by people elsewhere, will vary in accordance with the contexts and specific circumstances in which specific groups of Liberians find themselves; and this too needs to be understood in establishing processes of constitutional reform.

■ How Context Frames Constitutional Choices

Human beings live their lives in specific ecological conditions and in social contexts defined by culture, history, and other attributes of society. Physical and material circumstances do impose constraints as well as offer possibilities for constituting governance arrangements and pursuing development initiatives. For example, for people who live on arid lands and for whom water may be a very scarce resource, institutions organized for the provision and use of water may be among those people's most important governance arrangements. Community monitoring of use of water may be strict and sanctions imposed for misuse may be severe. Whereas communities that exist in the tropical rain forest may confront a different set of challenges, stemming from abundant rainfall, and may place greater importance on a different set of institutional arrangements having to do with water resources. In such circumstances, crafting institutions for flood control may be among a community's principal concerns. It would therefore be unwise to construct identical rules and regulations having to do with water rights and usages for both communities.

Cultural and social circumstances also play important roles in shaping institutions and defining their place in the life of a community. Religion and cultural values are among factors that undergird norms and affect the making and application of rules. Such attributes critically influence how individuals and groups identify themselves and others and how they create and utilize opportunities to cooperate with others. Ethnic identity does become a basis upon which groups are organized for collective action. Principles of organization associated with ethnic groups do foster or hinder their interactions with other groups. For example, people from cultures with principles of matrilineal descent are likely to face substantial challenges when confronted with the circumstance of working out property rights in settings in which those rights are assigned on the basis of patrilineal descent patterns. In many societies, systems of justice do become skewed against women and minority groups as a result of cultural values and practices. In some governance arrangements, centralized government institutions are relied upon to safeguard the rights of minorities with the expectation that, over time, appropriate social capital would be developed so that a community of shared understanding could be broadened to include such minorities.

Community attributes can themselves be perverse. For example, practices of female genital mutilation associated with rites of passage do pose danger to the health and well-being of women and are harmful to society generally. Personal attributes of narrow self-centeredness and shortsighted selfishness do detract from the development of trusting relationships within communities and reduce the prospect for collective action. Similarly, certain networks may also inherently promote objectives that have a retarding influence on collaboration. The role of these attributes among individuals and the role of such networks and associations of individuals should be fully understood in constitutional discourses, and ways of minimizing their effects should be a primary concern in the design of governance institutions. Thus, understanding the constraints and possibilities posed by physical and material conditions and by culture and social attributes of a community are indispensable for the crafting and implementing of appropriate institutions of governance.

Taking diversity of contexts into account in the crafting and implementing of governance arrangements does not mean accepting and perpetuating inequities and perversities that are frequently present in diverse situations. To the contrary, the homogenization of communities through one-size-fits-all governance arrangements could exacerbate inequities that frequently lead to tension and conflicts. Differences in physical and material conditions and in cultural and social attributes define the uniqueness of specific contexts and bear significantly on possibilities and choices in processes of social ordering.

Attaining local knowledge is vital to understanding context and local problem situations. For example, people who live in communities rich in alluvial soils would probably not need to spend as much money and time on soil-enrichment activities as would those who live in semiarid regions and those who till lateritic soils. A good understanding of local conditions and the nature of available resources is fundamental to crafting institutions appropriate for addressing local challenges. Several centuries ago, individuals in Dutch communities in the lowlands of river deltas in Europe were able to devise ways to control the encroachment of the ocean. Institutions organized for this purpose were central to the survival of such communities. In the Kalahari Desert of southern Africa, San hunters long ago discovered a cactus plant that suppressed hunger and thirst, enabling them to undertake long hunting treks across inhospitable terrain without food or water. Thus, it is important in processes of constitution choice to first ensure a full understanding of local conditions and practices. Building upon local knowledge by drawing upon experiences from elsewhere does improve possibilities for problem solving. Only a process of constitutional choice that involves local people can fully provide local knowledge and make for a true understanding of the context within which governance institutions are to be designed.

Finally, with respect to the importance of understanding context, it is important to understand that patterns of established governing orders and the outcomes they produce over time do, in turn, impact the physical and social conditions of society, making for dynamic interactive processes between governing orders and their environments. Governance arrangements having to do with the use of natural resources, for example, may impact the ecosystem in profound ways that, in turn, may impact future governing arrangements. There are abundant cases, for example, where central government cedes property rights in mineral resources to private companies without consideration of such externalities as the impact of pollution from mining on the streams and waterways that are resources for local as well as distant communities. Quite frequently in such situations, affected communities, by themselves or in collaboration with national governments and international institutions, would have to organize further institutions to address this problem and its consequences.

Thus, as can be understood from this discussion, the process of constitution making or constitutional reform for democratic governance cannot proceed under the assumption of uniformity of biophysical conditions and sociocultural attributes. Biophysical conditions do vary and cultures and subcultures do bear distinct differences. These underlie the diverse nature of the experiences of people in a country and need to be fully understood. Acquiring this understanding is an indispensable task of constitutional discourse that is integral to processes of constitutional choice. Processes of constitutional choice do not take place in a vacuum. The ecological and social characteristics define their possibilities and are in turn affected by governance choices. To assume that these are not important considerations and to design governing institutions for uniform application is to reduce the prospects of attaining a workable system of democratic governance.

■ African Indigenous Patterns and the Possibilities for African Constitutional Choices

An understanding of patterns of indigenous social organization is critical to mastering the context and challenges of constitutional choices for establishing systems of democratic governance in African countries. Some of these patterns can constitute foundations upon which self-governing democracies can be built. Since colonial times, anthropologists have described hierarchical and segmentary social formations as the two dominant indigenous patterns found in African societies. Until Meyer Fortes and E. E. Evans-Pritchard, hierarchies were more often seen as higher forms of complexity (Fortes and Evans-Pritchard 1940; Evans-Pritchard 1940). This perception has changed as social scientists and archeologists have now shown the existence of enormous complexities in acephalous societies and the diversity of patterns displayed by various mixes of hierarchies and segmentation (see McIntosh 1999; Southall

1961; Middleton and Tait 1958). However, state building in Africa has been essentially a process of hierarchization that frequently ignored the various mixes of patterns that characterized African social formations and more often strengthened hierarchies where they existed and created them where they did not exist. Understanding how indigenous patterns were organized in Liberia provides clues as to how local people are likely to craft governing institutions if they are allowed to do so. It also provides further clues as to the nature of social capital from which a system of democratic governance can draw.

In the Mano River basin area of West Africa where Liberia is situated, pre-colonial social formations were dominated by the Malinke and Fulbe, who organized centralized states and imposed their order on others. Besides Malinke and Fulbe, there were also smaller formations of other Mande-speaking communities in the area that is now Liberia that included the Kpelle, Mende, Mandingo, Vai, Loma, Mah, and Dan. In addition to Mande-speaking communities, there were Mel- and Kwa-speaking groups. Mel formations included the Gola and Kissi; and Kwa formations included the Kru, Bassa, Dei, Krahn, Grebo, and Sarpo. These tropical rain forest communities became the indigenous formations over which the Liberian state was built. Mande and Mel formations of the rain forest were typically hierarchical with the Poro as the ultimate authority. However, because these communities were small, they were constrained to forge patterns of strategic alliances among themselves. Some Mande communities that were situated in close proximity to Kwa groups evolved heterarchical formations. Kwa patterns were largely segmentary; each town was essentially an autonomous political community. Patterns of alliances also existed among Kwa political communities.

Despite discernible differences in social patterns, certain features were common to all indigenous communities of the rain forest region that is now Liberia: First, whether predominantly hierarchical or segmental in their social organization, as political communities they were all small in size and they frequently formed alliances, including multiethnic alliances. Many of them were multiethnic political communities. Second, in all of them there were opportunities for upward mobility through achievement. None was rigidly castellke. In many of them, individuals demonstrating extraordinary skills in management and administration were often co-opted into leadership roles. Ascendancy to leadership within the military, for example, could be achieved through demonstrated skills. In a sense, all displayed varying degrees of heterarchization. These features should be understood and appreciated because they constitute vital building blocks. Building upon the multiethnic character of communities, learning from patterns of alliances, and strengthening traditions of achievement orientation are uses of social capital provided by indigenous patterns for increasing democratic governance in Liberia.

Liberian state authority co-opted some of these patterns and deployed them in service of a greater hierarchy. Although the Liberian state's manipulation of chieftaincy arrangements, for example, enhanced central control, such manipulation was not unknown among indigenous communities themselves. The dynamics of political life in the area prior to the formation of the Liberian state were replete with conquests, mergers, and accommodation among communities. Machinations within these patterns included the creation of fictive lineage connections and the use of subterfuge and other contrivances as vehicles for ascendancy to power. Thus, as in social orders everywhere, a variety of organizational principles and governing institutional forms are constitutive of Liberian social patterns even as the hierarchy of the state strengthened its control. Some of these patterns are underpinned by principles of self-organization that have potential appropriate for democratic governance and some are not. In some, there were significant participatory roles for women and an array of age-set groups in decisionmaking at the highest levels; others were gerontocratic and dominated wholly by males.

These patterns cannot be wished away in the process of establishing democratic institutions of governance. Those that are themselves consistent with patterns of democratic governance can contribute to foundations to be built upon; for others that may not be supportive of democratic patterns of governance, appropriate institutional responses will have to be designed to address the challenges they pose. What is important is that these communities themselves become participants in processes of constitutional choice and therefore designers, along with others, of institutional arrangements for a new age. The important point here, and as stressed in Chapter 3, is that all of the indigenous and cultural patterns need to be understood at a deeper level and considered within processes of constitutional choice that involve local communities themselves in crafting rules as institutional designs for democratic governance. It is therefore important that we understand the place of rules as institutional designs.

■ Rules and Institutional Designs

Understanding the nature and place of rules in establishing governing institutions is critical where people seek to undertake the task of constitution making or constitutional reform. Human society is replete with complex patterns of rule-ordered relationships. Elinor Ostrom (2005) has defined rules as shared understandings about "enforced prescriptions about what actions are required, prohibited, or permitted." Knowledge of and adherence to rules impose constraints that make human behavior predictable and enable individuals to engage in collective action (North 1990; E. Ostrom 1990). This is why rules are so important when thinking about political reform; they pattern our interactions in the numerous and diverse situations in which we live our lives. Rules are essential tools in any effort to improve the outcomes that we obtain. A conceptual distinction is made between institutions and organizations such that the former have to do with rule-ordered relationships and the latter with groups of individuals interacting within or about these rules. An organization exists when individuals bring together resources that are available to them and adopt coordinated strategies to achieve certain objectives. All organizations are characterized by patterns of institutional arrangements, but not all institutions are organizations (Buchanan 1977; E. Ostrom 2005). The family, school, clan, football team, business organization, and age-set club are all organizations interacting within complex configurations of rule-ordered relationships.

At the core of governance is the question of who makes rules and whether rules that are formally made are enforceable. Enforceable sanctions distinguish rules as tools of governance from cultural norms.[2] And yet there are rules-in-form and rules-in-use. It is not unusual that rules may be written but not enforced or that rules enforced may not appear in written statutes, ordinances, or constitutions. A most critical governance challenge is to ensure consistency between formal rules and rules that are in use. Consistency between the two establishes rule of law. In some African countries, constitutional and statutory laws (laws on the books) depart substantially from rules-in-use, undermining any claims to the existence of a consistent pattern of "rule of law."

As discussed earlier, the crafting of rules requires knowledge of and sensitivity to ecological variations and special circumstances. Rule of law is frequently misconstrued to mean uniformity of law. This is a misconception that pervades Africa, where the search is for uniformity of laws, including dogmatic adherence to majoritarian principles even where the principle of consensus building or other formulations might be more appropriate. This is precisely the dilemma confronting Rwanda and other societies where ethnicity has become a lethal political weapon. Liberian fixation on an overly powerful presidency, despite the violent conflicts it has invited over the years, demonstrates insensitivity to self-evident circumstances as is the case in so many situations where old ways have failed and rules need to be changed.

Institutions of governance consist of configurations of rules of several types. Elinor Ostrom (2005) has identified at least seven types of rules that affect collective action. These are *boundary rules,* defining membership; *position rules,* having to do with who holds what office; *authority rules,* dealing with prerogatives to take action; *scope rules,* specifying the nature and limits of outcome expected from action taken; *information rules,* having to do with the availability of knowledge and the flow of information; *aggregation rules,* concerning how actors configure their interactions; and *payoff rules,* having to do with the sharing of benefit and cost that result from patterns of interaction.

Considering the range and contents of these rules reminds us of how inherently complex the most routine pattern of interaction is. Human beings engage in multiple patterns of interaction simultaneously as participants in schools, families, religious bodies, political parties, clan organizations, and so on; we assume varied identities, occupy different positions, have variable access to information, and aggregate in various vertical and horizontal modes with different incentives for collective action. Considering these, we can appreciate the diversity and complexity of governance institutions. That is why when we seek to compact and compress these complex configurations of institutions that structure our lives into simple hierarchical and pyramidal institutional arrangements, they do not hold; in some cases, they unravel in violence and human tragedy.

In addition to rules that explain how inherently complex and diversified patterns of interaction in rule-ordered relationships really are, there are rules having to do with the levels of interaction entailed in rule-ordered relationships. Human beings create and sustain governance orders by first crafting rules that are constitutive of those orders and then, within such foundation or constitutional rules, establish or craft collective choice rules that are constitutive of policy. These are then applied in operational situations.

Thus, collective endeavors occur on three levels of governance: constitutional choice, collective choice, and operational choice (see Kiser and Ostrom 2000).[3] There are rules that govern on-the-ground or day-to-day patterns of interaction (operational rules); they are derived and nested in policies or collective choice rules, which are themselves rooted in rules of constitutional choice. Those who craft and enforce rules of constitutional choice exercise sovereign authority. When such authority is exercised by individuals in their various communities and townships, and in the array of self-organized associations and other collectivities, sovereign authority is then said to reside in patterns of self-governance.

In many parts of Africa, as was the case in Nigeria, constitutional law (on the books) was crafted or approved by the parliament without any reference to the people. In Ghana, despite progress in establishing parliamentary independence, only the executive can propose legislative bills for enactment by the parliament. Such cases demonstrate not only the sovereignty of the government but also the role of the president as the ultimate source of law—at least policy. Democratic self-governance requires that citizens become the source of constitutional law; that their representatives function in multiple centers of authority as the sources of most policy or laws of collective choice; and that an array of functionaries formulate operational rules. Coherence and consistency among levels of choice ensure both integrity and efficiency of governance order. In such systems of democratic governance, coordination is absolutely crucial.

Finally, regarding rules and institutional designs, it is important to understand that configuration of rules creates governance arrangements of different scales or domains—local, provincial, national, and supranational. The existence of various centers of authority at the different scales of governance underscores the democratic character of polycentric arrangements and, again, emphasizes the importance of coordination among scales of governance.

■ Institutions as Social Capital

Another important consideration that needs to be understood about rules where processes of constitution making and constitutional reform are concerned is that rules are social capital to be deployed in the construction of order. Processes of constitutional choice are enhanced when institutions or rules on which interactions are patterned are seen as social capital. Coleman (1988, 2003) has shown how social capital can be generated in both formal and informal organizations. Relationships of trust, solidarity, and reciprocity among individuals do have implications for the outcomes of collective action. Rules, networks, and personal qualities of trustworthiness are constitutive of social capital (E. Ostrom and Ahn 2003). Social capital can reduce or produce free riding and other perversities and, therefore, should be closely examined. We have seen in Chapter 3 how forms of social capital became ordinary people's instrumentalities for survival during years of violent conflict in Liberia.

In most African countries, it is the networks and associations formed for collective action that give local communities their vibrancy. Failure to use such social capital in the construction of patterns of local governance detracts from the overall initiative to constitute systems of democratic governance. This failure accounts for the gap that can be seen in many African political orders between local government typically established by the central state and the configuration of networks and associations that constitutes local or community governance organized and operated by local people to meet local needs. Theories of constitutional choice for African countries and the institutions crafted from them will be inadequate if the role of ethnic-based and other networks is not fully understood and their potential as social capital is not explored. Adebayo Adedeji speaks to this question when he stresses that for Africans the challenge is to be able to craft "ethnic-prone" institutional arrangements that are capable of yielding "ethnic-proof" constitutional orders.[1]

Thus, in undertaking constitutional reform in Liberia and elsewhere in Africa, the full stock of social capital should be displayed—those things that strengthen bonds within communities, build bridges between communities, and create the basis for harmonious and productive relationships among peoples, as well as those that work against these processes. There is a need to understand the patterns and internal logics of this pool of capital and to assess their suitability as building blocks for a new democratic order. This is all part of a wider need of those who engage in processes of constitutional choice for the purpose of establishing systems of democratic governance to understand the nature and diversity of the contexts within which people make choices, the nature and place of rules as institutions, and how these rules configure and sustain arrangements with multiple centers of authority. After all, people typically live their lives in far more complex relationships than can be reflected in a monocentric system.

■ Polycentric Governance as a Democratic Alternative to Monocentric Government

What distinguishes self-governing democracies from autocratic rule is that in self-governing systems, citizens, interacting through appropriate institutional arrangements, are the ones engaged in rule making at all levels of decision-making (operational, policy, collective choice, and constitutional) and at all scales or domains (neighborhood, township, district, province, national, and supranational). The concept of polycentricity recognizes multiple sites and multiple scales of decisionmaking—each relatively autonomous, each vested with limited authority, and each interconnected to others in a system of governance in which citizens functioning as governors exercise choice (V. Ostrom 1999).[5] If people live their lives through configurations of institutions that are horizontal and vertical, theories of constitutional choice compatible with these circumstances cannot produce solely monocentric or unitary orders. Complex systems of governments with multiple and overlapping jurisdictions are truer expressions of patterns of human interaction even though they pose a significant challenge of analysis. Polycentric systems of governance have several advantages over monocentric government: They can better address diversity of preferences and circumstances, and their multiple jurisdictions may allow for variation and innovation and, in some instances, even healthy competition among jurisdictions. They are resilient and hardly ever suffer total breakdown or collapse in times of crisis as happens often with monocentric arrangements, especially when the sovereign president is at the center of the crisis. Normatively, liberty and efficiency are enhanced through multiple arenas of sovereign authority (Elazar 1987); and communities of citizens have the opportunity for genuine and effective participation in governance. All of these make for democratic self-governance.

Polycentric Governance and Public Goods and Services

A particular strength of polycentricity is that it allows for citizens' participation in providing, producing and consuming public goods and services in variable ways. In their path-breaking work, Vincent Ostrom, Charles Tiebout, and Robert Warren (1999) drew a distinction between the *provision* and the *production* of goods and services. The former has to do with how goods and services are chosen, paid for, and made available, while the latter concerns how the goods are fabricated or produced. Provision of goods and services addresses questions as to who needs them and how they are paid for; production concerns who makes them and how they are made. This distinction is crucial to a deeper understanding of patterns of governance because of the variety of institutional arrangements that can be designed and crafted for attaining public goods and services in a variety of situations. For example, a community of citizens may provide (pay for) refuse disposal, while a specific vendor may produce such service; or the community of citizens may both provide and produce such a service by purchasing or leasing equipment and organizing neighborhood teams to collect and dispose of community refuse.

The nature of the good or service may suggest a variety of ways in which provision and production can be handled. Public choice literature has shown analytic distinctions among goods that go beyond distinguishing between private goods and public goods. Using exclusion and jointness of use or consumption as the initial defining characteristics, goods can be better understood and institutions appropriately designed for their provision, production, and consumption (see Figure 5.1). Exclusion refers to the feasibility of denying others the use of a good. Jointness of use has to do with whether the use of a good by one person subtracts from its simultaneous availability to others. Some goods are excludable and others are not. Similarly, some goods can be used jointly by several people while other goods become subtractable once used. When both characteristics of excludability and jointness of use are considered together, a more complex typology emerges such that purely private good, toll good, common pool resources, and public goods can be distinguished as types of goods (Ostrom and Ostrom 1999).

A pair of slippers, for example, is a purely private good. It can be acquired and used by a single person to the exclusion of others. Transactions involving its acquisition and use can be wholly subjected to the domain of

Figure 5.1   Types of Goods

		Jointness of Use or Consumption	
		Alternative Use	Joint Use
Exclusion	Low cost	*Private goods:* a pair of slippers, bicycle, book, haircut, etc.	*Toll goods:* cinema, telephone service, night club, etc.
	High cost	*Common pool resources:* water pumped from a groundwater basin, fish taken from a lake, tribal land holdings/reserves, etc.	*Public goods:* peace and security of a community, streets, national defense, public health, fire protection, mosquito abatement, etc.

Source: Adapted from Ostrom and Ostrom (1999).

market exchange. Using a telephone service or attending a movie in the cinema hall are examples of excludable but not easily subtractable goods, since use by one person does not subtract from the simultaneous availability of such services to others—until, of course, a cinema hall reaches its capacity or a telephone service nears a point of congestion. Such goods are toll goods. Those who do not pay a toll can be excluded from the use of such goods. Common pool resources, such as the fishing grounds of lakes and oceans, community rangelands and forests, and creeks and streams that supply water to communities can be subject to exclusive use only with enormous difficulty and are subtractable when consumed. Their management requires an appropriate set of institutions, preferably organized by user groups themselves.

Public goods such as peace and public safety are nonexcludable and nonsubtractable. My enjoyment of peace and safety does not detract from the supply of these goods available to others. Thus, crafting institutions for the provision of public goods is at the heart of the challenge of governing public economies; and by using polycentric approaches, a variety of institutional arrangements can be put together for the provision, production, and consumption of a range of public goods and services in diverse circumstances. The availability of an array of institutional designs through polycentricity dispels the often held view that centralization and its variations and privatization are the only institutional options available for constituting governing arrangements in African countries.

What gives polycentric arrangements their special character is not simply the fact that they allow for multiple jurisdictions but, as Michael McGinnis (1999b, 6) points out, polycentric arrangements of governance open up "multiple opportunities by which participants can forge and dissolve links among different collective entities." Self-organization is a vital feature that allows individuals to take collective action, crafting and enforcing rules and changing them as necessary—"forging and dissolving" patterns of collective action. Because of such inherent flexibility, polycentric arrangements are better able to respond to variability. However, as Vincent Ostrom (1999) has pointed out, polycentric systems of governance must consist of the full range of compatible legal, economic, and political institutional arrangements; otherwise, such arrangements cease to be a system of governance.

Coprovision, coproduction and joint consumption offer the possibilities for crafting a vast array of institutional arrangements for public services. Private firms, voluntary associations, and consumer collectives can all function in various mixes as provision and production units within public economies. Ostrom and Ostrom (1999) have referred to these mixes as public service *industries,* recognizing the complex configuration of autonomous institutions that are involved in the provision, production, and consumption of public goods and services such as health care services, public transportation networks, and educational systems.

The notion of coprovision and coproduction is significant for understanding different ways in which citizens can participate in governing public economies. For example, citizens engage in the provision of public security when they decide to organize neighborhood and community watches or to establish and generate funds for the support of a community police force. Citizens also become coproducers of public security when they go out and participate in neighborhood and community watches, just as police officers produce public security when they produce the vast variety of services associated with policing; these could include providing foot patrols, regulating traffic on roadways, and investigating crimes. Each of these may require a different type of production arrangement. The pattern of organization essential to investigating crime may be very different from that needed for regulating highway traffic. Citizens provide educational services when they pool their resources to build a school, or to collect money and other goods to pay teachers. Parents coproduce education when they help their children with homework; in this way, teachers, students, and parents together are producers of education. These are complex arrangements with challenges that must be properly understood and addressed.

Ronald Oakerson (1999) reminds us that in organizing citizens into provision and consumer units, there are challenges of setting boundaries or defining jurisdictions, deciding how to match up services needed with available resources (fiscal equivalence), and meeting transaction costs in organizing and operating such units. He also emphasizes the importance of not underestimating coordination and production costs and determining questions associated with economies of scale (Oakerson 1999).

Then there is the problem of free riding. Because public goods are by their nature subject to joint consumption and pose difficulty for exclusion, supplying them poses challenges. If their use is not regulated but left to voluntary choice, free riding occurs. Excessive free riding undermines successful collective action. This is why sanctions are necessary. Consumers are challenged to organize collective units to provide such goods in a manner that reduces the prospects of free riding. Courts, arbitration boards, and other mechanisms of dispute resolution are typically established to handle such contingencies. Despite these challenges, citizens' collaboration as coproviders and coproducers in public economies is not only essential in attaining desired outcomes; it is especially important because it reveals the true character of democratic participation that gives self-governance its distinctive quality.[6]

General Purpose and Task-Specific Governments

In polycentric governance arrangements, limited authority resides in each jurisdiction. Citizens are the source of rules and therefore the foundation of sovereign authority in all jurisdictions. Jurisdictions may take a variety of forms and serve a variety of functions.[7] There are typically two mutually inclusive types of polycentric or multilevel governmental arrangements. Liesbet Hooghe and Gary Marks (2003) have analyzed both types and shown how they complement each other.[8] One type is the general purpose, multilevel governmental arrangement. The other is the special purpose, task-specific governmental arrangement. General purpose, multilevel governments are typically referred to as federalism. In such arrangements, constitutional prerogatives reside in a national or federal government and a limited number of permanently fixed, mutually exclusive, multitask jurisdictions. They typically comprise three levels of governments: local, state or regional, and national or federal. In these arrangements, jurisdictions are largely permanent fixtures and are required to perform multiple tasks. The essential ingredient of federalism is to be found in the fact that individual citizens remain the unit of analysis and the repository of sovereign authority in all domains or jurisdictions.

Special purpose, task-specific governments are configured differently. They are typically organized for the provision of specific public goods. They consist of numerous task-specific, territorially overlapping, flexible jurisdictions. Citizens who share a particular collective action problem may organize a specific jurisdiction to address that problem. Most significant in this arrangement is that governance jurisdictions are largely determined by the nature of the public good or, more precisely, the nature of component elements of the public good at issue. Typically, police services, for example, could be provided by a multiplex of jurisdictions as best suited to the various constituent components as discussed above. As circumstances change, so also could jurisdictions. For example, new technology could allow for economies of scale in the provision of communications services or distant education. Improved technology could similarly enable several police districts to operate a single communications dispatch service. Determining what should be an appropriate scale or jurisdiction is a persistent question in polycentric arrangements. One way that has been proposed to determine what should be the appropriate jurisdiction for the provision of a public service is to deem a jurisdiction appropriate if it has the capacity to internalize the externalities associated with providing the public service in question (McKinnon and Nechyba 1997).

How can permanently fixed, multitask jurisdictional governments that constitute classical federal arrangements coexist and interface with special purpose, task-specific jurisdictional governments in a system of democratic self-governance? Hooghe and Marks (2003) have sought to demonstrate how this works. They argue that the latter can be crafted and function efficiently at junctures where the former are inappropriate for the provision of efficient services. There are junctures at which the establishment of special purpose governments is appropriate. Where do such junctures appear? They argue that such junctures appear at (a) national and international frontiers where certain dilemmas such as climate change present externalities that can only be internalized at an international or supranational scale; (b) cross-border locations where managing such dilemmas as cross-border ethnic disputes poses special challenges for fixed jurisdictions; (c) locations where local governance intersects with community associations where local initiatives can invigorate local governance processes, as is the case where women's organizations and other local groups that provide services and contribute to the vitality of community life are left out of local processes of political governance; and (d) the public sector–private sector frontier where self-regulating market-based entities can produce services on contract as is the case of refuse disposal and telephone services, for example.

Hooghe and Marks's analytic categories are not exhaustive; obviously, each country or governance situation provides a unique set of circumstances that could create other categories or illuminate these. In the case of Liberia, where violent collapse of the state ignited a system of subregional conflicts and created a special security situation, resolving governance dilemmas requires a range of governance jurisdictions that has to include supranational institutions such as those that operate at the Mano basin–wide level and the West African subregional level, as well as local, provincial, and national-level institutions. Certain security challenges can be addressed properly only at supranational levels, whereas others require intensive local involvement. (More is said about the security and other critical challenges in Chapter 6.) Let me briefly return to the resilience of polycentric systems because of its obvious importance in the face of state failure and state collapse in Africa.

▪ Building Resilience Through Polycentric Governance

One of the most important but infrequently mentioned advantages of polycentric governance systems is their ability to adapt to change while remaining stable. Diversity of institutional arrangements, overlapping jurisdictions, and multiple centers of authority are common properties of polycentric systems that provide the capacity to cope with change and to absorb shocks without collapse. Processes of self-organization through which citizens engage in the provision and production of public goods and services do involve learning. People are able to cope with change by generating knowledge—often through trial and error—spreading risks, heeding early warning signals, and so on. Small changes are co-opted and transformed into new opportunities as polycentric systems adapt and sustain themselves. This is why complex systems of governance may suffer strains and partial collapse but hardly ever totally collapse (see, for example, Folke et al. 2002; Walker et al. 2002; and E. Ostrom and Janssen 2002).[9]

When monocentric government fosters an open public realm, a process of learning takes place that provides opportunities for some measure of adaptation;

however, not much diversity can exist in such arrangements due to the inherent nature of a monocentric system. By its own dynamics, an open and active public realm encourages self-organization; in complex societies, this leads to the creation of multiple centers of decisionmaking. With an open public realm, monocentric governments are faced with a choice to either accept new actors and patterns of participation or resist such pressure for change. Both courses are strewn with uncertainties; the latter, however, could ultimately end in destructive conflict.

The increasing number of FM radio stations and transistor radios are transforming communications and impacting participation across Africa. In rural areas, community problems concerning schools, health care, farm implements, and the like are being discussed on the radio in local languages. In urban areas, animated discussions take place on all issues in an interactive manner made possible by telephone. Governments are hard pressed to not only listen but also respond in a manner that reflects a sense of accountability. These forums are stimulating or reinforcing neighborhood and community-scale discussions. The net result is that the structure of authority relations is then put under stress. Though fraught with uncertainties, new patterns of authority relations are emerging in some places; yet in others, resistance is stiffening. Through the prudent exercise of constitutional choice, new institutional arrangements of multiple centers of power can be established to cope with pressures for change, thereby building resilience instead of creating conditions for destructive conflicts. Constitutional reforms that establish polycentric governance do improve the chances of avoiding breakdowns because such reforms do ensure the construction of numerous centers of participation in decisionmaking, thereby foreclosing the existence of a monopoly of power and the dangers of breakdowns and collapse that are possible when a monocentric system comes under pressure.

■   ## Appreciating the Need for Public Entrepreneurship

Elinor Ostrom (1990) has told us that collective action does not necessarily occur spontaneously. We cannot count on people to engage in collective action simply because a problem or need exists. Collective action results from entrepreneurship. The role of entrepreneurs as innovators and catalysts of collective action is often overlooked. It takes entrepreneurial skills to create or discover an opportunity, to identify preferences, and to devise strategies and mechanisms amid uncertainties to achieve desired outcomes (Kuhnert 2001). In villages, towns, cities, and other settings, it takes enterprising individuals to create conditions for change.[10] The ingenuity of public entrepreneurs engaged in civic education and democratic consciousness-building endeavors in hierarchical and repressive societies is extremely important for the creation of an open public realm.

Entrepreneurship in creating strategies for the crafting and implementation of multilevel governance arrangements is critically needed where institutions of democratic governance are to be established. Strategies for nesting local and subnational units of collection action compatibly within units of national scale are in short supply. Since those who wield authority on a national scale are typically unsupportive of governance arrangements that foster multiple centers of authority, what incentives can be provided and what kinds of institutional arrangements can be designed to reduce their tendency to monopolize power? For example, one who raises the question of how African leaders can be encouraged to promote polycentric governance arrangements is confronted with a complex puzzle. We know that when there is a single center of authority and citizens cannot sufficiently exact accountability from such leaders, internal institutions can hardly offer adequate incentives to encourage them to retire. Citizens can do so only by rising up in nonpeaceful ways. This is why only those who exercise prerogatives over the means of violence—that is, the military and security forces—are often the organizers of regime change.

Quite frequently, external actors are capable of offering stronger incentives to encourage accountability than can national populations. Can there be an attractive alternative to the prospects of sitting tight pending an undignified and inglorious eviction from office and possible harm? Are there incentives that can be built into systems of governance that could reduce the perceived costs of leaving office or, better still, increase the attractiveness of honorable retirement from office by political leaders? Substantial public entrepreneurial skills are required in designing institutions that can provide a variety of incentives to address various aspects of complex governance dilemmas.

■ The Impact of the International Order

Finally, those who attempt to establish polycentric governance need to be aware that such a system itself is to be nested in a larger international order or, better still, several international orders. A polycentric governing order established in any part of Africa becomes a constituent element of a range of African regional and international governance arrangements and needs to be able to take advantage of positive externalities and to address negative externalities (public bads) that flow from other arenas of the larger international orders.

Globalization presents challenges to countries trying to establish democratic systems of governance just as it does to other countries. International trade regimes operate in favor of developed countries and to the disadvantage of developing countries.[11] Tariff barriers imposed by the European Union, the United States, Japan, and Canada, for example, against imports from developing countries are four times higher than those imposed by developing countries on the imports from developed countries or those imposed by developed countries among themselves.[12] The most glaring case of biased rules can be seen with respect to market access to agricultural products. The international trade regime insists that developing countries adopt policies of open market access. The International Monetary Fund (IMF) and World Bank have not only set this as a conditionality but have also insisted on the termination of subsidies to local farmers in developing countries, whereas in Europe and the United States, both farmers' production costs and the export costs of agricultural products are subsidized.[13] Biased rules concerning intellectual property rights also threaten to worsen the condition of smallholder households. Intellectual property rights laws established by the World Trade Organization allow transnational corporations to obtain patent rights to genetically modified seeds but fail to grant royalty to those from whom such seeds were obtained.[14] Thus, food security can hardly be ensured in many countries partly because of such biased rules of international trade.

The most damaging impact of globalization on efforts to constitute self-governing democratic orders in Africa is to be found in the proliferation of small arms and light weapons.[15] The breakdown of order as a result of governance failure in the wake of the ending of the Cold War, coupled with the liberalization of trade, has invigorated the market for such weapons. Rebel wars and rising criminality are fueled by the vast supply of small arms. Trade in minerals, especially diamonds, has been linked to the supply of such arms to create war economies that service conflict systems in the Mano River basin areas of West Africa, in the Democratic Republic of Congo (DRC), in the Great Lakes region of central Africa, and (for at least two decades) in Angola. The role of oil in the continuing conflict in Sudan is still to be fully assessed (Human Rights Watch 2003; Dupraz 2002). It is impossible to think about ways of crafting institutions for democratic governance in Liberia without first considering the security environment within Liberia and the larger Mano River basin area, which has been engulfed in a system of violent conflicts.[16]

The point to be made here is that governance regimes in Africa and elsewhere in the developing world are nested in or otherwise linked to a global order whose dominant actors are often direct actors in the coprovision and coproduction of food and other agricultural products, community security, and other goods and services in local public and private economies in developing countries. These actors make and implement rules that often weaken certain segments of the society—smallholders, for example—rather than assist in their empowerment. These interactions are often counterproductive to a country's effort to establish and sustain a self-governing democratic order.

All of this suggests that a significant and appropriate change is essential in the rules under which international regimes operate vis-à-vis African countries so that such international regimes can play a more helpful role in assisting African peoples in their task of establishing democratic orders in their societies.

■   Guideposts for Framing an
    Alternative to Monocentric Government

In this discussion, I have used the language of institutional analysis to intro-
duce a way of thinking about setting on course constitutional processes that
can yield democratic governance in Africa generally and Liberia particularly.
I have attempted to identify and highlight issues critical to the creation of a
polycentric governance alternative to the overcentralized state with its sovereign president. Polycentric governance arrangements can be designed for the
range of circumstances experienced in human society. While this discussion
does not provide a complete framework or a theory of constitutional choice
for Liberia, the elements of polycentricity discussed do provide critical guideposts for the constitution of self-governing democratic orders for African
countries generally, but especially Liberia.

In summary, this discussion emphasizes seven essential guideposts critical to the creation of a governance framework for constituting a paradigmatic
shift away from presidential and monocentric government to polycentric democratic governance in the African, especially Liberian, context.

Demystifying the Process of
Constitution Making and Constitutional Reform

The first of these guideposts emphasizes the need to demystify the conception
and process of constitution making and constitutional reform. Constitutions of
democratic orders are foundational rules of governance put together and used
by ordinary people to create structured and predictable relationships in dealing with the exigencies of life. They proceed first of all from informed and
enlightened discourse in an open public realm and not simply as artifacts
crafted by experts or special commissions. As an open process to be engaged
in and sustained by ordinary people, the making and sustaining of constitutional arrangements for democratic self-governance entails a major commitment to the creation and sustaining of an open public realm, even at the level
of the village and township, where local newspapers and radio stations operate and where face-to-face discussions take place among ordinary people.
This constitutes the enabling environment for the exercise of constitutional
choice. Public enlightenment is impossible without mass education, especially mass literacy. This issue is more fully addressed in Chapter 8.

Understanding Context

The second important guidepost has to do with the relevance of context within
which a constitutional order is to be established and sustained. The ecology of

a society is its natural endowments or natural capital, its social and cultural patterns are its social capital, and the knowledge and skills of its people are its human capital. All of these should offer possibilities and impose constraints in shaping and sustaining governance arrangement. Knowledge about them should be harnessed and utilized to the best advantage of the society in creating and sustaining constitutional orders of democratic governance.

Understanding Rules and Institutions

The third guidepost emphasizes the importance of a deeper understanding of the nature of institutions. Institutions of governance are complex configurations of rule. Decomposing them and understanding constituent components are crucial processes. Rules determine what is imperative, allowed, and prohibited; they carry sanctions that must be enforceable. Knowing the difference between rules that are in use and formal rules that are on the books but not applied and understanding how rules and norms intersect are very important for processes of crafting and sustaining governance institutions. The existence of unenforceable rules or the inability to enforce rules is the surest way of undermining governance arrangements. These are among considerations that must feature critically in the constitution of order for democratic governance.

Appreciating Complexity

Fourth, processes of constitution making or constitutional reform must be guided by the knowledge that human beings typically live their lives under multilevel or polycentric governance arrangements that are inherently complex. Voluntary associations, age-set groups, educational and religious institutions, court systems, and market institutions are all structured differently; nonetheless, we function in all of them. The nature and variety of human endeavors consist of such complexities, and these complexities can provide resilience to governance arrangements. That is why we have the capacity to cope with crisis, to regroup, and even to thrive. We must learn to understand and appreciate complexity and be guided by the fact that the exercise of constitutional choice is the search for the most appropriate governance arrangements, not necessarily the simplest. The patterns that order our lives are complex, not simple. Quick fixes may satisfy short-term needs but may undermine long-term success.

Overcoming Path-Dependent Resistance

Fifth, as we live our lives in society, we should be guided by history and nested in culture but not enslaved by our background. Rituals and meaning must be reassessed with changing circumstances. Valuation cannot become captive of path-dependent processes. Refurbishment and renewal are essential for survival; adaptation and innovation are required in meeting new challenges. Change must take place within a framework of stability and continuity. Thus, the ultimate value of the "good old days" is revealed when it becomes a building block for the future and not a stumbling block to progress. The challenge of constitution making and constitutional reform requires that we constantly assess our institutions, ferreting out or modifying those that we increasingly find no reasons to value and crafting new and appropriate ones where necessary in the light of new circumstances.

Coping with Adverse External Conditions

Sixth, the notion of national sovereignty is of ever declining usefulness. External actors, acknowledged or not, provide significant inputs and bear considerable influence on governance processes at national and subnational scales. Those who engage in processes of constitution making and constitutional reform must be aware that such processes involve externalities that require the patterning of relationships at scales beyond national boundaries. Challenges of security, trade, and environmental issues are typically more frequently addressed at scales beyond the national jurisdiction. Understanding and addressing externalities in collaboration with others elsewhere is an important element of constitution making and constitutional reform.

Encouraging Entrepreneurship

Finally, because innovations and good ideas do not drop from the sky and collective actions do not occur spontaneously, entrepreneurship is required. The appropriate development of human capital is indispensable to the promotion of entrepreneurship. Creating conditions and developing capacity in local knowledge and linking such knowledge with experiences of others elsewhere encourage people to begin to think about new ways of solving problems. Educational systems, training programs, and social norms need to be supportive of human artisanship. The generation and reproduction of knowledge and the promotion of human creativity must be both the ingredient and the product of processes of constitutional choice.

■   Notes

1. See Second Quarterly Report of the Governance Reform Commission, September 30, 2004.
2. Crawford and Ostrom (2000) have drawn a distinction between rules and norms, contending that the former are prescriptions that impose sanctions, whereas the latter are moral prescriptions typically without sanctions.
3. The term *level* is used here with reference to layers of decisionmaking and not scales of governments.

4. See "Summary of Discussion, Workshop on New Approaches to the Constitution of Order in Africa," Consortium for the Self-Governance in Africa, at www.indiana .edu/~csga.

5. Here, the terms *level* and *scales* are not used interchangeably but rather to convey specific meanings.

6. Studies of metropolitan police services in the United States have shown how different types of institutional arrangements can be crafted for the coproduction of the various components of such services. Community patrol, communications dispatch, criminal laboratory facilities, and training are among the components of policing services, each lending itself to a different mode and scale of organization (see E. Ostrom and Whitaker 1999; and Ostrom, Parks, and Whitaker 1999). Applying such analysis to the management of local public economies of metropolitan areas in the United States, Oakerson (1999) has demonstrated how various patterns of coprovision and coproduction of public goods are possible.

7. This is what Frey and Eichenberger (1999) have called functional, overlapping, competing jurisdictions.

8. The term *multilevel* as used by Hooghe and Marks and repeated in this section and in subsequent chapters has the same meaning as *multiple scales* or *domains* as used elsewhere in this book.

9. I am grateful to Marco Jenssen who brought to my attention a body of literature on resilience and development as published by the Resilience Alliance and other scientific groups.

10. In acephalous societies, local entrepreneurs are known to move away from established towns and found new settlements. In situations of conflict, public entrepreneurs are known to create or strengthen social capital that bridges communities. In Chapter 3, I noted the entrepreneurial role of the offspring of mixed marriages of Mano and Mandingo and Gio and Mandingo in initiating peace-building and reconciliation interactions among ethnic communities of northern Liberia. The contribution of educational entrepreneurs in providing educational services has been indispensable in many places where public schools run by government are failing or in short supply.

11. There are aspects of globalization that are supportive of democratic self-governance and development. Information technology is one such aspect.

12. It is estimated that tariff adjustments that would lead to an increase of 1 percent in Africa's share of world trade could generate income of $70 billion for African societies. This is the equivalent of five times the continent's receipt in aid (see Oxfam Report 2002).

13. Subsidies made to European and U.S. farmers by their governments are estimated at $1 billion a day. European and U.S. agricultural products are sold at prices more than one-third lower than production costs (see Oxfam Report 2002).

14. Some experts have argued that royalty fees of 2 percent could earn as much as $5 billion (Oxfam Report 2002).

15. For analyses of the supply of small arms and light weapons and their impact on conflicts in Africa, see IANSA (2001); and Eavis (1999).

16. UN Security Council reports have documented how illicit trade in diamonds is linked to gunrunning and how the Liberian regime headed by Charles Taylor was involved in such acts. See Report of the UN Security Council Mission to Sierra Leone, October 16, 2000 (S/2000/992); and UN Security Council Resolution 1343, March 2001.

CHAPTER 6

Creating a Context of
Peace and Security

N O MATTER HOW THOUGHTFULLY CONSIDERED, AN APPROPRIATE DESIGN FOR DEM-
ocratic governance in Liberia cannot be implemented unless there is
peace and security. In Chapter 2, I discussed the nature of the violent conflict
that engulfed Liberia and turned that country into the epicenter of a Mano
basin-wide network of conflicts where armed gangs plundered and pillaged
local communities from Geugeudou in the forest region of Guinea to Guiglo
in the western reaches of Côte d'Ivoire. In this chapter, I discuss the challenge
of putting in place an immediate postconflict security regime and undertaking
peacebuilding activities that are compatible with the objective of establishing
democratic governance over time. I argue that the nature of initial security and
peacebuilding measures have a profound impact on the nature of postconflict
governance arrangements to be established—especially on the possibility of
building a democratic system of government.

In the first part of this chapter I discuss the importance of a constitutional
choice approach to creating an environment for peace and security—tasks
typically clustered under the rubric called peacebuilding. The critical point
made is that peacebuilding activities must be seen as foundations for long-
term governance and not as an assortment of vital activities undertaken eclec-
tically for postconflict recovery and as donor resources become available.
They must be designed to constitute foundations for democratic governance,
and if they are to truly become foundations for democratic governance, the
people of the country must be central to the processes of designing and implementing such activities—they must be coproviders and coproducers as well as
consumers of peacebuilding activities and of the outcomes of such activities.
Local people cannot be left as spectators in design processes and beneficiaries of implementation processes and yet be expected to later take over and
then build and sustain democratic systems and development programs on

137

foundations that have been laid by others. I then discuss how through polycentric approaches, an appropriate security architecture can be constructed
and other peacebuilding activities undertaken so that they become foundations upon which democratic governance is established in Liberia.

■   Peacebuilding and Constitutional Choice

Postconflict peacebuilding involves some fundamental and difficult challenges, such as those associated with creating a secure environment, repatriat-
ing and resettling the displaced, reconciling and healing fractured communities, and reconstituting the basic initial institutions of political, economic, and
social governance. It is not atypical that these peacebuilding activities are
undertaken in an eclectic and compartmentalized manner as donor support
becomes available and as external expertise directs. For example, resettlement
of the displaced is typically directed by the technical and administrative personnel from the United Nations High Commissioner for Refugees (UNHCR)
with financial support usually provided by European countries, the United
States, and Japan, among others. On a separate and often unrelated track, the
reorganization of security forces proceeds with bilateral and multilateral financial and technical support. Each peacebuilding activity proceeds in a separate
compartment.

What is sometimes not taken into account is that these activities are
related parts of the challenge of reconstituting order and must be situated
within a broader framework that defines an overall approach to peacebuilding.
Understandably, there is always urgency to certain aspects of postconflict
recovery, especially those having to do with humanitarian relief; however,
even humanitarian relief must be arranged as part of a coherent set of activities organized to lay foundations for long-term governance. Michael Maren
(1997) has shown how some strategies for providing humanitarian emergency
relief can encourage dependency and erode the capacity of individuals and
communities to become self-reliant. Viewed with long-term governance in
mind, peacebuilding immediately invokes questions regarding the nature of
the order to be constituted: What kind of governance arrangements is envi-
sioned? What theory of governance is to undergird such arrangements? How
are such governing structures to be designed? If the constitution of foundations for a democratic order is the goal, which is the idea driving this book,
then addressing these questions would require a deliberative process more
inclusive than the one that could have been provided during the negotiations
of peace agreements or within a caretaker transitional government. If self-
governance is the goal, then the people of the society must be central to shaping the foundations of governance. And this process must begin with an
appropriate diagnostic assessment and an assessment of the capabilities people bring to their own processes of recovery. Without the exercise of consti-

tutional choice, peacebuilding processes may end up contributing to reestablishing orders similar to those that have failed or pursuing great ideals without framing them in appropriate institutional arrangements.

It is therefore important in establishing a democratic order that peacebuilding processes be seen as processes of constitutional choice and that peacebuilding activities be implemented as interrelated and well-coordinated collective undertakings constitutive of a conceptualized order of democratic governance.[1] This is why a polycentric approach to the critical tasks entailed in peacebuilding is crucial to enhancing the prospects for establishing a democratic order.

■ A Polycentric Approach to Peacebuilding

Considering the fact that the conflict engulfed much of the Mano River basin area, linking numerous flash points in several countries, any viable and effective approach to peacebuilding must be informed by and respond to this reality. Movement of men and war-making material and the flow of displaced people and illicit trade across the area underscore how the basin-wide area was transformed into a single theater of conflict. Yet there were other levels of conflict. The collapse of individual governments and the unraveling of national security systems highlight the country-specific dimension of the conflict. At local levels, local boys sometimes turned on their communities, and interethnic conflict resolution mechanisms of long standing broke down. Clearly, in such circumstances, there is no one-size-fits-all or single-level approach to creating security, putting in place a system of transitional justice, and undertaking any of the other tasks associated with postconflict peacebuilding. What is needed is a multilevel, polycentric approach that analyzes each task, identifying its components and seeking appropriate institutional remedies.[2]

■ Creating Basin-Area Security Arrangements

Creating appropriate arrangements for physical security is of primary importance. Due to the nature of the conflict, an appropriate arrangement for physical security has to be basin-wide in scope and not narrowly constructed to cover only Liberian territory. Appropriate basin-wide security architecture will have to consist of a complex mix of institutions designed to address each aspect of every set of security challenges. Certain security challenges, such as those having to do with the flow of small arms and light weapons, require the construction and involvement of a mix of institutions that operate at various levels: from institutions that regulate and monitor the sale of such weapons in international markets, to local truckers who are hired to bring them across borders, to community and neighborhood watches whose members are concerned about community security.

Other security challenges of basin-wide scope include those having to do with disarming and demobilizing fighters and creating early warning and early response systems. Some security challenges, such as those having to do with the security of cross-border communities, may require specific cross-border mechanisms. Yet others, having to do with community policing, may require wholly internal if not only local mechanisms. Table 6.1 illustrates how security challenges span various levels of governance and need to be addressed through a polycentric arrangement. It is important that the array of security challenges presented by the conflict be identified and analyzed so that there is proper understanding of the various contexts, arenas, and actors involved and the proper levels at which these challenges can be effectively addressed. Needless to say, not only security challenges but all peacebuilding and governance challenges need to be subjected to analysis so that they can be properly understood and addressed.

Key dimensions of the security challenge discussed in the following sections include those having to do with disarming and demobilizing armed bands, establishing early warning and early action systems, constructing post-conflict security architecture, and dealing with related transitional justice issues such as reconciliation and the question of impunity.

Disarmament and Demobilization

Disarming and demobilizing all armed groups is one of the primary tasks in ensuring a secure environment. Since members and former members of Liberian and Sierra Leonean armed groups were known to roam and plunder communities in the Mano basin subregion, disarming and demobilizing them must be seen as a basin-wide challenge. Other groups with whom they interacted, such as the renegade soldiers in the Guinean forest region and rump elements of Ivorian rebel forces, would also have to be disarmed and demobilized if disarmament and demobilization in Liberia and Sierra Leone are to be successful. Although such broad disarmament and demobilization may not deter criminality, it will reduce the prospects of the resurgence of such groups as readily available instruments of political violence, domination and control. To effectively accomplish this task, a United Nations–mandated stabilization force would need to operate throughout the basin area, especially in Liberia, in Sierra Leone, in the forest region of Guinea, and in western Côte d'Ivoire, an area that now defines a conflict system. These forces would need to remain available, though in diminishing numbers, for several years—certainly for more than three years.

Under Chapter VIII of the UN Charter, the stabilization force established to ensure initial security in Liberia can be expanded and given enforcement powers within the basin area. Admittedly, claims of sovereignty could be raised to oppose the expansion of the scope of operation of this force, but fail-

141

Table 6.1   Illustrative Polycentric Approach to Postconflict Peacebuilding

Peacebuilding task	Local Level	Mezo Level	National Level	Basin-wide Level	Subregional-Regional Level	International Level
Disarm and demobilize				Basin-wide coordinated mechanisms	ECOWAS peacekeepers	UN peacekeepers
Reintegrate excombatants			Government and civil society organizations	Basin-wide coordinated mechanisms		
Uncover hidden weapons	Local and community-based organizations	Pan-ethnic organizations	Government and civil society organizations	Basin-wide CSOs and panethnic organizations	ECOWAS peacekeepers	UN and INGOs (small-arms action networks)
Create early-warning system	Local and community-based organizations	Pan-ethnic organizations	CSOs	Basin-wide CSOs	ECOWAS and AU observatories	UN and INGOs
Resolve ethnic-based conflicts		Interethnic and interreligious organizations	Government, interreligious and women's NGOs	Cross-border interethnic organizations and basin-wide CSOs	ECOWAS council of elders and Eminent Persons Group	INGOs
Address impunity			National Truth and Reconciliation Commission		African Court on Human Rights	International Criminal Court and special UN tribunals
Create national reconciliation mechanism	Local and community-based organizations	Interethnic and interreligious organizations		Basin-wide Eminent Persons Group	ECOWAS Eminent Persons Group	UN and International contact group support

ure to deploy a well-coordinated basin-wide stabilization force will not reduce opportunities for the basin-wide movement of fighters and weapons and will make the task of consolidating disarmament and uncovering hidden weapons in Liberia and Sierra Leone more difficult. The authorities of the Mano River Union countries and Côte d'Ivoire would need to consider working with ECOWAS, the United Nations, and the major international powers to coprovide and coproduce such a force.

Local communities throughout the basin area will have to play a vital role in uncovering hidden weapons. This requires encouraging people-to-people interaction, especially in cross-border communities. Interethnic associations and panethnic organizations are critical social capital for assisting with this task. A special effort would have to be made by the Liberian, Sierra Leonean, and Guinean authorities to facilitate such interactions—or at least not to prevent them.

Demobilization can be ensured only when disguised structures of command and control are dismantled and ex-combatants are engaged in alternative productive activities. Rehabilitation and training in productive skills are essential activities that must be closely associated with successful demobilization. Demobilization and rehabilitation initiatives need to be integrated into strategies for human resource and socioeconomic development and not treated as measures intended only to take guns from young fighters and sever their ties with leaders of armed groups. A national and basin-wide initiative backed by the international community using NGOs and INGOs and an assortment of competent institutions is appropriate for successful demobilization and rehabilitation of ex-combatants.

Early Warning and Early Action Systems

To have effective early warning capabilities requires a good understanding of the causes and dynamics of disputes, constant vigilance in observing and heeding warning signals, and prompt and careful analyses of such signals. Effective early warning without prompt and effective early action does not help dispute resolution. Effective (especially local) mechanisms for monitoring the gathering storms and for dispute resolution are critical. One of the major challenges of early warning and early action in the Mano basin area is to address the numerous local-based ethnic disputes that have been caused or exacerbated by over a decade of violence (see Chapter 3).[3] Some of these involve cross-border ethnic communities, such as the conflicts between Loma and Mandingo communities that straddle both sides of the Liberian-Guinean border. Panethnic and interethnic associations, community-based organizations, and, where appropriate, religious bodies are all needed to assist in this task.[4] These need to be linked to observatories equipped with monitoring and analytic capabilities that could be established at provincial and cross-border locations. The early warning observation centers established by ECOWAS provide a good beginning; however, they need to be linked to local, county, and transborder communities in ways that allow for greater direct involvement of groups at these levels on both sides of the border. The ECOWAS observatory, as established, relies too heavily on monitoring done by national governments to meet the requirement of effective early warning.[5]

Constructing an Appropriate Security Architecture

The assumption that effective security forces can be organized by merging warring groups to form an army or by bringing them into an already established military is, at least in the experience of the basin region, questionable. In Liberia, where armed bands were adopted as government security forces, a variant of this strategy has been taken to criminal extreme. In Sierra Leone, despite professional training by the British, the military has not convincingly demonstrated its commitment to supporting constitutional rule and respecting civilian authority.[6] In many cases, African militaries have been instruments of control and predation over African societies (Hutchful and Bathily 1998). The militaries of the three countries of the Mano basin area have functioned more as forces of pacification against local populations than as protectors of territorial integrity and national sovereignty.[7]

The question of what type of security force is appropriate to meet the needs of the people of Liberia clearly needs to be the subject of discourse in the public realm. Does Liberia need a national army, or can a constabulary force perform the same services that an army is supposed to perform? Should local communities play a role in providing for their own security? If so, what should be that role and how best can it be performed? For more than a decade, leaders of armed groups have routinely recruited the youth of local communities into rebel bands. Can local communities themselves organize properly trained and disciplined community defense units, and can these units be linked and properly coordinated in a network of community defense units and integrated into a system of societal defense? Thus, against the background of the profound tragedy experienced by ordinary people in local communities of the basin area, the question of local communities' coproducing their own security protection must be considered an appropriate subject of debate.

One of the delicate challenges in this respect is how to involve local people in local security arrangements without militarizing their communities. Local security units and militia forces constituted by local people as part of more complex security arrangements are known to exist in many countries.[8] Though ineffective, county militia forces had existed in Liberia until the military takeover of 1980. In view of contemporary security dilemmas, a strong case can be made for the reorganization and appropriate modernization of these militia units as part of Liberia's overall security architecture.

The presumption that responsibility for the security of the people of a country should be left solely to the state, though proven to be questionable, still prevails but needs to be reconsidered in the light of contemporary experience and in the face of the challenges to constitute systems of democratic governance. Liberians and basin-area authorities and experts need to undertake serious analyses of the security needs and capabilities of the basin area and, based on such analysis, specific security tasks need to be defined, scales of effective task performance determined, and a complex, task-specific, multilevel security arrangement established. This arrangement may well include security organizations that range from local police and community militia units, to nationally organized constabulary forces, to basin-wide rapid deployment specialist units and subregionally organized peacekeeping units. At the West African regional level, ECOWAS's decision to maintain ECOMOG as a standing peacekeeping force provides for an important dimension of the West African regional security architecture, which itself is a part of an emergent Africa security system. The critical challenge is to ensure that all of these security entities are professionally trained, synchronized and coordinated, and, above all, committed to protecting ordinary citizens rather than preying upon them.

Addressing Impunity

The clearest indications of the interconnectedness of conflicts in the Mano basin area are revealed in investigations that identified those who bear the greatest responsibility for atrocities committed in Sierra Leone. The report of a UN panel of experts and the indictments issued by the chief prosecutor at the Special Court in Sierra Leone assert that certain individuals not only bear the greatest responsibility for egregious crimes but have also, for over a decade, maintained a ubiquitous presence in every phase and flashpoint of conflict in the basin area. Some, such as Charles Taylor and Foday Sankoh, were rewarded with positions of authority as a trade-off for ending the fighting and still continued to pursue agendas of terror and plunder. Prosecuting Taylor and his principal collaborators for crimes against humanity addresses several challenges that are critical to the creation of a security arrangement and the successful pursuit of peacebuilding in Liberia and the wider basin area. First, it confirms the international community's responsibility and the emergence of appropriate mechanisms to protect the humanity of all human beings from those who so outrageously violate that humanity. The indictment of Charles Taylor sends a strong signal against impunity in high places in Africa. It serves to elevate the rights and dignity of ordinary people over interpretations of principles of sovereignty that legalize such abuse of authority. It provides a legitimate means of curtailing the agency of those who pursue ambitions to exercise control through terror and continuously pose obstacles to the creation of environments of peace and security. Much like Savimbi in Angola, Charles Taylor, until his expulsion from Liberia, had demonstrated for over a decade that he was not prepared to be an instrument of peace and stability in Liberia and the Mano basin area. While it is true that he was elected president of Liberia in 1997, his abuse of the Liberian presidency transformed that office into an instrument of criminality and repression against Liberians, Sierra Leoneans, and others in the Mano basin area and requires investigation by both international legal tribunals and Liberian courts when practicable.

Second, the prosecution of Taylor and others who commit such crimes will serve to build local people's confidence in the integrity of the new postconflict security arrangements and legal regimes. People who over the years have not had their rights protected by systems of justice are not likely to have confidence in any new system of governance that purports to protect their rights until they see evidence that the new arrangements do work and are applicable to the powerful.

In addition to the indictment of those who bear greatest responsibility for atrocities committed in Sierra Leone, there is a need to address impunity with respect to crimes committed in Liberia. Besides generalized killings in firefights, there were specific incidents of mass killings, some considered genocide-like or of the magnitude associated with war crimes and crimes against humanity. Pursuing retributive justice in such situations will be more effective in promoting reconciliation than allowing impunity to continue and rewarding perpetrators of crimes with positions in government and high status in society. A special United Nations–led investigative commission needs to be established for this purpose. Its findings should lead to criminal prosecution by an appropriate international tribunal.

A further measure in addressing impunity should involve an effort to ensure accountability on the part of all those who served in successive transitional governments and in the Taylor government and who were entrusted with the management of public resources. The question of how public resources were used was never an important concern during efforts to achieve peace. Timber was harvested and sold by armed groups, offshore maritime funds were received and used by successive interim governments, and contracts of various kinds were awarded by these governments. Some of the interim governments even intervened in private disputes, confiscating products without accounting for them. There should be a full assessment of the use of Liberia's natural resources during the periods of conflict, an assessment of the revenue intake by all armed groups, and audits of the accounts of all interim governments as of 1990. A special initiative that involves forensic accounting will have to be established, preferably under the auspices of the United Nations.

Processes of Reconciliation

Reconciliation is an important aspect of peacebuilding that requires strong leadership from the transitional government and later from the central government when a system of democratic governance is established. Since the beginning of democratization in South Africa in the early 1990s, reconciliation has become associated mainly with the work of truth and reconciliation commissions. Such mechanisms have become important both in terms of the opportunities they present for national soul-searching and for their symbolic value representing a new beginning. Yet national reconciliation can only be achieved through processes that involve many institutions working together over time to address a range of relationships that are considered by various segments of the population to be inequitable and unjust. In this sense, every peacebuilding initiative should be designed to contribute to the goal of reconciliation. The concept of self-governance itself implies that people engage each other in respectful, informed, and sympathetic interactions to arrive at mutually beneficial solutions to problems. A system of democratic self-governance provides opportunities for citizens to establish and constantly refurbish institutions and mechanisms essential to the resolution of societal conflicts. The reconstitution of Liberian political order along lines capable of enhancing democratic self-governance is the best self-sustaining approach to reconciliation that can be conceived.

How should the desire for reconciliation be translated into action? The answer to this question takes specific forms depending on the issue and the circumstances. In postconflict situations, society faces a variety of delicate issues that need to be addressed in specific and sometimes unique ways if the overall process of reconciliation is to succeed. The quest for reconciliation is likely to be successful when accompanied by a quest for justice. The quest for justice takes different forms and pursues different goals as may be appropriate for individual and societal needs. There are issues and disputes that are more appropriately addressed by the regular court system established as a normal part of systems of governance. Such courts are much more suitable when the goal of reconciliation is to achieve retributive justice through the application of punitive measures to address impunity. The examination of facts, application of legal prescriptions, determination of guilt, demands for restitution, and imposition of punishment are activities typical of courts that are suitable for addressing a variety of wrongdoings, especially those in which the ends of justice are to ensure that retribution is achieved. However, Archbishop Desmond Tutu (1999) and other peacebuilding practitioners have argued that there are circumstances where courts that deliver retributive justice are unsuitable for attaining reconciliation and healing. There are circumstances where restorative justice must be pursued over and against retributive justice.

The challenge of every conflict-torn society is to determine which wrongdoings should be addressed in courts and tribunals—where retributive and punitive measures define the outcome of the search for justice—and which ones should be addressed through other mechanisms, especially mechanisms that seek to achieve justice through equity or through healing and restoration.[9]

The violent conflict in Liberia embodies an array of issues, events, and circumstances that could be considered wrongdoings that need to be addressed if the ends of justice are to be served. Some of these have roots in the country's history, while others arose during the course of conflict. Peacebuilding initiatives that seek reconciliation must ensure that each is treated in a way that serves the ends of justice as appropriate for the needs of victims and society as a whole. The transitional government, and later the national government, must be seen to be showing leadership in addressing these critical and delicate issues and not avoiding them by deploying slogans such as "let bygones be bygones."

In the search for restorative justice, one measure that needs to be taken is the reconstruction of the historical narrative and national symbols of Liberia, with the view to truly reflecting the contribution of the various communities that constitute the Liberian mosaic. This point is more fully discussed in Chapter 8. Also in the quest for restorative justice, a serious effort should be made to account for all the victims of violent conflicts over the last quarter-century, to determine their identities and the circumstances of their death or disappearance, and to construct a fitting memorial to them. The national government, working with county authorities and local and community-based associations, should establish an appropriate mechanism to lead this reconciliation initiative.

■ Beyond Physical Security: Local Communities as Crucibles for Peacebuilding

Jean Paul Lederach (1997) has observed that once physical security has been minimally taken care of, peacebuilding initiatives tend to turn immediately to economic and political transitional issues, giving less attention to the psychosocial state of individuals and communities. There is an unspoken assumption that the provision of opportunities for training and employment and of an open public realm where people can have their say eases the impact of postconflict trauma. One can assume the pervasiveness of unattended conflict-related trauma among Liberians, given the paucity of facilities for healing in what has been an ongoing conflict for twenty-five years. It is important that peacebuilding initiatives be designed to provide for individual therapeutic treatment as well as community-based healing while creating employment opportunities and establishing rudimentary political institutions. It is also important to first locate and integrate these initiatives within local communities before moving on to other levels. Doing so establishes local communities as the crucibles of immediate postconflict recovery and foundations for long-term governance (Spence 1999). Local community ownership of short-term peacebuilding provides solid foundations to support democratic governance over the long term. Elinor Ostrom and her colleagues have suggested that local ownership of community development activities enhances local people's capacity to articulate needs, contribute to projects, enhance the benefits that flow from them, and contribute to sustaining or transforming projects (E. Ostrom et al. 2002).

Peacebuilding activities designed to revitalize community-based economies, reconstitute local conflict resolution mechanisms, and provide for individual and community-based therapy cannot but strengthen local communities and kick-start the process of constituting a postconflict democratic order. The coordination costs of achieving the integration or coordination of various initiatives can be high in view of the vast array of actors who provide support or are otherwise involved in the many dimensions of these peacebuilding undertakings, but the benefits can be even greater.

■ Children, Youth, and the Elderly as Fundamental Peacebuilding Challenges

A final point about transitional peacebuilding processes in postconflict situations is that peacebuilding activities must be organized principally to attend the plight of vulnerable populations. In the Liberian conflict, as in such conflicts elsewhere, children, women, and the elderly were the most vulnerable and greatest victims. Together they constitute the majority of the population; therefore, addressing their plight must be central to transitional peacebuilding initiatives.

Children-Centered Peacebuilding

Societies that meet the needs and promote the rights of children are the societies that build the stock of capital most essential for development and democracy. Peacebuilding strategies should be organized to prioritize the health care, education, and other survival needs of children; to promote their dignity; and to enhance their role as participating members of society. Values of tolerance, belief in the inherent equality and dignity of others, and participation in community life are foundational values that children must be taught at an early age. Concerns about the well-being of children need to permeate every peacebuilding initiative, including the design of shelter, the rehabilitation of towns and villages, the use of natural resources, care of the environment, and every other aspect of physical and social infrastructure reconstruction.

Liberia faces the grave circumstance where all of its children have been traumatized by war.[10] Thousands saw their parents brutally killed or tortured, were abandoned, were separated from their families, or were otherwise abused. Several thousands were forcibly recruited and exploited as child soldiers. Countless teenage girls were abducted as "war wives." The rehabilitation of child soldiers into families and communities poses a particularly delicate challenge, especially since many of these children have known nothing except war and have committed atrocious acts themselves. The need for appropriate psychosocial rehabilitation cannot be overstated. Considerable international support is needed, since addressing this challenge requires various types of individual, family, and community-based therapy—in some cases, for a long period of time. Special educational and training programs and a system of juvenile justice sensitive to the needs of former child soldiers are also needed.

The international community has established numerous programs to meet the needs of Liberia's children. UNICEF is the lead agency in these efforts and has ensured proper coordination among participating organizations. Like most of the current transitional peacebuilding initiatives, children-related programs are essentially of the type that can be called humanitarian emergency initiatives. While coordination is strong among IGOs such as UNICEF and INGOs such as Save the Children Fund, Liberian groups are marginally involved in the conceptualization and design of such initiatives. Thus, very little capacity building is taking place and, therefore, very little preparation for transition from the phase of humanitarian emergency to development. The implied expectation is that the Liberian government will ultimately take over these programs and shape them to meet the long term developmental needs of the country.

Also noticeable is the lack of content coordination. The content of school curriculums is not always informed or reinforced by the initiatives in, say, community health care programs. Ensuring continuity of initiatives after the humanitarian emergency phase will pose a serious challenge unless these programs are community-based, with local people integrally involved in their design and implementation, and, where local expertise is unavailable, capacity-building projects will have to be integrated into all of them.

Rescuing Youth

In Chapter 2, I discussed, among other issues, the role of youth in armed conflict and the erosion of institutions that are responsible for the intergenerational transfer of knowledge. The young people who constituted the largest group of fighters are part of a larger pool of youth who have had little or no education, home training, or training in skills for gainful employment. Growth of Liberia's lumpen youth has accelerated since the late 1970s as a result of a population increase of youth that was greater than growth among other population groups. This shift in Liberia's demography comes at a time of a steadily declining economy, a failing educational system, and increasing unemployment.[11]

The crisis of youth goes beyond the problem of ex-combatants and others who had seized power in an environment dominated by armed bands. Even youth who were not combatants or of such character have been traumatized and gravely affected by prolonged armed conflict. Many who attended school during this period have received an inferior education. Large numbers remain unemployed. What is required is a multifaceted policy designed to address all dimensions of the crisis of youth, including the problem of ex-combatants and others in similar categories.

Because ex-combatants may well constitute the more difficult of the dilemmas associated with youth, they need to have access to rehabilitation programs immediately upon their demobilization. Such programs need to involve training in skills for gainful employment and in other types of productive entrepreneurship. If such training programs are designed to go hand in hand with productive labor, ex-combatants and other youth can become the largest pool of productive workers for the reconstruction of the physical infrastructures of towns and villages throughout war-torn Liberia. Reconstruction projects on which ex-combatants are coproducers, working side by side with the people of local communities, can offer opportunities for reconciliation and healing. Ex-combatants and other youth can give their labor, local entrepreneurs can provide leadership, and, through labor and discourse, communities can reconstruct and also reconcile.

The paucity of initiatives designed to effectively train young people to be producers in agriculture is a noticeable shortcoming of postconflict peace-building in Liberia. The fact that young people constitute the largest number of those being rehabilitated suggests that unless they are trained for agriculture-related enterprises, they are likely to gravitate to urban and periurban areas. Most of these young people were not farmers before the conflict began and would need to be brought into agricultural production activities with elders who have local knowledge about agriculture. If creative ways are not found to rescue Liberian youth, they are likely to be the source of a continuing threat to the peace and stability of Liberia and the Mano basin region for years to come.

Youth programs that are being implemented have shortcomings similar to those seen in children-related programs. Those organized for ex-combatants are not necessarily connected to long-term training and are designed largely by INGOs and international contractors whose commitment is short term. It is highly likely that community-based participation of this type will come to an end as soon as donor funding dries up. Youth educational and skill development initiatives are not undertaken within a larger human resource development strategy, one formulated with a view to ensuring sustainability as well as promoting self-reliant development and self-governance. Civic education for youth is not only in short supply but, where available, is inadequate if not inappropriate. More is said about education in Chapter 8.

Rehabilitating Elders

Changing property rights and state predation are among the factors contributing to the changing role of elders in African governance.[12] Ongoing processes of modernization and the introduction of new technologies are eroding their role in the transmission of knowledge. In addition to declining status, elders in areas of conflict are among the most vulnerable members of society. In Liberia, they were more vulnerable to the harsh conditions of violent conflicts, especially the predatory behavior of armed men.[13] Both Charles Taylor and Samuel Doe before him strove to co-opt and manipulate gerontocractic institutions, such as the Poro, which have always played a critical role in the transmission of values and knowledge in many rural societies. During years of violent conflict, armed men's assaults on elders in rural communities became commonplace eliciting a response of withdrawal by elders from participation in community affairs (Sawyer, Wesseh, and Ajavon 2000). The declining role of elders has contributed to the erosion of values. Local knowledge, especially about agriculture, handicraft production, and blacksmithing, is being lost. Large numbers of young people are growing up without grounding in the values taught by the institutions of their subcultures or by the Western-oriented institutions. A critical peacebuilding initiative has to be designed to safeguard the health and well-being of the elderly and assess the potential of institutions they control. Such an initiative will contribute to national recovery, especially with respect to conflict resolution and the transmission of values that build productive social capital for collective action.

There are very few peacebuilding initiatives organized to address the plight of the elderly. Most elderly people are only assisted to the extent that assistance is provided to the general population. And most of such assistance comes in the form of humanitarian relief. There are very few programs designed to help the elderly return to productive lives and help restore their dignity and place in society such that they can become important actors in the building of a system of democratic governance.[14]

■ The Struggle for Gender Equality as a Fundamental Peacebuilding Challenge

The 1995 Human Development Report, prepared for the Fourth World Conference on Women, in Beijing, calls the struggle for gender equality "one of the defining movements of the twentieth century." It gravely asserts that "human development, if not engendered, is endangered" (Human Development Report 1995). Empowering women through strengthened capabilities and access to opportunities so that they can exercise choices is of fundamental importance in itself. Recognizing women as individuals with their own rights and needs is the first step to empowering and protecting them. In addition to being of intrinsic value, empowering women bears enormous dividends for children, families, and society generally. Claims to democracy are compromised where women's participation is not meaningful, is curtailed, or is forbidden. Development initiatives remain stunted where they are not aimed at cultivating the potential of women and fully employing their skills and resources. Thus, peacebuilding initiatives designed to advance gender equality provides the surest strategy of contributing to the attainment of durable peace through democratic governance and self-reliant development.

In recent times, the conditions under which women in Liberia have lived have been made worse by years of violent conflict. Peacebuilding initiatives have to address issues related to the violence perpetrated against women during the conflict. Rape and related offenses that are considered war crimes should be addressed as such. The practice of holding women as "war wives" and forcibly conscripting girls as fighters and otherwise using them as support providers needs to be fully investigated and punished. The experiences of women during displacement are gender differentiated and should be recognized and addressed. The violence that causes women to flee in the first place was often related to their sex and gender roles, so rape is disproportionately against women and girls. Reports show that even in safe havens, displaced women are not always safe. They are sometimes coerced to barter their bodies to protect their husbands and children or to get needed food, shelter, and medicines. Yet, in these circumstances, men expect women to maintain their traditional responsibilities and take on new ones. Displaced men, embittered by their disempowerment brought about by their lack of status, frequently respond by being more oppressive of women.[15] Reintegration programs need to be sensitive to these experiences of women and girls and to respond to their special needs.

Additionally, and as elsewhere in Africa, efforts for gender equality in Liberia face other significant challenges. A fundamental challenge can be found in the tri-system of customary, Islamic, and statutory laws that define the rights and duties of women. There have been some efforts to standardize the laws, but there are still discriminatory provisions, particularly in the area of family law where under customary and Islamic laws, rights of inheritance are biased against women and, in certain circumstances, women themselves are considered to be inheritable property or disposable with abandon through perfunctory divorce proceedings. Unequal restrictions on travel, discrimination in access to bank loans, and inarticulate laws regarding landownership exist in each domain of the tri-system of laws in Liberia. As a result, women are forced into relationships they might not choose to be in. Gender-based inequality forms a continuum that begins with denying girls their rights and advantaging boys, thus setting the social path to gender-based violence and institutionalized oppression. Peacebuilding initiatives designed to review legislation and address discriminatory provisions or unintended effects need to be fully supported, among other measures.[16]

Access to education is also of critical importance. Making educational opportunities available is insufficient without enabling girls and women to take advantage of those opportunities. Reducing the adverse social and cultural constraints enables girls to take advantage of educational opportunities. It is worth restating that the multiplier effects of investment in women's education and quality of life are enormous, and the results benefit the entire society. This investment has implications for women's ability to participate in society and for fertility. Helping women to stay healthy and to control the amount of time spent in childbearing and child rearing enables them to increase their choices and thereby contribute in larger measure to uplifting the entire society.

Removing barriers and creating capabilities for economic entrepreneurship of women are also critical. The extraordinary entrepreneurship many women display in the informal sector should be encouraged and reinforced. Stories of female economic entrepreneurship in West Africa are well known. The vigorous role of Liberian women in West African trade has become apparent in recent years. Women pay back loans at a much higher rate and save and invest money relatively more often than do men. Nontraditional collateral and customized loan requirements are necessary to enable women to take advantage of entrepreneurial opportunities. Thus, to treat gender equality as a fundamental peacebuilding challenge requires the development of strategic initiatives that will not only remove barriers but also build capabilities to create and access opportunities.

The best way to ensure that the transition process lays solid foundations for longer term democratization is to have it address issues of gender equity right from the start of that process. There is much truth in the saying "educate the women and you educate the community." Programs of education, primary health care, food production, and food security are likely not only to succeed but also to have considerable multiplier effects when organized around the core issue of the empowerment of women. While many programs are organized to address the numerous dimensions of women's empowerment, these programs, like most other peacebuilding initiatives, are not sufficiently integrated to inform and reinforce each other; neither are they organized within a larger framework that places women's empowerment as a central element in an overall process of self-reliant development and democratic self-governance.

*   *   *

While it is true that during Liberia's postconflict transition, peacebuilding activities may not have all been organized as discrete initiatives (many are implemented through clusters known as thematic groups—for example, groups dealing with children's issues or agriculture), one can easily observe that there is insufficient coordination across thematic groups and linkages among them. Moreover, these initiatives are provided and produced largely by external actors, with Liberians playing mostly marginal roles in their production and primarily becoming consumers. Hence, the prospects for their sustainability is questionable.

Finally, peacebuilding in Liberia is proceeding on a course that does not substantially contribute to long-term democratization. Preparations for elections seem to be driven by donor timetables and not by a governance reform agenda of which elections should be a part. Ordinary Liberians are essentially beneficiaries of peacebuilding activities provided by others; yet they will ultimately be expected to sustain those activities in the future. Unless corrective measures are taken, the opportunity to use these peacebuilding activities to establish a process of constitutional choice and to build foundations for democratic governance that depart from patterns of government predation, repression, and governance failure will be missed.

▪ Notes

1. For example, postapartheid peacebuilding in South Africa and postconflict peacebuilding in Sierra Leone present two contrasting approaches, despite the fact that both established truth and reconciliation commissions. In South Africa, as a result of extensive public debate, South Africans evolved a vision of a nonracial, culturally diverse society to be governed by multileveled institutional arrangements that should derive their authority from and promote the well-being of individuals and communities. Sierra Leone's postconflict debate focused much more on how to promote "a culture of peace" as a human value than on how to create appropriate institutional arrangements based on a vision of a new Sierra Leone. See Lamin (2003).

2. In this chapter and the following chapter, I have drawn upon the analysis of Liesbet Hooghe and Gary Marks (2003) and have used the term *level* as they have, that is, with reference to scale or size of jurisdiction.

3. Notable among these are conflicts between the Grebo and Krahn in southeastern Liberia, and between the Mano/Gio and the Mandingo communities of Nimba. See also Sawyer, Wesseh, and Ajavon (2000).

4. Poro leaders and Mandingo imams have been able to restore trust among Mandingo and Loma people who live together in many multiethnic communities in northwestern Liberia. Such indigenous peacemaking mechanisms are hardly ever acknowledged for their contribution to peacemaking, nor are they incorporated in multileveled peacebuilding strategies.

5. See West African Observatory, ECOWAS website, www.cedeao.org.

6. The military overwhelmingly supported Johnny Paul Koromah in the 2000 elections, and its reported reluctance to engage residual and cross-border forces from Liberia have created suspicion as to its fitness as a national army (ICG 2003a).

7. An exception was when the Guinean military repulsed a Portuguese-backed invasion in 1971.

8. Switzerland and Israel are two well-known examples. In the United States, in addition to federal military forces, there are national guard forces organized at the state level. These are typically coordinated with the federal forces when they are needed to perform federal security duties.

9. As South Africa has shown, the major objective of truth and reconciliation commissions (TRCs) is to expose the facts as seen by both the perpetrators and victims of brutal repression and to arrive at a basis for restoration. The pursuit of restorative justice as the central objective of TRCs is not incompatible with the indictment and trial of those who bear the greatest responsibility for egregious crimes if both are pursued in appropriate proportions. South Africa has shown how a balance can be

ensured. Rwanda's dilemma with the trials of *génocidaires* is an example of a difficult quest for "victim's justice" on the one hand and a balanced approach to reconciliation on the other. See Mamdani (2001) and Tutu (1999).

10. At a workshop on war-affected children held in Monrovia in 1999, children were asked the question, "Who are war-affected children?" Some of their responses are as follows:

- children who go without food because of war
- children whose parents have been killed
- children who witnessed horrible killings
- children who disrespect older people
- children whose minds are disturbed and cannot do their school work well
- children who are too old for their grades
- children who became parents before their time
- children who took part in war as fighters
- children who engage in prostitution
- children who do not receive proper education
- girls who have been raped.

11. The term *lumpen youth* has been borrowed from Abdullah (1998).

12. See Ensminger (1990) for a succinct analysis of how changing property rights and other factors increased the costs of decisionmaking by councils of elders and contributed to their co-optation by the African state.

13. Although it is not known how many among the elderly perished as a result of the conflict, it is reported that life expectancy at birth fell from fifty-five years in 1980 to as low as thirty-five in 1997. See GOL (2000b, 45).

14. My research in 2002 identified only two programs wholly devoted to addressing humanitarian emergency needs of the elderly. Both are NGOs that serve as transmission belts between IGOs and INGOs and the elderly poor.

15. I thank Joyce Mends-Cole of the Gender Department of UNHCR for this perspective.

16. The Association of Female Lawyers of Liberia (AFELL) has taken the lead in addressing property rights issues affecting women.

CHAPTER 7

From Theory to Practice

A S STATED REPEATEDLY IN THIS BOOK, THE CONSTITUTION OF ORDER IN A SOCIETY relies upon much more than the prescriptions written down in the document called the constitution of the country. Order in any society is patterned by configurations of rules. As also stated, social scientists know all too well that not all rules are written and not all written rules are used as working rules. Political scientists have long studied discrepancies between laws on the books and rules-in-use. Elinor Ostrom (2005) has stressed that closing the gap between formal (written) rules and rules-in-use (working rules) is one of the most critical challenges for successful collective action. Embarking on a process of democratic change requires the establishment of appropriate written rules and a sustained effort to close the gap between formal rules and prevailing behavior. Thus, the establishment of written rules is a foundational activity.

The very idea of a single person proposing a set of institutional arrangements for democratic self-governance runs contrary to the fundamental thesis of this study. As stated repeatedly, only the Liberian people, through processes of constitutional choice, can organize their own patterns of democratic governance. What follows is a practical effort to show what a polycentric democratic governance arrangement designed for Liberians could look like within the context of the wider Mano basin area.[1] I first discuss a way of thinking about a polycentric approach to democratic governance in that region and then turn to how such patterns could be laid out for Liberia.

■ Framing a Polycentric System in the Mano Basin Area

Systems of polycentric governance differ from arrangements of centralized government and situations of command and control in that polycentric systems foster the establishment of multiple centers of limited or shared authority at multiple levels of governance. This is precisely the type of governing arrangements that can meet the needs of interrelated societies such as those of the Mano basin area. The fundamental task in making such systems work is to determine what should be the appropriate jurisdictions of governance for the provision and production of the array of public goods and services that people want. This involves appropriately mixing and matching institutions and public goods. Principles of subsidiarity, fiscal equivalency, and rules that address externalities and economics of scale are among the technical tools to be used to assist those who organize processes of constitutional choice in designing institutions of polycentric governance in diverse ecological and social contexts. Hooghe and Marks (2003) have shown how these principles apply in polycentric governance arrangements that consist of general purpose, multiple-level government jurisdictions and task-specific regimes such as in the European Union. While the model of the European Union need not be duplicated in the Mano basin area, lessons can be learned from that approach and from experiences elsewhere.

The Idea of a Mano Basin Federation

The violent conflict that engulfed Liberia and its neighbors has shown that country-specific governance institutions are not always appropriate for providing every essential public good. As shown in Chapter 6, the provision of security for Liberia requires a mix of regimes that includes institutions that operate at the basin-wide level. The need for basin-wide governance institutions is not one that has only recently been recognized, nor is it confined to the question of security. The Mano River Union was established in the 1970s as an instrumentality to advance certain basin-wide developmental activities. Among the services that were already being provided at the basin-wide level by the Mano River Union before the outbreak of violent conflict in 1989 were air traffic control services and capacity building in maritime operations and in forest conservation.

There are other areas in which basin-wide regimes are already needed. The cross-border location of certain natural resource endowments gives reason for organizing governance arrangements that should involve basin-wide as well as other levels of governance. For example, the rich deposits of iron ore of the low mountain range that straddles the border of Liberia and Guinea and the hydroelectric potential of the Mano River, which marks the border between Liberia and Sierra Leone, can best be developed under governance arrangements that include basin-wide governance institutions.

Language and ethnic groups overlap national borders, and indigenous governance institutions such as the Poro link transborder communities in Liberia, Sierra Leone, and Guinea. Transborder catchment areas of trade and culture have existed among the three countries for centuries and remain robust today, despite colonial divisions and state formation. These, along with the existing Mano River Union, are among the building blocks of what could be thought of as an emergent Mano basin federation.

The idea of a Mano basin federation may strike some as being reminiscent of several unsuccessful attempts at forming federations in Africa, especially in West Africa. The Mali Federation of Senegal and Mali; Senegambia, the federation of Senegal and The Gambia; and the union of Ghana, Guinea, and Mali are well-known examples of ill-fated postindependence West African federations. One of the shortcomings of these attempts to form federations is that they were driven largely, if not solely, by heads of states and by single-party parliaments. Because they involved almost no processes of constitutional choice in which the people of the various countries participated, their success depended to a large extent on the nature of personal ties between heads of states. Moreover, except for the initiative to form Senegambia, all of these initiatives took place within the ambit of Cold War global order and, as such, were connected to the politics of global bipolarity.

The context within which a Mano basin federation is to be thought of is quite different. Liberians and Sierra Leoneans have now seen how supranational-level governing institutions are a very important part of the mix of governance institutions that affect their lives. The international stabilization forces and the special court on war crimes are entities that are of service to the people of the basin area. ECOWAS has already adopted ECOMOG or a successor force as a standing West African regional rapid deployment force and, as such, an important coproducer of security in the basin area. More importantly, there is significant evidence of self-organization among the people of the basin area. Civil society groups of the three countries have been working together very closely for at least a decade on issues of conflict resolution and peacebuilding in the basin area. Womens' organizations of the three countries formed the Mano River Women's Peace Network and pressured leaders of the three countries into establishing a dialogue for peace. The Inter-Religious Council of Sierra Leone and the Interfaith Council of Liberia were both architects of peace formulas in the two countries and close collaborators in the search for peace in the basin area. The civil society movements of Liberia, Sierra Leone, and Guinea—which include organizations of teachers, students, journalists, trade unions, and a range of other groups promoting women's empowerment, rural development, and other concerns—have formed a common platform for peace and postconflict peacebuilding in the basin area. These are people-driven organizations evolving a sense of shared community across national borders.[2] Thus, one can say that there is already a substantial foundation on which to build a Mano basin federation.

Emergent governance patterns among the people of the Mano basin area are situated in a larger context of growing cooperation among West African countries. ECOWAS has now established the West African Community Court of Justice, the West African Parliament, and the West African Monetary Institute. With the establishment of the West African Monetary Institute, ECOWAS has moved closer to the establishment of a central bank and the issuance of a single currency—the eco.[3] While it is true that these institutions are best provided under the leadership of national governments, a shortcoming is that they are being established largely as undertakings of national governments with little input from the people of West African societies. The Community Court, for example, accords standing to individuals but only through national governments. A council of elders established to assist in conflict mediation in West Africa consists solely of individuals directly appointed by governments. West African institutions that govern on the regional level can deepen their legitimacy and grow robust only if those who are to be the beneficiaries are involved in their establishment and functioning. Regional systems of justice, security, and lawmaking, among other systems that affect local populations, need to be considered legitimate by local people if they are to work well. Polycentric arrangements arrived at through processes of constitutional choice offer the best approach to establishing or ensuring legitimacy to these regional governance arrangements. Contemporary European experience supports this observation.

It is hopeful that the increasing collective action among ordinary people of Liberia, Sierra Leone, and Guinea leads to basin-wide processes of constitutional choice for the crafting of institutions of democratic governance of the basin area. Although establishing systems of law and bridging language gaps are formidable challenges, the potential for addressing these challenges can be found in the language communities that cross-cut borders, in the common experiences and traditions of the area's peoples in problem solving, and in the experience of peoples elsewhere. It may not be far-fetched to envision a Mano basin federation in which the three countries become province-like or canton-like jurisdictions.

The growing demand for basin-wide institutions is linked to the demands of the people of the three countries for greater internal processes of democratic governance. Let me demonstrate how democratic governance based on a polycentric system of governance could work for one of the countries—Liberia.

■ Creating General Purpose and Task-Specific Governmental Institutions for Liberia

What Liberians generally think of as "the government" is in fact a set of centralized institutions headed or otherwise dominated by the president. They include the cabinet; county administrators, such as superintendents, district commissioners, and paramount, clan and other chiefs; and an assortment of executive functionaries. Also included in "the government" are the legislature, which has for more than a century been dominated by the president and his party; and the judiciary, which has also been under the influence of the president. In transforming this model of government, a multiple-level general purpose governmental arrangement will establish several levels of constitutionally mandated, independent, and coordinated governments. Task-specific jurisdictions would also be established that would in many cases cross-cut general purpose jurisdictions.

Establishing General Purpose, Multiple-Level Governments

General purpose multiple-level governments will include cities and township governments, county governments, and a national-level government, all functioning as autonomous but interrelated and coordinated political authorities with limited or shared sovereignty enshrined as provisions in the national constitution, in county constitutions, and in city and township charters. Townships and cities will be the basic general purpose governmental jurisdictions; counties will comprise several townships and cities; and, though limited in its authority, the national governmental jurisdiction will span the entire country.

Townships as Basic Jurisdictions of Governance

Villages and towns in various mixes headed by general town chiefs constitute the smallest administrative jurisdictions in Liberia today. Several of these villages and towns constitute a clan, with the clan chief as its administrative head. Svend Holsoe (2002) has rightly observed that over the years of Liberian state control, clans have become much more a territorial jurisdiction than a kinship-based unit, and their chiefs have become functionaries of the Liberian government "elected" by local people but paid by the national government and beholden to it.[4] Notwithstanding, clans are the most active and widely acknowledged units of community-based development throughout Liberia. Clan members who do not reside within clan jurisdictions are still recognized as such and are expected to participate in clan-based developmental activities. I follow Holsoe's proposal that, since clan jurisdictions have been transformed from purely kinship-based jurisdictions, they be reconstructed as territorial jurisdictions of townships.[5] Thus, where clans consist of clusters of villages and hamlets, they become townships; and where there are single towns and associated half-towns, those also become townships. In this way, townships become the basic jurisdictions of general purpose governance and membership, or citizenship becomes open to all residents, including nonkinsfolk who live in such townships. To some extent, this proposal follows trends, since the Tubman era of creating townships as administrative units within county jurisdictions; however, it departs significantly from those trends since it seeks to empower townships with constitutional authority.

Township councils. Political governance would be organized through township councils whose members would be elected or otherwise selected through processes of democratic choice agreed by the people themselves. Patterns are expected to vary as local culture differs. One would expect that in southeastern Liberia, members of township councils will be selected in ways that reflect *panton* or equivalent representational patterns, while it is likely that in some parts of northwestern Liberia, Poro standing and relations to owners of the land may influence patterns of selection. Whatever the arrangements, it is important that they are designed to support processes of choice at this basic level of governance so that the new governance patterns can depart both from local boss rule as well as from the domination and control of the national government. It is expected that as constitutional authority becomes shared with townships, many more educated sons and daughters of those areas will become directly involved in local processes of governance. Being a member of a township council will then become more prestigious and meaningful as the township becomes a locus of political authority and development initiatives.

A chair or chief commissioner will serve as administrative head of the township council for a defined tenure. Townships will have the authority to levy taxes and expend such resources on township needs. Through processes of subsidiarity and fiscal equivalency, certain functions of governance will be mandated to township governments. Among these could be the provision of services, such as community refuse disposal, maintenance of market grounds and of wells and public toilets, and the settlement of land disputes that fall within the jurisdiction of the township. In view of Liberia's postconflict security realities, townships could also organize community-based early warning networks and community security units. Age-set groups would be particularly suitable for this purpose. Linked to similar groups in other townships, such networks could also perform policing services and become units for local defense.

Township courts. Township courts will be established as part of a system of county courts. These courts will be guided by a harmonized system of laws, a project that would have to be undertaken at the national level. Judges of township courts will be appointed by township councils from among candidates certified by a county judicial service commission that would be established within the bar association of the county. Dispute resolution through equity jurisprudence and other arrangements compatible with the principle of due process of law will be encouraged; however, courts of chiefs and "native governors" will be abolished.[6]

Township development associations. Township development associations will now become the crucible of community development, the basic organizations in which the array of networks and organizations will officially interact for community development purposes. Currently, the status of such bodies is ambiguous; in many places they operate parallel to and are frequently in conflict with national government-created development authorities. Their leaders are frequently selected through inclusive processes of constitutional choice reflective of the broad array of networks and organizations that constitute associational life in townships. Such organizations are typically all-inclusive. Their challenge will be to remain so and to ensure that their internal processes are democratic. Township councils will be expected to draw upon the institutional resources of township development associations, making the latter coproducers of township development undertakings thereby further enhancing the participatory nature of township governance.

Abolishing Paramount Chieftaincies and Districts

Clans are the only local political and administrative jurisdictions constructed upon formations previously organized by the people themselves. Paramount chieftaincies and districts were created entirely by the national government to enhance its control over interior populations. Sandwiched between clan and county jurisdictions are paramount chieftaincies and districts, which are administrative units used by the national government for the implementation of its policies.[7] Such instruments of command and control are hardly compatible with the horizontal and upwardly vertical patterns of aggregation that are characteristic of and required by self-governing institutional arrangements; therefore, they need to be abolished.[8] As discussed subsequently, townships, as constitutionally created jurisdictions, may combine among themselves to form special jurisdictions for the provision of specific public goods and services.

A final word about the future of chieftaincy formations in Liberia: At this historic juncture, most indicators critical to the future of Liberia present chieftaincies as being of diminishing relevance if Liberia is to develop a system of democratic governance. With increasing demographic shifts in favor of youth, only a diminishing percentage of the population of rural Liberia (perhaps those above forty years old) are likely to have an appreciation of the role of the paramount chief, let alone loyalty to that position. Unlike chieftaincy formations in Ghana and Nigeria, for example, those in Liberia have not only been subjected to sustained abuse and political manipulation over years of state predation and repression, including the brutal repression of Samuel Doe, but they have also been dealt the coup de grâce by fifteen years of violent plunder and carnage.

■ Counties as Jurisdictions of Shared Sovereignty

In Liberia's unitary system of government, counties are the divisional hubs from which executive decisions are implemented and public goods and services that are organized from the top trickle down to local people. County officials are also the intermediaries through which local people articulate and transmit their concerns to the central government. These centers, characterized largely by a downward flow of the central government's directives and services, will have to be transformed into jurisdictions of shared sovereign authority if self-governance is to be established. The establishment of counties as sites of shared sovereignty is at the core of the constitutional reform essential to establishing institutions of democratic self-governance.

Creating and Rationalizing County Jurisdictions

Since the early 1960s, the creation of counties and the demarcation of their territorial boundaries have been based largely on political decisions made by the president, with the support or at the urging of influential local leaders, and have been approved by the legislature. Some of these decisions were widely accepted because they had implications for fostering national harmony. For example, the creation of the counties of Bong, Grand Gedeh, Lofa, and Nimba in the mid-1960s was popularly acclaimed and seen as advancing the process of political unification and integration. The creation of these counties brought the total number of counties to nine. However, the creation of four new counties in the 1970s drew muted displeasure from sectors of the population of the counties that lost territory and from others. The four new counties of Bomi, Grand Kru, Margibi, and River Cess were previously county subjurisdictions called territories and were administered as semiautonomous entities within their parent counties. Still later, during Charles Taylor's presidency, two new counties were carved out of existing counties. River Gee County was carved out of Grand Gedeh County and Gbarpolu County out of Lofa.

Although narrow political considerations sometimes come into play in the creation of new counties, there are cases in which such action has been an important means of resolving unhealthy ethnic rivalries and conflicts or providing growth opportunities for certain remote and inaccessible areas. Whatever the political motive, the creation of River Gee County addressed longstanding political feuds between Krahn and Grebo elites of the parent Grand Gedeh County, and the creation of Gbarpolu County established a new political and socioeconomic catchment area in what was the underdeveloped nexus of three counties. The creation of Grand Kru County two decades earlier sought to establish a socioeconomic catchment area in the southeast in what were remote communities in Sinoe and Maryland counties.

In a new polycentric governance system in Liberia, there might still be calls by local elites for the creation of new counties; however, such calls are likely to gain the support of local people only where patterns of local self-governance are "nested" in unsupportive county-level governance arrangements or where such local communities are unable to establish vital and mutually rewarding horizontal relationships with neighboring communities. What is important in such cases is that local people—those who would aspire to establish new jurisdictions as well as those who are to remain within the original jurisdictions—be involved in making such decisions through processes of choice. This, of course, is a challenge for the future.

One of the immediate challenges in reconstituting counties as jurisdictions of shared sovereignty is to rationalize within them the subjurisdictions called statutory districts and the awkward combination of scattered settlements sometimes called "cities." Many of these were created by the central government for purely partisan or personalized reasons.[9] While not detracting from the freedom of people to form new communities and to amalgamate old ones, as has been going on for years among people of both southeastern and northwestern Liberia, there is a need to address situations where anomalous jurisdictions have been created as a means of providing government positions as spoils to faithful partisans—thus misusing a vital constitutional process. Therefore, all statutory districts would have to be abolished and the towns and villages within them reorganized as townships and where practical, cities.

Organizing County Governance

County governance must be established through the mix of institutions that pattern order in the townships and cities of the county. These would include horizontally aggregated institutions through which townships and cities cooperate in collective actions (such as sanitation districts) as well as others organized only at the county level (such as county councils). To ensure that county governance assumes and maintains a self-governing democratic character, it is important that institutions organized through horizontal and vertical aggregation within a county dominate governance relationships within that county. People solving problems through community-based collective actions must constitute the foundations of county governance. Actions of county governmental institutions must be both a reflection of and a response to locally based initiatives. Townships and cities must be the energizers of county governance and must aggregate in appropriate patterns to solve county-based problems. County-level institutions will also have the responsibility to ensure equity and rights of participation to all individuals and groups that live in townships and cities within the county, especially those individuals and groups that are ethnic and religious minorities, are subject to gender discrimination, or are disabled. This is a vital responsibility that will be shared with appropriate national-level institutions.

County council or assembly. A major pillar of Liberia's self-governing democracy will be the county council or assembly—a countywide, broadly representative, deliberative, and decisionmaking body—whose members will be elected from electoral and other constituencies of the various townships and cities of the county. County councilors or assembly members will serve fixed terms of office. Each county, through a process of constitutional choice, will decide its own pattern of democratic governance: to have an elected county executive independent of, but reporting to, the council or assembly; to select one of its members as managing councilor or assembly chair; or to have a rotational chair and hire a qualified technician as county manager. Each county will fashion its own internal democratic processes to meet its needs and circumstances. Whatever the case, county executives will not be considered vicegerents of the president and county councils and assemblies will not be beholden to the national government; they will be responsible to the people of the county. However, they will be obliged to coordinate the affairs of the county with the national government and will be accountable to that government in specific instances and under specific circumstances that would be specified by law. One such circumstance will be to ensure the protection of the fundamental rights of individuals and groups (especially women and ethnic minorities) at local levels of governance against adverse local practices and exclusion.

Shared sovereign authority. The council will have the power to levy taxes and, through subsidiarity and other appropriate and agreed arrangements, disburse county revenues to townships and cities and special jurisdictions and receive disbursements from the central government. A critical aspect of the council's or assembly's work will be to identify strategic and optimal levels of county governance at which certain goods and services can best be provided and to encourage and empower townships and cities to engage in certain types of collective actions at that level. In addition to sharing responsibility with national institutions to ensure equity and rights of participation of minority groups at local levels, county-level government will also constitute a residual authority where township and city jurisdictions are inapplicable. County authorities will develop strategies and programs for the development of the county. Two or more counties may combine their efforts in development undertakings. Under principles of shared sovereignty and subject to coordination with other counties, counties will have the right to team up with national government and, under the rules laid down by the latter, negotiate external trade relationships and leverage foreign investments in a manner consistent with Liberia's foreign policy enunciated by the national government. The allocation of property rights in natural resources between central government and the counties will be a critical issue that will have to be addressed on an ongoing basis. Each county will have to establish a special commission or set of instrumentalities to attend this question.

County commissions. Counties may choose to set up a variety of commissions as implementation mechanisms as well as to provide technical and other types of support services for local jurisdictions. For example, a commission on education may, in coordination with school authorities and other organizations of the townships and cities, design, monitor, and evaluate educational services provided in the county.

County judicial system. County courts will be an integral part of the national judicial system; however, county jurisdictions will play an important role in the appointment of judges and the creation of an environment within which they can function with integrity and credibility. A county judicial system will include township and city courts of common pleas and specialized courts. The harmonization of laws is critical to the dispensing of justice; therefore, the effort to address incompatibilities between customary and statutory laws needs to be sustained through institutional processes at both the county and national levels of governance. A judicial mechanism could be established at the national level to address this question and to be available to provide advice as an ongoing service.

County auditing office. The position of county auditor will be established and charged with the responsibility of undertaking periodic and special audits of the use of county resources by any county-associated organization. The county auditor will be appointed by and responsible to the county council or assembly. The tenure and remunerations of the office will be set in a manner to ensure the autonomy, integrity, and security of the office.

■ Reorganizing National Government

The character of the national government will change in view of the establishment of a polycentric system of governance where powers are shared with township and county levels of governance and with special purpose jurisdictions, and also in view of emergent patterns of Mano basin–wide governance. Change in power relationships between the national government and the counties will, in turn, require significant changes in the configuration and functions of institutions of the national government. To begin with, the character of the executive will be transformed as the expansive powers of appointment of the president are curbed. Under new resource-sharing arrangements, the national government will not be able to exercise exclusive control over the country's subsoil and other natural resources. The national government will no longer have monopoly over decisions that determine the political, social, and economic development of the country; these will be shared with several county, city, and township decisionmaking centers around the country and with specialized jurisdictions, including some that operate at Mano basin–wide level. Despite such dispersal of powers, the national government will still have a critical role in governance.

Critical Responsibilities of the National Government

There are some responsibilities that will be performed by the national government only or under its leadership. Some of these are described in the following paragraphs.

Articulating vision and mission. National-level institutions will have to take the lead in shaping the vision and framing the mission of the new Liberia and ensuring that that vision and mission permeate all levels of governance. The core values to which Liberians aspire, as expressed in the fundamental rights provided for in the constitution, must be promoted and protected by the national government over and against all countervailing views and actions that may emanate from county and local governments and from elsewhere in the society or abroad. The national legislature and supreme court, along with the president, must be the chief articulators of these rights and the president their chief enforcer.

Setting standards, ensuring coordination, monitoring, evaluating, and enforcing. Patterns of uneven development are not unusual in any social situation or system of governance. The challenge is to ensure that some minimum standards are agreed and that sufficient efforts and resources are available to make sure that all jurisdictions attain at least the minimum acceptable standards of public goods and services. This is particularly important in areas such as security, education, and health care. The national government must set standards regarding what is considered minimally acceptable educational and health care systems, for example. It must monitor the activities of educational and health care systems and evaluate their performance, and in certain cases, it must seek rulings of courts and enforce certain sanctions upon subnational jurisdictions where access to public goods and services are denied or made available inequitably.

Formulating foreign policy. Only the national government will be able to structure a framework for Liberia's interaction with foreign countries. County jurisdictions must interact with external actors within a national foreign policy framework and in partnership with the national government—a partnership in which the latter is the lead partner. The president, in consultation with the national legislature, would have the responsibility of formulating foreign policy.

Determining responsibility for security and defense. The provision of internal policing can be shared among local, county, and national jurisdictions and with specialized jurisdictions, and the proportion of involvement of each level would be determined by specific situations. However, the ultimate responsibility for the safety and security of the people of society rests upon the people themselves, and it must be exercised through the national government ultimately. Defense against external aggressors must be the responsibility of the national government. Protection against illicit trade, including drug and arms trafficking, will be a responsibility shared at multiple levels but under the leadership of the national government. While local communities must play a role in providing for their own security, through organized policing units, and early warning and early action mechanisms, for example, the national government must coordinate and buttress these initiatives.

Protecting minority rights. Inherent in self-governing arrangements is the potential that local majorities may marginalize and mistreat local minorities. The national government must have a very important role to play in ensuring the protection of the rights of local minorities against the potential tyranny of local majorities. In addition to the role of national courts in addressing this problem, there would be special executive agencies set up at the national level to monitor and ensure the protection of the rights of local minorities. These are illustrative of areas in which only the national government can appropriately take leadership.

Strengthening National Institutions

Creation and transformation of institutions to enhance accountable performance. The establishment of shared responsibilities and resources at three levels of governance provides the opportunity to restructure national government and strengthen its institutions, especially its mechanisms for ensuring accountable performance in its spheres of activities. Many of the reforms proposed in the 1983 draft constitution could be applied at this time. For example, the task of ensuring standards and strengthening accountability within the national government—and at other levels, for that matter—will be enhanced through the establishment of a number of national-level autonomous commissions. Bodies such as a national judicial service commission, a public service commission, an electoral commission, and an office of auditor general would also function at county and township levels where national government's resources are used. Some agencies will have to be abolished or their responsibilities changed. The ministry of internal affairs, for example, has been one of the important instruments of presidential control over the counties; with the introduction of shared sovereignty, it will have to be abolished or its role substantially changed. Within a streamlined national bureaucracy, it could be assigned the task of addressing issues having to do with the protection of the rights of local minorities.

Technical offices such as the bureau of state enterprises and the national investment commission will have to be reorganized to reflect the principle of shared sovereignty and, as such, to also become accountable to county authorities as the latter's interests would require.

National legislature. As counties become constitutionally independent actors, the burden of restraining presidential authority will not rest entirely on the legislature. Counties will also have interest in protecting their constitutional authority. Notwithstanding, the legislature's responsibility to act as coparticipant in policymaking, to respond to constituencies, and to ensure presidential accountability remains critical. This responsibility can be properly exercised only when the legislature itself becomes independent of presidential control and develops appropriate capabilities. To achieve autonomy, the legislature must first gain control over its own resources. Constitutional rules must be established to give the legislature control over its own operational budget, which must be managed in accordance with the same professional standards and subjected to the same auditing requirements as expected of executive and other agencies. The legislature will also have to establish internal rules that will enable it to carry out its constitutional duty to participate in policymaking. It must recruit a highly competent technical and professional staff and develop the capacity to access information and generate independent research rather than rely on the executive for information and research.

Legislative participation in budgetary and financial matters is of particular importance. Constitutional rules will be needed to ensure that the legislature's participation in budget matters is broader than its current role of debating and passing the national budget. New rules will empower the legislature to participate with the executive in making certain implementation decisions, such as those regarding interagency transfers of budgeted allocations and related fiscal transactions over which the president now exercises sole constitutional control. The discretionary account that is administered solely by the president will be limited in both the amounts it contains as well as the purposes for which it could be used. The auditing of executive agencies, including the presidential discretionary account, will also be as much an exercised prerogative of the legislature as it is of the president.

Under this new arrangement of county empowerment, national institutions such as the legislature and the executive must provide a counterbalance to the upsurge of county assertiveness to ensure that this new dispensation does not become an instrument to dismantle the body politic through undue fragmentation, confusion, and breakdown of a sense of national identity. One of the ways in which the legislature could be helpful in this respect is to make sure that as competitive multiparty politics take root, electoral rules are crafted to prevent political party recruitment to legislative positions and to keep county councils from being skewed in favor of representation from any particular segment of the population.

Supreme Court. Since the coup of 1980, there have been more efforts to strengthen the Liberian judiciary than there have been to improve any other institution of national government. The provisions of the 1983 draft constitution that called for substantial increases in the salaries and benefits of judges were retained in the revised and approved constitution and have been implemented. Since the promulgation of the constitution in 1986, various external actors have provided law libraries and judicial equipment and have sponsored numerous legal seminars and a variety of capacity-building projects, all in the hope of strengthening the competence, integrity, and independence of the judiciary. Yet, the Liberian judiciary has remained the weakest link in Liberia's national governmental arrangement. While on rare occasions over the years the legislature has displayed spasms of independence, the supreme court has largely remained an available tool for the purposes of the president.

The lack of judicial independence is not caused by lack of legal education, inadequate remuneration, or capacity deficiency. Members of the judiciary suffer the same sense of insecurity and vulnerability that pervades Liberia's president-dominated system of government. Lawyers with a keen sense of personal integrity have routinely declined judicial appointments. It has become so obvious in recent times that one cannot have a judiciary that lacks independence and integrity in a postconflict situation where criminality and war-related offenses require serious attention, where multiparty political competition is gaining ground, and where human rights awareness and advocacy are on the rise.

A strong, independent, and competent judiciary is at once an essential requirement for successful implementation of the type of governance reforms under discussion here as well as one of its most important outcomes. Judicial independence can only be achieved as a result of widespread governance reforms and the cascading impact each reform measure will have on others. For example, curtailment of presidential excesses through institutional reform that includes the establishment of independent commissions, constitutional empowerment of county-level governing institutions, and increased citizens' demands for accountability and protection of their rights will all have reinforcing impacts that are bound to improve the judiciary. Competent lawyers with integrity will now find incentives to take up judicial appointments. In a system of shared sovereignty, the court's function of judicial review becomes critical in resolving disputes between jurisdictions. Also, as local-level institutions exercise constitutional prerogatives, the courts become an indispensable mechanism for the protection of the rights of minorities. This is why courts at all levels of governance must be linked to the supreme court through appellate processes, and access to such processes must be within the reach of all and without inhibitions of cost when questions affecting the fundamental rights of people are at issue.

Other institutions. Clearly, this brief discussion of national-level institutional reforms does not begin to address the full scope of executive, legislative, and judicial reforms needed, let alone reforms in other areas of national-level governance. There are several areas, including the full range of agencies that function under the control of the president, that should be studied and reformed. The nature of the national bureaucracy will be completely changed. The electoral system will also be reformed. A significant challenge will be to determine which services would more appropriately be provided at which level of governance and how suitable institutions for those purposes might be crafted. Questions of revenue sharing and equity will pose huge challenges. Defining taxing authority and the authority to raise grants and loans, and agreeing on formulas for revenue allocation among various jurisdictions, are among challenges that will need constant attention and for which special institutions will have to be crafted. Examining the experiences of South Africa, Switzerland, and the United States, among others, would be very helpful in addressing these issues.[10]

■ Establishing Task-Specific Regimes

As Hooghe and Marks (2003) explained, the advantage of task-specific regimes is that they provide institutional flexibility in response to a variety of governance situations. When it comes to the provision of goods and services, such regimes can be created to cut across fixed jurisdictions, including those that are extraterritorial to a country. They can be crafted to respond to the nature of the good and to service more than a single fixed jurisdiction at any given time. Task-specific organizations will be appropriate to provide a variety of goods and services under a new arrangement of polycentric governance in Liberia. Many of the current public corporations that have been operating as entities of the central government will be reconstituted as special purpose jurisdictions. The challenge is to know which are more suitable for privatization and which can best be managed as task-specific regimes. This requires analysis specific to each situation. Such studies will enhance understanding of the nature of the good or service to be provided, the social and physical environment, and any special or unique circumstances that might exist. Based on such studies, a determination would be made as to whether or how such entities fit within the context of shared sovereignty and self-governance. While it is beyond the ambition of this book to prescribe detailed institutional arrangements, one can see broad outlines as to how task-specific regimes might function in a mix with general purpose jurisdictions. The following examples of how the reconstitution of public corporations that produce electricity and manage forest resources might be worked out illustrate how general purpose and task-specific jurisdictions could interact.

Producing Electricity Under Task-Specific Regimes

Public corporations such as the Liberia Electricity Corporation would be reconstituted to make electricity available as toll goods. A variety of provision, production, and consumption arrangements are possible. Provision could be done by a task-specific regime composed of several counties acting together or in partnership with private business, or by private business alone acting as a single provision unit. Production of the several aspects of electric power (generation, transmission, distribution) could similarly be done by private entities and, in the case of transmission and distribution, any mix of private and other arrangements. These special purpose jurisdictions could cross-cut county boundaries as well as national borders. In a similar manner, local communities could organize consumption units and purchase electric power, as could individuals or households. It is possible, for example, that several counties of the southeast, working in cooperation with regions of western Côte d'Ivoire, could constitute a task-specific jurisdiction to exploit the electric power potential of the Cavalla River. This, of course, may require the involvement of national governments and the private sector—especially with respect to financing the project. Similarly, the hydroelectric potential of the Sinoe River could also be exploited to provide electric power through arrangements that could involve both private and public participation. National, county, and township governments would participate with private enterprises in arranging the capital and other production costs, while townships, cities, and other fixed jurisdictions as well as other task-specific regimes and private sector firms would contract for purchase of the electric power. The point here is that a variety of arrangements can be crafted to establish task-specific jurisdiction for the production of electric power and that such autonomous task-specific regimes would interact with autonomous general purpose, fixed jurisdictions and other organizations in a variety of ways that can be mutually beneficial.

Governing Forest Resources

The Forestry Development Authority (FDA) will be reorganized to become one of several coordinated task-specific regimes that involve participation of townships and county-level jurisdictions, along with the national government and private entrepreneurs, in the coproduction of a variety of forest resources. Special basin area jurisdictions can be established to manage forest resources, such as parks, that may transcend national borders.

Until recently, Liberia's tropical rain forests were among the remaining patches in West Africa not overexploited by aggressive logging. The appropriation of property rights in forest resources by the national government has had a significant impact on communities of forest users. It has reduced accessibility of farmland; destroyed sacred groves, wildlife habitat, and sources of herbal remedies; and reduced the supply of game as a source of protein in the diet of rural dwellers—even though it has also provided seasonal employment and seasonally usable roads to some communities. State-dominated governance of forest resources has regularly ignored communal claims or typically compromised them when exercised by government-appointed chiefs who cannot enforce claims or may not be disposed to do so. In most cases, relationships between local communities and private concession holders are characterized by suspicion, mistrust and even violence. Rural flight has been exacerbated, in part, because people of rural communities have not been able to benefit substantially from the major resources of their environment. Forest user communities are important conservers of forest resources. Multiple and coordinated use of such resources under conditions of sustainability is possible through appropriately designed task-specific regimes that involve the joint participation of local townships, county government, and others in arrangements that secure the interest of local people in the use and conservation of these resources (see Gibson, McKean, and Ostrom 2000).

Governing Mineral Resources

Under principles of shared sovereignty, new property rights regimes regarding subsoil property will be required. The national government will not have sole control over the mineral resources of the country. New task-specific jurisdictions will have to be constituted. The shape of such task-specific regimes will be determined by the nature of the resource and the biophysical context and social circumstances within which such regimes are constituted and are to operate. In some cases, local townships, county governments, and national government may all be considered co-owners of subsoil rights, coproviders of services derived from exploitation of such resources, and cobeneficiaries of the outcomes that flow from the exploitation of those resources. Exploitation of the resources will also be organized in a variety of institutional mixes that could involve private sector participation wholly or in part as prevailing circumstances require. The impact of externalities both negative and positive, but especially negative, will have to play a significant role in provision, production, and consumption calculations.

Experience in Liberia has shown how mineral resource–rich local communities were brought close to destitution once the mines closed down. Tubmanburg in Bomi County is a classic case. Not only has there been massive loss of jobs, there have also been substantial problems of environmental degradation. Mineral resources were exploited under arrangements in which the national government, the sole owners, formed joint venture partnerships with international corporations or granted concession agreements to foreign private entities. While it is true that much of Liberia's social and physical infrastructural development was supported from the intake by the exploitation of these resources, there is no denying that the net impact of externalities on many mineral-rich communities has been devastating. Tubmanburg has never recovered from the closure of the Liberian Mining Company about thirty years ago. A similar fate could befall the port city of Buchanan, which serviced the iron ore industry of Nimba, and, more recently, the rapacious activities of the Oriental Timber Company.

The point being made here is not that local people should have exclusive rights to the control of mineral resources found in their communities. Obviously, there are considerations extending far beyond local communities that come into play in resource production and use. Local communities are not islands existing in isolation from the rest of society. The condition and fate of others who may not be so richly endowed do impinge upon the well-being of communities so endowed, making the sharing of the benefits of such resources a social imperative, a proposition that is in the best interest of all, including those in whose communities these resources are to be found. Besides, local communities cannot alone provide the productive capacity needed for the exploitation of such resources or the absorptive capacity for the potential outcomes or benefits that flow from the exploitation of such resources. The point here is that where these resources have been the sole preserve of the national government, arrangements related to how they are managed have been subject to the same shortcomings and challenges that obtain in other areas of governance under Liberia's system of unitary sovereignty. This is why new arrangements are necessary. Clearly, it is not possible to prescribe what these new arrangements should be. One can only say that they would be founded in the principle of shared sovereignty and be appropriate for the nature of the resource and the specific contexts and circumstances.

Establishing Other Task-Specific Transboundary Jurisdictions

As discussed earlier in this chapter, patterns of cultural, social, and economic interactions, developed long before colonial penetration and the founding of Liberia, have remained resilient. These transboundary catchment areas consist of ethnic communities that have developed robust patterns of trade, effective conflict resolution mechanisms, and reliable safety nets for their members on Liberia's borders with its neighbors. Systems of monocentric government in Liberia and in neighboring countries have routinely found these governance arrangements threatening to state sovereignty and to efforts to develop a sense of national identity and have sought to impose upon them central government institutions. Yet these patterns have continued to exist in spite of state resistance. It is important that such de facto transboundary jurisdictions be seen as the valuable resources they are and be incorporated into the system of polycentric governance. Emergent Mano basin institutions are likely to address questions pertaining to such transborder community relationships that obtain among communities in Liberia, Sierra Leone, and Guinea. These, however, are not the only such communities.

Along the Liberian-Ivorian borders, Gio communities, such as those of Gborplay and Butuo in Liberia and Danane and Man in Côte d'Ivoire, have built upon long-standing patterns of trade and have established welfare networks and security corridors for their members. Krahn communities, such as Tai and Guiglo in Côte d'Ivoire and Zleh Town and Toe Town in Liberia, have also strengthened their links.[11] Institutions created by these people to mediate conflicts between them and promote their mutual interests cannot be ignored. No amount of nationalistic suasion can break these ties. The issuance of national identity cards has not bridged the gulf between antagonistic groups within the same country nor broken the bonds between kinship groups that are divided by national borders. Only in wider polycentric systems can such regimes be treated as task-specific jurisdictions and their contributions to the governance of society fully appreciated and utilized.

Other Task-Specific Jurisdictions

Task-specific regimes can be established to provide a variety of other services, especially where economies of scale suggest that such services can best be delivered through jurisdictions that do not coincide with township, city, and county jurisdictions. Specialized education and referral health care are services that can more efficiently be delivered through task-specific jurisdictions. For example, two or three counties may find it an efficient use of resources to jointly establish a technical college, a regional university, or a regional medical referral center with certain advanced diagnostic or curative capabilities. A single appropriately outfitted and maintained criminal investigation laboratory established in Bopolu, for example, could service a jurisdiction that includes Garpolu and Bomi counties. A single unit of expert investigators of crimes could be established to service this area. What is important to get across is that task-specific jurisdictions can be created for a variety of contingencies and can operate complementarily with general purpose, fixed jurisdictions in a polycentric system of democratic governance.

■ Expanding Opportunities Through Polycentric Governance

What we have seen in this chapter is how polycentric arrangements based on principles of limited sovereignty are capable of expanding opportunities for entrepreneurship in a country. With a single center of authority, a system of unitary sovereignty can foreclose certain opportunities. Survival in such systems too frequently requires the mobilization of the creative genius of human beings for sycophancy and manipulation rather than for constructive productive outcomes. In such a state of Hobbesian sovereignty, no degree of moral suasion ultimately counts, because the stakes are high and individuals often find themselves locked in numerous noncooperative games. Distrust and suspicion abound. Some anthropologists who have observed this phenomenon play itself out in Liberia have ascribed it to the nature of human character and to culture in Liberia (Yoder 2003; Ellis 1999). Yet several scholars have written about the generosity of Liberians, their ability to get along socially, and the lack of a sense of ethnic particularism among most of them. Despite such characteristics, Liberians become distrustful in the realm of politics. Social congeniality does not translate into political accommodation, because there is plenty of social space in Liberia's social order, but political space remains narrow and controlled under its highly centralized governmental system.

A shift in governance paradigm opens up entrepreneurial space of all types. For example, the central government's control over commercial licenses and registrations will no longer exist. Enterprising young people will find it profitable to return to local townships and counties where laws are made and opportunities created rather than remain in Monrovia trying to find patrons. Many individuals who spend their time trying to become president may find it attractive to pursue leadership positions at the county level where they will be able to use their talents and energies in developing educational, health, and other services for society. Some of these individuals who may now be locked in debilitating competition among themselves will find it mutually rewarding to undertake cross-county collaborative ventures in education, health, public works, and even in private sector business ventures. Thousands of Liberians who are professionals in such fields as health care, agriculture, engineering, and education have left the country over the years. Not all of them left to seek greener economic pastures. Many left to escape the suppressive environment created by overcentralized, predatory, and repressive government; the malaise it spawned in society; and the subsequent violent breakdowns. The possibilities of unlocking human potential and engaging the creative and constructive energies of Liberians will be vastly expanded in a reconstituted governing order that departs from monocentric government and embraces a polycentric model of governance.

■   Understanding Entrenched
    Resistance to Polycentric Change

Any undertaking that proposes a new way of doing things is bound to encounter resistance. Entrenched interests and old habits often pose obstacles to the introduction of new ideas. Liberia is no exception. Liberia is not a tabula rasa. A century of presidential sovereignty has deeply influenced Liberian thinking about political order. Similarly, fifty years of what James Scott (1998) calls "high modernism" has dominated thinking about development. Accompanying both of these is a psychological orientation of dependency on the United States, a constant quest for American approbation. Understanding these factors is essential to confronting entrenched resistance to the constitution of a polycentric system of democratic governance in Liberia.

Monocentric Mind-Set and Top-Down Governance

The monocentric mind-set that permeates Liberian thinking about political governance is not uniquely Liberian. To many Africanist policy analysts and African political practitioners, order and hierarchy are synonymous. Simple and parsimonious arrangements are typically considered "natural" and easier to analyze and administer. In the aftermath of state collapse, the search for somebody to take charge of reconstituting order typically supersedes every other consideration except the provision of humanitarian assistance. The question of who takes charge is often posed even before a diagnostic assessment is made of the situation. Where the task becomes establishing a system of democratic governance, the preoccupation turns to electing a president.

Establishing rules is subordinated to identifying personalities; empowering people to be their own governors is subordinated to establishing a central authority from the top. The question of transforming unitary government has never dominated the reform agenda. The major discourse has focused on who should become the next president. This kind of discourse inevitably degenerates into shouting matches and unproductive rivalries as the spirit of narrow partisanship takes hold and battle lines are quickly drawn. In this environment, monocentricity's inherent dilemmas are hardly ever investigated. After elections, disgruntlement grows louder as increasing numbers of people become dissatisfied with the exercise of unbridled presidential authority. Battle lines get reinforced and the zero-sum nature of politics become manifest in pristine form.

The monocentric mind-set that pervades discourse about governance in Liberia is reinforced by what Liberians learn about governance in their schools. Civics courses teach about the president as the source of authority; the superintendent as his vicegerent; the district commissioner as a subordinate of the superintendent; and paramount, clan, and town chiefs as successive subordinates of the district commissioner. All political order is perceived in this way, making for a clear hierarchical order in thought and action regarding governance. The complex mix of horizontal and vertical patterns of association that is constitutive of community life is hardly ever discussed, because these patterns are not considered to be important to processes of political governance.[12] Thus, successive generations of Liberians are taught to conceive of political processes largely in terms of structures of hierarchies.

High Modernism

Along with thinking of political governance through monocentric forms, Liberians have also gotten used to thinking of the governance of public economies as a task that must be undertaken by government through grandiose projects that deliver services in uniform patterns throughout the country. A candidate for president in the 1997 elections promised to demolish the shanties of Monrovia and replace them with high-rise buildings to serve as homes for the poor. This is the orientation that propels the search for comprehensive solutions and great accomplishments using problem-solving strategies and means that typically ignore local uniqueness and downplay the importance of local knowledge. "High modernism," as Scott (1998) calls this orientation, fosters a preference for things grand and foreign over things local and suitable to local conditions. Foreign expertise is preferred over local knowledge. Six-lane highways that lead nowhere are preferred over compact farm-to-market roads; massive concrete, prefabricated, uniformly constructed, low-cost rural shelters crammed together are preferred over fire-burned mud-brick houses designed to meet the needs of rural dwellers. As Scott put it, this is "planning for abstract citizens."

The notion that the government and foreign experts can "bring development to the people" has had currency in Africa. It fosters a distorted and dysfunctional view that the state is the provider and producer of development and citizens the faceless beneficiaries. When this orientation becomes as prominent as it has in some African countries, including Liberia, it can distract local people from struggling to muster their own initiatives and appreciate and improve upon what they have. Quite frequently, schools and universities reinforce this orientation. During the early 1970s, a professor of economics at the University of Liberia proposed to invite an illiterate trader as guest lecturer to discuss trading patterns in what is called the informal sector. Departmental authorities were enraged; the professor was not allowed to do so. Besides the fact that the workings of the informal sector remained unknown to students of economics, the rejection of the proposal sent a negative signal, potentially deepening the divide between academics and the poor. Both become poorer.

Years later, and under different university leadership, a similar development occurred. A professor of music invited a number of traditional artists to assist in creating new arrangements of indigenous songs and to perform them with the university choir. The performance electrified the audience. Mixing local knowledge appropriately with other expertise enriches both and benefits all. High modernism is to the governance of public economies what the monocentric mind-set is to political governance. They reinforce each other and together create powerful resistance to efforts to shift governance paradigms.

A deliberate and sustained effort is required through education and the design and implementation of self-governing institutions to break this orientation.

Liberia's U.S.-Dependent Psychology

The direct involvement of former colonial powers in African governance has been integral to the configuration of governance institutions in ways constitutive of scales of governance rather than of distinct patterns of interactions characteristic of so-called state-to-state relationships. For example, governance patterns in many francophone African countries have involved the direct participation of the French government as actors in "national" decisionmaking, often in ways reflective of a higher scale of decisionmaking. Countries such as the Central African Republic and Niger have been dependent on French government budgetary support, which is obtained annually through resource allocation and budget review processes similar to those employed typically within configurations of governance dominated by supranational scales (O'Toole 1986). During the thirty-year presidency of Houphouët-Boigny in Côte d'Ivoire, the French ambassador was a key member of the "kitchen cabinet" of the Ivorian president (Harshe 1984). In the 1980s, there were as many as 1,700 French government "advisers" holding positions in the Ivorian government (Matloff 1996). Patterns of governance in many African countries reflect the reality of a vital level of "national" or country-specific decisionmaking that is wholly external (Schraeder 1997). Although these patterns have been changing since the end of the Cold War, they still exist in substantial forms (see Renou 2002.)

In the case of Liberia, the history of its involvement with the United States has bred among Liberians an unhealthy psychology of dependency. Right from its founding, Liberian leaders depended on the threat, and often the use, of U.S. gunboats to ensure the security of Liberian settler communities, U.S. diplomatic interventions to prevent absorption by the British and French, and U.S.-constructed loan packages to keep the country financially solvent. Since the mid-nineteenth century, the Liberian elite has perfected the art of appealing to the United States to solve its problems. Throughout the twentieth century, in every national crisis, appeals for American intervention have been the central approach to problem solving. Protagonists to disputes after every contested elections have called for U.S. intervention.[13] In every national crisis, Liberians, in their desperation, have marched to the American Embassy in Monrovia to petition the Americans to "do something." It is not unusual for those who seek elected office to first seek the approbation of U.S. officials and use that as the most important qualification for public office. The ultimate and decisive question is always, "What do the Americans say?"

For decades, such U.S.-dependent psychology was encouraged by the U.S. government because it served American interests.[14] Pronouncements of "special relationships" adorned discourses between Liberians and U.S. offi-cials.[15] Although these suddenly ceased with the disintegration of the Soviet Union, Liberians have remained mentally entrapped. Debilitated by the psy-chology of dependency and the burden of a tortuous history, many among the Liberian elite find it difficult to muster a sense of efficacy, overcome a desire for recrimination within their society, and adopt a constructive approach to collective soul-searching with a view to solving problems.

These are some of the obstacles that will have to be studied more closely and addressed over time if a self-governing order and a self-reliant approach to development are to be successfully established.

■ Notes

1. Yarsuo Weh-Dorliae (2004) has made a substantial contribution to ways of thinking about redesigning governance arrangements for Liberia. His book has been helpful to me.

2. Since 1995, I have worked in several capacities with many of these groups in all three countries and have firsthand knowledge of the increasing solidarity and work-ing linkages among them.

3. See ECOWAS website: www.ecowas.int.

4. This point is also made in Sawyer (1992, 199, 358).

5. This formulation of townships as the basic governance jurisdiction has drawn from Svend Holsoe's paper "Liberia Transformed: Locally Empowering Rural Politi-cal Institutions," May 1994 (revised September 2002), and from the discussions it stimulated during a meeting of the Liberia Governance Working Group held at Indiana University in February 2003.

6. Although not much research has been done on the performance of the courts of tribal governors, it is well known among Liberian lawyers that such courts are not only of uneven quality but are also largely a mechanism for shakedown.

7. In the late 1970s, the Rural Development Task Force recommended that district-level jurisdictions become the fulcrum of county development activities because district commissioners were state-appointed officials who function between indigenous leaders—that is, paramount and clan chiefs—and the central state. This recommendation was not fully implemented, as many of the task force's recommen-dations remained pending until the coup occurred in 1980.

8. Holsoe (2002) has recommended that paramount chieftancy jurisdictions be kept as electoral districts for county councils or commissions. My sense is that elec-toral districts need to be drawn from time to time based on the ebb and flow of the pop-ulation, the vicissitudes of townships and cities, and other factors.

9. The existence, for example, of Kpanyan, Juarzon, and Tarjuarzon as statutory districts within Sinoe County; and Bua and Barrobo as statutory districts within Mary-land County; and the combining of settlements or towns that are miles apart into a sin-gle city, as was the case in the creation of St. John River City in Grand Bassa County that brought Fortsville and Harlaansville together as a single city.

10. I thank Byron Tarr for raising these issues with me and for recommending research reports done by the Public International Law and Policy Group, www.publicinternationallaw.org. I thank Paul Williams and his colleagues for sharing with me studies done by the group.

11. I thank Bai Gbala for helping me crystallize this point.

12. Claude Ake (1993) was foremost among contemporary African scholars in calling for the constitution of African democracies through what he called "consocietal arrangements" using ethnic and other constituencies in ways that constitute order in bottom-up configurative patterns.

13. In 1925, 1955, and 1985, opposition candidates, being unable to reach a satisfactory settlement with the president, had sought U.S. intervention.

14. In the 1920s, Liberia became the major source of rubber for the United States after the British reduced U.S. access to British-controlled Asian supplies. During World War II, Liberia was important as a strategic fueling stop en route to the war front in southern Europe. In Cold War competition, Liberia was the location of significant U.S. diplomatic and security communications facilities.

15. U.S. operational involvement in financial administration in Liberia continued well into the 1950s, it then took on a more indirect form as the concession economy and parastatals gained dominance. International firms and foreign donors, especially the World Bank and International Monetary Fund, became powerful actors in financial, and therefore political, decisionmaking in Liberia. Some observers have claimed that in the 1970s, President Tolbert's efforts to diversify Liberia's financial and political relations, thereby reducing the impact of American engagement in Liberia, contributed to a cooling off of relations with the United States and led ultimately to the vulnerability of his regime. See, for example, Dunn and Tarr (1988). In the 1980s, the Doe regime could not have survived without direct U.S. engagement, which ranged from providing food assistance, funding the national budget, and helping forge agricultural and economic policies, to providing military hardware and advisers, and participating directly in security policymaking. By 1987, operational experts hired by the United States government and accountable to it were deployed to exercise control over Liberian government revenues.

CHAPTER 8

Rethinking Citizenship and Education for Democracy

THE EXTENT TO WHICH INSTITUTIONAL ARRANGEMENTS WORK TO SUSTAIN DEMOCRATIC governance turns critically upon the role to be played by ordinary people in the processes of governance. People who function as subjects in political orders may at best enjoy the material benefits of governance arrangements but cannot be considered the architects of their own future. The people of the Mano basin area have been living in countries in which there have been years of government predation, repression, and governance failure. In order to function as true citizens and reverse their ill fortunes, the people of the basin area would need not only to construct institutional arrangements for democratic governance but also to be able to sustain democracy by strengthening their capabilities for democratic citizenship. This entails developing the capabilities for participation as governors or decisionmakers at township, local community, and other levels of governance, including the basin area level, rather than simply acting as petitioners to the state, as has largely been the case.

How can the people of the basin area empower themselves to become true citizens and governors? What capabilities do they need? What dilemmas must they resolve? The development of citizenship capabilities within the context of the Mano basin area calls into question the role of language, education, and issues of identity, among others. We need to understand these issues within the context of specific countries and the larger basin area in order to explore the possibilities for nurturing citizens who can sustain processes of democratization in the basin area.

Although this chapter, like most chapters of the book, focuses on the Liberian experience, the challenges discussed have relevance for the basin area as a whole. I first articulate a conception of citizenship that is foundational to democratic self-governance. This is followed by an explanation of how the experience in state building in Liberia has not been able to support

183

the nurturing of citizens to function in a democracy—how it has instead implanted a notion of citizens as subjects of the state. I then discuss the role of literacy and education in nurturing citizens who can be relied upon to sustain a system of democratic governance in Liberia and build upon already established linkages in the basin area and ECOWAS. I close with a discussion of the place of local language and the importance of an open public realm in enhancing citizen enlightenment through public discourse.

■ Citizenship and Governance

The concept of democracy is often used with reference to electoral processes and associated activities having to do with representative government and basic freedoms, especially freedom of expression and association. It is sometimes forgotten that at the foundation of a system of democratic governance are *citizens who are governors*. When the process of building and operating democratic institutions ceases to be driven by citizens and becomes the prerogative of the state solely, problems of sustaining these institutions are then exacerbated, and the character of the institutions is then called into question because such institutions are likely to become authoritarian if not repressive.

Success in sustaining institutions of democratic governance depends upon the effectiveness of initiatives designed to enable people to empower themselves as true citizens capable of, and willing to participate in, the vital decisionmaking institutions and processes of their political order instead of being subjects of the state and accepting whatever flows from its institutions.

Self-governing democracies demand much more of citizens than do capable states. In the latter, citizens are expected to make demands on the state and provide support for it. In the former, citizens are the instruments of governance; they participate in running the affairs of society—through neighborhood councils, local school boards and town councils, county commissions, provincial and national assemblies, and the array of institutions that are entrusted with public affairs in a society. They also function as governors in public affairs that link societies in joint endeavors. Democratic governance does not simply require that leaders be accountable to citizens; it requires that citizens also participate as leaders. Participation is critical to citizenship, but participation cannot meaningfully enhance individual and societal well-being *and* demonstrate ownership prerogatives without enlightenment.

Citizenship for democratic governance therefore imposes on citizens the responsibility to prepare for and engage in enlightened contestation. Liberia will not be able to sustain a democratic system of governance unless it is able to nurture empowered citizens. This is why an examination of how citizens have been made in the Liberian political order is an important question. A similar question needs to be raised with respect to the other countries of the basin area.

■ How "Citizens" Were Made in Liberia

The processes of state formation in Africa have made more complex the question of identity—especially where it pertains to citizenship. Who are citizens and what are the prerogatives and responsibilities of citizenship? Mahmood Mamdani (1996) has shown that in postcolonial governance, African countries have adopted a bifurcated conception of citizenship that confers special rights and protection on individuals who are urban dwellers while maintaining institutional control, through native authority structures and the application of what is called "customary law," of individuals and groups in rural areas. Pressing the point further, Mamdani (2001) argues that even within such bifurcation, governance dynamics and state law—especially those associated with property rights—have further fragmentized identities and citizenship beyond the urban-rural distinction, occasionally with profoundly tragic consequences as in the case of Rwanda.[1]

But even where citizenship confers more privileges on some members of a political community than on others, such privileges typically fall short of empowering citizens to participate meaningfully in public affairs. In highly centralized political arrangements, those who participate meaningfully in public affairs constitute a small core; and it is these who are allowed to exercise the full prerogatives of citizenship. All others may be subjects, even though some may enjoy certain material privileges.

In Liberia, the process of citizen formation has not led to the empowerment of people to serve as governors. At the founding of Liberia, the first identities that were created distinguished settlers from those who were called aborigines. The former included freed slaves and their descendants and recaptives. Aborigines subsumed all indigenous groups without differentiation. These were essentially cultural identities that distinguished the "civilized" from the "uncivilized"—the latter being entrusted to the tutelage of the former. It is these cultural categories of civilized and uncivilized that first defined political identities and constituted the basis of citizenship. Liberia's state-building processes articulated power relations such that freed slaves and their descendants exercised prerogatives of power and property rights. Aboriginal identity decomposed into several ethnic identities that, through legislative enactments, assigned to all such ethnic groups the political identity of subjects of the state (see Huberich 1947, 2:1015–1016).

The creation of state administrative jurisdictions in the interior froze cultural identities and transformed them into political identities with prerogatives and duties determined under customary law. The politicization of cultural identity constituted a fundamental element of the system of indirect rule that consolidated the distinction between subjects and "citizens" in Liberia. Citizens would own land in fee simple; subjects would have entitlements within ethnocommunal arrangements. Citizens would live in cities and upriver towns; subjects would live in rural towns, villages, and hamlets or in cities as clients of citizens. Citizens would hold office in government and undertake the civilizing mission; subjects would manage other subjects and supply labor and other resources.

For an individual, the passage from subject to citizen required transcending the system of indirect rule and engaging in a socializing process that entailed acculturation through "apprenticeship" training in the households of "civilized" people and a process of formal Western education. In 1882, the first individual of wholly indigenous background was considered sufficiently civilized to be elected to the Liberian legislature from a predominant settler community. It was possible for select communities to be accepted into limited forms of citizenship if they engaged in patterns of sustained cooperation with settler communities of proximity (Akpan 1968; Sawyer 1992). In such circumstances, laws were enacted allowing these communities limited representation in the legislature and some forms of enfranchisement. In some of these communities new municipal and other political jurisdictions were established, enabling them to transcend the system of indirect rule.

To the extent citizenship conferred rights to meaningfully participate in decisionmaking in the political process, only a small group of largely male settlers could exercise such rights. Clarence E. Zamba Liberty (2002) has referred to this group as the "upper echelon settlers." It was this group that pressured both President Coleman in 1900 and President King in 1930 to resign from office. The influence of this group waned steadily as the powers of the president increased. By mid-twentieth century, this group constituted little more than a support cast to the president, even though it remained materially privileged.

After his election as president in 1944, Tubman proposed the enfranchisement of settler women and some ethnic communities—the latter, under conditions of hut tax payment (see Appendix 1). Women of indigenous communities remained disenfranchised as a result of customary law. By 1954, Tubman accelerated the pace of citizen identity formation in indigenous communities with the launching of the Unification and Integration Program. Two significant undertakings of this program were (1) the restructuring of the administrative jurisdiction of the country so as to elevate the political status of the hinterland from that of a protectorate; and (2) the expansion of education—especially primary and elementary education. While the creation of new counties put hinterland jurisdictions on legal parity with coastal administrative jurisdictions that were dominated by settlers, it did not significantly alter the nature of native authority and the subordinate system of justice under customary law. However, it did create expectations and increased pressure for inclusion as citizens on the part of educated members of indigenous communities.

The expansion of educational opportunities as a result of both government and private (largely missionary) initiatives gave momentum to the quest for political inclusion and individual autonomy. Pressures increased throughout the late 1960s and 1970s, with students and workers often leading open protests. Regime response turned increasingly repressive. The core issues of protestation had to do with the desire of people of various sectors of society to have decisionmaking roles in the institutions in which they functioned. Workers wanted collective bargaining rights, students wanted improved educational conditions and the right to organize and run student associations, and political entrepreneurs wanted the right to organize opposition political parties. This broad thrust for citizenship participation overwhelmed a resisting autocracy, leading ultimately to the collapse of the regime.

Thus, what we have seen here is that citizens were made in Liberia as a result of incremental processes of entitlement that involved acculturation, graduated enfranchisement, and the bestowing of land alienation rights. Presidential sovereignty and oligarchic rule resisted a broadening of the prerogatives of citizenship to include meaningful participation as decisionmakers in public affairs. It is this conception of citizenship that is required to sustain the system of democratic governance discussed in this book. The question is how, then, can such citizenship be nurtured?

■ Building Citizenship for Democratic Self-Governance

While the national government must play a substantial role in shaping citizenship identity, that identity cannot be a solely vertical identity that enables citizens to see themselves as belonging to a national collectivity, engaging its officials, and striving to participate in national-level activities. Citizenship nurturing for self-governance must also include linking communities in horizontal relationships, establishing a sense of common identity and interest across diverse groups, and engaging in collective action across such groups. It is not good enough that Kru people and Bassa people, for example, establish identification with Liberia as a country; they must also nurture a bond with each other. The establishment of horizontal relationships enables people to act upon mutual interests and develop trusting relationships across social divides without necessarily being policed by a central authority. Polycentric governance relies as much on the establishment and successful functioning of horizontal institutions as it does on centralized institutions.

Polycentric governance arrangements will also make possible the creation of special purpose, task-specific jurisdictions that cross-cut townships and county boundaries and serve as bridges between diverse communities, thereby closing horizontal gaps between ethnic communities that have been functioning as subjects of the state. In this way, people of adjacent local communities can think about establishing joint initiatives for managing forest resources, providing schools, and building and maintaining roadways and other facilities. During the 1970s and before the outbreak of violence, the existence of agricultural cooperatives in multiethnic townships such as Saclapea, Bahn, and Karnplay constituted critical bridging institutions that went a long way in enhancing interethnic cooperation. Many of these failed as the country became engulfed in violence.

Thus, a major challenge of citizen making for a self-governing order in Liberia is to have individuals and communities forge a common national identity and a common set of values, so that they can pursue their various interests within the framework of communities of shared understanding. To accomplish this, the nurturing of citizens must proceed from both the bottom—by developing bridges across communities—and from the top—by developing a sense of national and regional identity. Citizenship built through a process of inclusive association among individuals and communities is more sustainable than a process that depends solely, or predominantly, on the capacity of the central government to deliver to local communities. Moreover, building patterns of inclusive association horizontally increases capabilities to leverage participation at vertical levels of aggregation.

Against this background, and with respect to the task of transforming subjects into citizens, one of the most critical steps that must be taken is to address the gaps between Western-based statutory law and customary law as well within each system of laws. This does not mean that cultural variations should no longer be appreciated; it does mean that cultural norms and practices that are incompatible with acceptable standards of fairness and justice need to be reexamined. As a whole, the customary laws under which ethnic communities are governed are of a subordinate order of rule of law and cannot foster equality and equity. Customary law's designation of women as inheritable property is an example of how customary law further diminishes the standing of women as citizens.

Nurturing a sense of common citizenship and shared values also requires redressing the disparaging of indigenous communities of Liberians, as is done in the interpretation of Liberian history as told in the history and civic textbooks that shape the perspectives of Liberians about themselves. It is an interpretation that presents a picture of two communities of Liberians: one of settler background—enlightened and benevolent; and the other of indigenous background—primitive and pitiful. A history textbook used in Liberian schools up to 1990 portrayed indigenous Liberians as follows: "Most of the Liberian tribesmen were well-built, averaging from 5 to 6 feet in height. They had dark brown skin, rather flat noses, fine white teeth and black hair. Their eyes also were black. Although they wore no shoes, their feet were usually small. They were a primitive people, but very skillful in providing themselves with food, shelter and a scant covering for their bodies" (Henries and Henries 1966, 16). This depiction of Liberians reads no differently from those written in colonial times to deride Africans.[2]

Not only do the history books erroneously present Liberians as consisting of two homogeneous blocks, they go on to portray interactions between these blocks as an epic struggle on the part of one to dominate the other and the other to oust or exterminate the dominant group. Accounts of wars between settler and indigenous communities are often presented not only with emphasis on a false or overstated dichotomy between homogeneous communities, but also without serious analysis of the issues central to the conflicts—issues that defined the interests and shaped the decisions of individual indigenous and settler communities. As a result, patterns of shifting alliances based on changing circumstances affecting the interests of individual political communities are hardly given the prominence they deserve; when mentioned, they are treated with derision or as acts of betrayal. For example, when Sao Boso, the leader of a major multiethnic confederation situated in what is now north-central Liberia, supported the settler government's efforts to secure the trade routes from the coast leading to his jurisdiction, his actions are seen in the history books as a betrayal of indigenous people, when they should have been seen to be typical of leaders in such circumstances acting to protect vital trade interests—the lifeblood of communities of people. Another example dates to a little over a half-century later, when members of settler frontier communities opposed the Liberian government's military pacification expeditions against surrounding indigenous communities. The government's assault on those indigenous communities posed serious threats to the security of nearby settler communities; the latter's opposition was not unpatriotic but protective of local interests. Portrayal of the story of Liberia solely as a struggle between two homogeneous and antagonistic communities diminishes the role of rational actors and misses the rich and varied patterns that unfold in the course of creative interaction among individuals and communities in Liberia.

Civics lessons taught in Liberian schools even now present a patronizing picture of a settler society, driven by benevolence, and an indigenous society given to insolence and free riding. The following passage shows how a civics textbook described relationships between the two communities and justified the imposition of hut taxes while presenting a distortion of both topography and demography:

Two regions of Liberia are inhabited by different groups of people. The coastal region is westernized to a great extent and has the appearance of many places in America and Europe. The majority of people in this region speak English. Forty miles back from the coast live numerous tribal groups who speak several diverse languages and dialects of African origin in addition to English. Primitive towns and villages are sprinkled over this hinterland region of our country. For a long time Liberians who lived along the seacoast assumed complete responsibility for developing a fair arrangement. In a democracy all citizens should share in meeting the needs of the country. Therefore, after World War I, the hut tax was imposed on tribal groups, giving them additional rights and responsibilities of citizens. (A. Henries 1980)

Compounding the impact of these distorted and divisive historical inter-pretations are Liberian national symbols that also project an image of division and exclusion among Liberians. For years now, some Liberian commentators have emphasized the need to change many of Liberia's national symbols—such as the motto and flag—because they reflect only settlers' heritage, and to adopt symbols that are inclusive and unifying.[3] Despite increased public pro-nouncements by leaders of government, religious bodies, and civil society about the need for reconciliation, there has not been a meaningful effort recently to address the question of divisive national symbols.

Perspectives that present the Liberian reality as an enduring struggle between settler and indigenous communities have become engrained in the consciousness of Liberians and have had a profound effect on the Liberian psyche. These perspectives detract from the society's capacity to sustain a system of democratic governance and therefore need to be transformed. The best way to begin transforming them is by initiating governance reforms that establish institutions of democratic self-governance, as discussed in previous chapters (especially Chapter 7) and through rethinking and reshaping Liberia's educational system such that it becomes capable of producing skills and values supportive of democratic governance and self-reliant development.

■   The Role of Education in Nurturing Citizens

An educational system that provides sound and appropriate education is indis-pensable in nurturing citizens. One of the major challenges with respect to nur-turing citizens in Liberia is to establish a relevant and aggressive literacy pro-gram that would provide the tools of literacy to all Liberians and ensure them access to a full range of educational and participatory opportunities. There is a critical need to create an educational system that integrates what is essentially a dual system of education—one indigenous based and the other Western ori-ented—into a well-rounded educational experience that is relevant for address-ing the challenges of life in African society more generally and in Liberian society more specifically. A system that draws on local knowledge as well as knowledge generated elsewhere is indispensable for self-reliant development.

Dual System of Education

Liberia, like most African countries, has had a dual system of education—one dispensing indigenous knowledge and the other providing Western-derived edu-cation. The two have not been harmonized. Spasmodic efforts have been made to integrate elements of the former into the latter. The so-called bush schools of Poro, Sande, and Kwee societies have operated in secrecy to nonmembers of those organizations and have passed down knowledge in certain specializations through patterns of ascription. Blacksmithing and herbal therapy, for example, were among professions often ascribed to particular lineages, while basket weaving and pottery were gender-ascribed. Much of this indigenous knowledge is being lost as a result of the nature of the two educational systems, the culture of secrecy that shrouds indigenous educational patterns, and the disdain with which Liberia's Western-based educational system holds this type of indigenous knowledge. The historic mission to civilize and Christianize has precluded taking a serious interest in indigenous education and training.[4]

The failure to integrate indigenous knowledge into the Western educational system adopted in Liberia denies Liberians a potentially expansive knowledge base for solving problems. Indigenous methods of child rearing and socialization, for example, are not sufficiently informing academic studies and training programs relevant to nurturing children; nor has the study of indigenous institutions of governance been incorporated into the study of political science or public administration. As a result, the impact of indigenous patterns of authority relations on the nurturing of children as citizens is hardly ever considered as part of the intellectual inquiry of institutions of learning. The fact that the very concept of citizenship varies from ethnic community to ethnic community has implications for the conception of Liberian citizenship generally. These have not been fully explored. Thus, there is a compelling need to provide a more organized and systematic explanation of local knowledge and practices and to incorporate these into the framework of an appropriate educational and training program if the educational system of Liberia is to serve as an effective agent in nurturing citizens and generating knowledge to enhance development.[5]

Until the mid-twentieth century, the Western-derived educational system of Liberia hardly provided the basis for livelihood and professional skill development or the basis for nurturing citizens respectful of, and functional within, a multiethnic context of citizen identity. Liberia's educational system was designed to mold "civilized" individuals and to build solidarity among them in an environment numerically dominated by the "uncivilized." Courses in Greek and Roman civilization, Christian doctrine, rhetoric, and English law dominated the curriculum of schools. The training of preachers was emphasized over the training of engineers and technicians (Azango 1968). Citizenship training required the shedding of African identity and the exclusion of the majority of inhabitants of the society.

Postconflict Crisis of the Educational System

Although educational philosophy and implementation strategies have changed and considerable progress has been made in the expansion of educational opportunities, there is still much work to be done in making the content of education more relevant to the needs of Liberia and in improving educational facilities.

Poor as the educational system was prior to the outbreak of war in 1989, things have become even worse since that time. A crisis of profound proportions exists today. Students attending primary and secondary school range in age from five to twenty-four; 48 percent of all students are at the primary level of education (grades one to three), yet the net enrollment rate of primary school–age children (ages five to eight) is 46 percent. This means a disproportionately large number of older children, and perhaps young adults, are struggling to obtain a primary-level education. Girls are further disadvantaged, accounting for only 35 percent of those attending school.[6] Qualified teachers are in short supply. Since 1999, more than 50 percent of students enrolled in Liberian schools have been taught by unqualified teachers (GOL 2000b). As noted in Chapter 3, performance on examinations administered by the West African Examination Council (WAEC) remains poor. Liberians have to work hard to ensure that the next generation does not turn out to be less educated than their parents.

Compounding the problem of poor-quality teachers is the lack of appropriate textbooks, especially those with direct relevance to citizenship training. Subjects such as Liberian history, civics, and social studies, which are essential to the development of a sense of shared identity, are being held hostage by a legacy of overcentralized and predatory government and the interpretation of history that supports its domination. Appropriate scholarly research is required to provide for Liberian schools a historical account that reflects the Liberian mosaic and thereby enhances a sense of inclusion and a basis to embrace and sustain a democratic alternative to autocracy.

The Importance of Literacy

A system of democratic governance cannot be sustained without a literate population. Designing and establishing democratic institutions only makes sense if members of the society can use, or are developing the capability to use, those institutions. Literacy unlocks the potential of individuals and, in a democratic system of governance, enhances an appreciation of the full range of rights and duties that comes with being a citizen. It also provides a tool for learning from the experiences of people elsewhere.

Although illiterate people throughout the world do engage in collective action, literacy provides access to a variety of patterns of collective action and to modes of sustaining, transforming, and assessing such actions and their outcomes. For example, learning numbers enables a person to read scales, keep records of stocks, and list and compare prices—all of which are fundamental to any form of business enterprise, no matter how small. Literacy of the family, especially of women and girls, has been found to be the best predictor of the state of family health and well-being and of the prospects for socioeconomic empowerment of the family and for the overall development of society.[7] A substantial literacy campaign is needed for post-conflict Liberia to support a system of democratic governance.

The problem of illiteracy in Liberia has to be addressed frontally, because it is an important obstacle to democratic governance and development. According to current estimates (see Table 8.1), Liberia's adult literacy rate stands at 38 percent, which includes 54 percent of males and 22 percent of females. A national literacy program has been going on for many years now, ebbing and receding with the vicissitudes of government policy and the generosity of external funding sources. More recent literacy campaigns ambitiously sought to lower illiteracy rates to 35 percent by 2000 but could not deliver.[8]

The difficulty of substantially reducing or eliminating illiteracy in Liberia is directly related to the role of literacy in the lives of individuals and communities and, consequently, the demand for literacy or the lack thereof.

Literacy is often seen almost exclusively as an intrinsic value, perhaps even as an ornamental artifact unrelated to people's day-to-day functioning. This is why, in rural areas mostly, newly literate adults sometimes relapse into illiteracy. Children and parents are not engaged in the intergenerational transfer of knowledge through literacy. Literacy must become a tool in addressing the puzzles of daily life as people interact in solving problems. This is what linguistic specialists refer to as *social literacy*. Literacy must have social meaning and, like education, generally must be transformatory and liberating (Freire 1970; 1998). How one communicates with neighbors, buys and sells food, functions in the workplace, and acquires information important to local and national life needs to be affected by the acquisition of literacy and should, in turn, influence the approach used in teaching people to become literate.

The social demand for literacy remains low in Liberia. However, if ordinary people are entrusted with governance decisionmaking responsibilities through establishing institutions of democratic governance, these people will immediately see the importance of literacy as an indispensable tool for functioning as citizens who are decisionmakers. By creating a demand for literacy,

Table 8.1   Adult Literacy Rate of Liberia and Its Neighbors, 2002 (percentages)

Country	Total Adult Literacy Rate	Male	Female
Côte d'Ivoire	49	57	40
Guinea	36	50	22
Liberia	38	54	22
Sierra Leone	31	45	18

Source: CIA, *World Factbook 2002* (cited at www.mrdowling.com/800literacy.html).

a literate environment will be created in turn, and ordinary citizens will sustain that environment because of its importance to their participation in governing their own affairs.

■ The Place of Indigenous Languages

Literacy as a tool must be linked to language, the conveyor of thought and meaning, if the objective is to enhance ordinary people's meaningful participation in governance. People are confronted with a profound dilemma when the language through which they make sense of their society is not the language that can enhance their opportunities. Most of the people of Liberia, like most of the people of other African countries, do not read or speak the official language of their political orders. President Chisano of Mozambique shocked colleagues and invited dignitaries at the July 2004 summit of heads of state of the African Union when he delivered his address to that body in Kiswahili. The question of the place of indigenous languages in the promotion of literacy has not been seriously addressed in Liberia and in many other African societies.[9]

There are several reasons why language policy has not been a priority on the national agenda of African countries; among them is the fact that, in view of the fragile ethnocultural mix that constitutes the body politic of most African countries, adoption of colonial languages—mainly English, French, and Portuguese—is believed to have spared African countries the tedious and delicate debate about making choices among local languages. Some have even suggested a conspiracy theory: that African political elites prefer to rule through European languages in order to retain language as an instrument of control (Obeng 2002).

There are those in contemporary literary circles in Africa who bemoan the lack of literary traditions in African languages, but they also stress that European languages have proven to be sufficiently learnable and can be used with appropriate adaptations and flexibility, to express the creative genius of African peoples—or any other peoples for that matter.[10] There is also the fear that instruction in indigenous languages may not sufficiently prepare individuals for competitive functioning in our ever changing technological world.[11]

Yet there is growing evidence that mother-tongue or first-language literacy yields considerable advantages in educational performance.[12] Linguistic specialists have often expounded on the link between language, culture, and thought.[13] As Ellin Scholnick (2002, 3) puts it, these three do not only "represent the world and the self, they represent each other." Thus, proponents of this view maintain that it is not possible to capture the depth of African ontology without using African languages.[14] Advocacy to impart literacy, first in local and national languages and then in European or global languages, has gained currency among literacy education experts. But there are several impediments, such as the fear of parents that their children may lose the competitive edge; the lack of a literary environment in indigenous languages; and the reluctance of political elites to face up to what amounts to a delicate question linked to culture and identity.

For most African countries, multilingualism creates a special challenge for mother-tongue and local-language literacy promotion. Nigeria, with its 400-odd indigenous languages and four official languages (English, Hausa, Igbo, and Yoruba), and Cameroon, with 250 indigenous languages and two national languages (English and French) are examples that underscore the complexity posed by multilingualism in the quest for indigenous literacy.

In the case of Liberia, speaking and writing in the English language was both an emblem of being civilized and an instrument of control. In 1861, Liberian patriot Alexander Crummell stressed that a critical part of the civilizing mission was to teach indigenous Africans to speak English (Crummell [1862] 1969). With a total population of less than 4 million, Liberia has sixteen ethnic groups. Although each constitutes a speech community and some are mutually intelligible, only one language, Vai, has a syllabary constitutive of a writing system known as the Vai script. According to Sylvia Scribner and Michael Cole (1981), the Vai script ranks high on the "developmental scale" created by historians of writing and applied to writing systems. Unfortunately, there is no connection between becoming literate in the Vai script and the acquisition of indigenous knowledge and skills in Vai society. Learning to read and write the Vai language through the Vai script is not a part of Vai socialization and the indigenous educational system. Individuals usually grow up and seek for themselves, or are persuaded by parents or others, to acquire literacy in Vai.[15]

Failure to integrate Vai literacy as an essential tool of Vai patterns of education and socialization has detracted from the importance of the Vai script as a means of empowerment in Vai society in particular and in Liberian society in general.[16] This failure underscores the acute need to link literacy to the everyday experience of people and to improve their prospects of a better life. Can a body of literature be developed in Vai? With Vai-language community as a member of the family of Mande-language community, can the Vai script be adapted in ways that provide harmonization and standardization to other languages of Mande speakers? If this can be done, more than 50 percent of Liberians would be able to acquire literacy in indigenous languages.[17] This is another important challenge for Liberia's intellectual community.

Besides Vai, only a few other Liberian languages have a system of alphabetics, a phonetic system developed mainly through the efforts of missionaries, whose primary motivation was to make the Bible available in local languages. Kpelle and Loma people have access to the Bible or substantial parts of it in their languages, but here again, literacy linked to the reading of the Bible is not associated with other endeavors of daily living. Kpelle and Loma women in rural villages who learn to read the Bible in their local languages have no incentive to use their literacy skills in selling the products of their farms, communicating with their relatives in Monrovia and elsewhere, or calculating and negotiating the costs of transportation, cotton fabrics and other items they consume. Nor can they use those skills to broaden their knowledge about other ethnocultures, such as those of the Kru, Grebo, or Krahn.

The challenge of promoting literacy in indigenous Liberian languages goes far beyond the task of creating syllabaries and writing systems and resolving technical problems associated with such undertakings, important as these are. There are some other critical questions that have to be addressed. For example, is multilingual literacy a practical proposition for Liberia? Even if harmonization and standardization are possible, this remains a question of constitutional choice and the subject for discourse in the open public realm.

■ Citizenship and the Public Realm

Karl Popper (1952) has told us that the defining feature of a democracy is the existence of an open public realm. Open critical discourse is indispensable to wise action, he asserts. Emphasizing this point, he quotes Pericles' assertion that "although only a few may originate a policy, we are all able to judge it." The role of citizens is to participate among the few who at any period through representative government may originate policy as well as among the many who judge. It is therefore the obligation of citizens to prepare themselves, to engage in such discourses to gain enlightenment through contestation, and to frame and assess issues of public concern. For as Pericles further asserts, "We consider a man who takes no interest in the state not as harmless, but as useless" (Popper 1952, 186). Citizenship is a call to assume personal autonomy and responsibility while acting in association with others to enhance one's own well-being and that of the community through thoughtful productive participation.[18]

Liberia faces a major task of developing a public realm that can serve as an effective forum for knowledgeable contestation among citizens on issues vital to the common good and as a platform for expressive culture generally. The effects of years of centralized, predatory, and repressive government have made for a public realm that is largely used for petitioning leaders, making sycophantic pronouncements and strident denunciations, and engaging in superficial debates. In such situations, public discourse, which is not always informed by facts and sound analyses, more often degenerates into insubstantial shouting matches without much potential for edification. The lack of a credible public realm leaves ample public space for demagoguery, which is typically countered by government repression. This is why newspapers, radio stations, and other mass media must operate with integrity and be disseminators of accurate information and platforms of enlightening contestation. In this way, they can contribute to productive public discourse. Their role in civic education is especially important. If properly used, local language newspapers, radio, and other media can be critical in nurturing citizens who see themselves as having the duty to be responsible governors.

However, the use of local languages is not only important for conveying meaning in intellectual discourse and political governance; it is also vital for communicating other kinds of information and for creating and conveying social and cultural meanings. Through songs, dance, and other expressive forms, local languages capture the spirit of life of a society. Literacy in local languages enables local communities to invigorate their heritage while contributing to a larger common heritage with others. Literacy in local languages is therefore critical to the many ways in which the use of local languages can unlock human potential. The open public realm provides such opportunities.

■ Notes

1. Mamdani (2001) has shown how processes associated with governance in colonial and postcolonial states have created categories of indigenous ethnics and settler ethnics, among others, as forms of identities and citizenship and how these can be manipulated in power relationships, as was the case in the Rwandan genocide.

2. A. Doris Banks Henries, the principal author and an African American missionary, was married to Richard Henries, a political influential who was a member of the House of Representatives of Liberia for more than three decades, serving as speaker for close to twenty years. Mrs. Henries was for many years head of the division of the Ministry of Education having to do with textbook publication and selection for Liberians' schools. She authored several books, including a civics textbook. For years her publications were prescribed by the Ministry of Education as standard history and civics textbooks for elementary schools throughout Liberia.

3. Abeodu Jones and Edward Kesselly were among those who in the late twentieth century delivered widely publicized speeches calling for a change in Liberia's divisive national symbols. At least one national commission set up by the government in the 1970s—and dominated by members of the oligarchy—to address the issue recommended its rejection. The Liberian motto, "The love of liberty brought us here," refers to the establishment of Liberia by immigrants from the United States. The flag, patterned after that of the United States, has eleven red and white stripes and a blue field with one star in the upper left-hand corner. Despite the assigning of historical symbolism to the number of stripes and the single star, the Liberian flag's resemblance to that of the United States is readily obvious even to the most casual or inattentive observer.

4. There are a few areas in medicine, such as the mending of fractured bones, where indigenous remedies are integrated into the teaching and practice of Western-based medicine. Unfortunately, the vast range of herbs used by indigenous practitioners are not being investigated and improved upon for possible use by medical programs in Liberia.

5. Edward Wilmot Blyden was the outstanding advocate of this view in nineteenth-century Liberia; Mary Antoinette Brown Sherman was its most ardent articulator of the twentieth century. For example, see Sherman (1982; 1989).

6. See Liberia National Transitional Government (2004).

7. See UNICEF, *State of the World's Children* reports (1980–2004), especially the 2004 report subtitled "Girls, Education and Development."

8. A three-part national campaign was launched in 1999, involving a public sensitization through the media, a national voluntary literacy transfer initiative called *Each One Teach One,* and the expansion of functional literacy classes at the community level. See Ministry of Education 1999–2000.

9. South Africa's policy of multilingualism and Tanzania's use of Kiswahili as the official language, a policy that has not been reversed, were among the exceptions.

10. See Wafula's (2003) excellent essay on the debate about the place of mother-tongue languages in African literature.

11. According to Obeng (2002), mothers in Côte d'Ivoire are unwilling to have their children study in indigenous languages fearing that they will not be able to compete fully in a francophone African society.

12. The Ife Six Year Primary Project is often cited as evidence. It showed that students who studied in their mother tongue language, Yoruba, and studied English as a subject performed much better even in English than their colleagues who studied in English. See Afolayan (1976).

13. Fishman (1985, xi–xii) locates languages not only as a part of cultures but also as "an index of cultures" and a "symbol of ethnocultures within which they are embedded."

14. Among African literary figures, wa Thiong'o (1986) is among the most tenacious adherents to this view.

15. As Scribner and Cole (1981) have pointed out, individuals who are literate in Vai can be useful in rural villages in Vai society, serving as community scribes and facilitating written communications between individuals in the village and others elsewhere.

16. Vai socialization proceeds with patterns of traditional socialization independent of Vai literacy, quranic schooling in Arabic (learned largely by rote), and training in English in schools run by the government or Christian missions. See Scribner and Cole (1981) for an excellent analysis of the interplay among the three strands of Vai socialization process.

17. I have seen no evidence that this is not possible.

18. Habermas (1992) emphasizes a variant of participation that involves reflection, contestation, public reasoning, and consensus building as the mode of decision-making.

CHAPTER 9

Toward a New Beginning for Liberia

IF THERE IS A THEORETICAL PUZZLE UNDERPINNING THE STORY OF LIBERIA AND APPLI-
cable to the Mano basin area and other parts of Africa, it is to be found in the
question posed by Alexander Hamilton as to "whether societies of men are
really capable or not of establishing good government from reflection and
choice, or whether they are forever destined to depend for their political constitutions on accident and force" (Hamilton, Jay, and Madison [1788]). Can
human beings, living in specific ecological conditions and cultural settings,
draw principally upon their own resources and transform their social orders
through processes of enlightened choice making? A little over a decade ago, I
pondered this puzzle regarding the place of force as an instrument of change in
Liberia. I wrote: "The use of violence becomes appropriate as an instrument
for removing the essential core of a tyrannical autocracy, not as an instrument
for social control or social reordering" (Sawyer 1992, 313).

There is no denying that both the military coup of 1980 and the subsequent violent plunder and pillage by armed bands were demonstrably excessive, going far beyond any conception of an essential core.[1] Moreover, in both
cases, the use of violence as an instrument of social control and social reordering has not only failed but also yielded an enormous tragedy.

This study has argued that reconstituting political order on foundations of
unitary sovereignty is not likely to yield patterns of relationships that can
unlock the potential of Liberians and give them a stake in their own governance and a basis for durable peace. Monocentric government has been a
source of predation, repression, and governance failure in Liberia, in the other
countries of the Mano basin area, and elsewhere in Africa. This study has
shown that it is possible to design and establish institutions of democratic
governance in Liberia based on a theory of shared sovereignty. The task of
shifting governing paradigms is fraught with uncertainties and risks for all. It

199

involves learning through what is essentially a process of trial and error. Outcomes cannot be precisely predicted—but learning does occur and can be used productively.

Transformation from a highly centralized governmental arrangement to a system of multiple centers of limited authority involves shifts in power relationships that could affect those who hold or seek to hold a monopoly of power as well as those who would never imagine that they could be challenged to become governors. This transformation may also affect international responses, since powerful external actors have helped shape monocentric governments in Africa, often finding it more convenient to deal with a single center of authority, even a single person—and sometimes losing patience with the messiness inherent in the democratization experience. Yet there is no shortcut.

Some may argue that processes of constitutional choice need not be rooted in local populations. After all, there are examples of democratic systems that have taken root after being introduced through written constitutions imposed from outside.[2] Even those who make this argument would admit that such systems are the exceptions. Democracy has seldom flourished without evolving through processes of contestation among a people themselves. Even when imposed from outside, it must be sustained by empowered citizens. Empowerment of those who have not had opportunities or cannot imagine being in control of their own destiny is the greatest challenge—but also the surest path to success—in the quest for democracy and development in Liberia and other African countries. Leaders cannot achieve this for their people; and people should not be led to expect that others can be the source of their empowerment. As stated throughout this book, a major question for Africans generally and Liberians in particular is how to establish governance arrangements that build on the capabilities of local people and advance their prospects of working together to build democracy and to attain development from the bottom up. The benefit of experience from past failure now becomes useful capital in shaping future governance systems.

One such lesson that should be learned from past experience is that the quest for a monopoly of power, no matter how tenacious, does draw resistance that can induce violence and cause human tragedies. It should also become clear to Liberians and others in the Mano basin area that no matter the magnitude of international support and the moralistic plea for probity in government, postconflict recovery is likely to remain tenuous at best if it seeks to rebuild upon constitutional principles and arrangements that have themselves been the source of failed governance. It is better therefore to seek to constitute order differently and in so doing rely upon the creative genius of African peoples, as such genius is extant in human society everywhere. It is this creative artisanship of the Liberian people that will have to usher in a new beginning in democratic governance.

■ Notes

1. As Albert Porte put it, the 1980 coup was analogous to a surgical operation in which the surgeons removed healthy tissue. See Porte's commencement address, delivered at the University of Liberia, 1981.

2. Germany and Japan are examples often mentioned.

Appendix 1:
Chronology of Events

Late fifteenth to early sixteenth century	Mali Empire disintegrates and population disperses deeper into the West African tropical rain forest.
Late sixteenth century	Assortment of Mande-, Mel-, and Kwa-speaking groups are noted in West African region later to be called the Grain Coast.
Sixteenth to seventeenth century	Poro institutions emerge from various Mel and Mande ethnic traditions.
Mid-sixteenth century	European trade, including the Atlantic slave trade, is introduced.
Mid-seventeenth century	Ironworking skills are noted throughout the coastal plains.
Late eighteenth century	Gola political communities establish dominance in area later to be known as western Liberia.
1787	British abolitionists establish Freetown as home for freed slaves.
1807–1808	Slave trade is outlawed in Britain (1807) and the United States (1808).
1815	Thirty-eight members of free black families immigrate to Sierra Leone from the United States under the sponsorship of Paul Cuffe.
1816	American Colonization Society (ACS) is founded in Washington, D.C.
1820	First groups of settlers arrive at Shebro Island, Sierra Leone.
	Board of managers of ACS creates a constitution for the government of the African settlement.

1822	Monrovia is established; other upriver and coastal settlements are established over the next two decades.
1825	ACS creates constitution known as Plan for Civil Government.
1838	First Apprenticeship Act, specifying relationship expected between indigenous youngsters and settler families, is promulgated.
1839	Settlements unite in a commonwealth and establish ports of entry and common customs regulations.
1846	With the influx of recaptives, the Second Apprenticeship Act is promulgated.
1847	Liberia declares independence amid failure of colonial powers and some indigenous communities to respect ports of entry laws.
1848	Liberia's independence is recognized by Britain, France, and the Hanseatic German Confederation.
1860s	Attempts are made to promulgate Settlements Policy as an instrument of integration.
1862	United States recognizes Liberian independence.
1869	True Whig Party (TWP) is founded.
1871	President Roy is deposed after hotly contested elections and charges of illegal activities.
1884	Hillary R. W. Johnson is elected president, beginning TWP political domination.
1885	Britain annexes the Gallinas, the western frontier of Liberia.
1892	France lays claims to portions of eastern Liberia.
1904	Arthur Barclay is elected president and develops a plan for interior administration.
1908	Liberian Frontier Force is established. Constitution is amended to extend presidential term of office to four years.
1914	Paramount chieftaincies are delineated as jurisdictions of interior administration; interior bureaucracy grows.
1920–1924	Short-lived relationship exists between government of Liberia and the Universal Negro Improvement Association (Garvey Movement).
1919–1923	President's control over TWP machinery and interior bureaucracy is firmly established.
1926	Firestone concession agreement is signed.
1927	Forced labor controversy begins.
1929	League of Nations Commission of Inquiry begins investigation into forced labor scandal.

1930	President King resigns; all forms of servile relationships, including pawning, are abolished legally; Edwin Barclay becomes president.
1933	Stringent sedition laws are enacted.
1935	Constitution is amended to extend presidential tenure of office to a single term of eight years.
1944	Tubman is elected president and enunciates Open Door economic policy and Unification policy.
1945	Women of settler society are granted voting rights.
1946	Limited voting rights are extended to members of indigenous communities.
	First iron ore extraction concession is granted to a foreign firm (several others follow over next fifteen years).
1951	Three seats in the House of Representatives are allocated to three hinterland jurisdictions.
	Constitution is amended to extend presidential tenure of office to a first term of eight years and additional terms of four years each.
1952	Liberia College (established in 1862) is transformed into the University of Liberia.
1954	First National Unification Conference is held.
1955	Elections are held, followed by violent suppression of opposition.
1964	Hinterland jurisdictions are transformed into counties.
1968	Treason trial of H. B. Fahnbulleh Sr. is held.
1971	Tubman dies in office; Vice President Tolbert becomes president.
1973	MOJA is founded.
1975	PAL is founded.
	Trial of Albert Porte is held.
1976	New legislative enactments strengthen sedition, criminal malevolence, treason, and criminal libel laws.
1978	Hotly contested electoral campaign for mayor of Monrovia is held.
1979	Rice riots take place in Monrovia.
1980	Military takeover is waged by noncommissioned officers; President Tolbert and thirteen senior officials of government are killed; Samuel Doe becomes military head of state; military purges and repression begin.
1981	National Constitution Commission is established to draft new Liberian constitution.
	Decree 2A bans all political activities and student and labor organizations.

1983	National Constitution Commission completes draft; head of state turns draft over to Constitutional Advisory Assembly for review and revision.
1984	Constitutional Assembly completes major revision of draft constitution and submits document to referendum. Sawyer and other leaders of LPP and senior military officers are arrested and accused of coup plot.
1985	Samuel Doe wins rigged presidential elections. Quiwonkpa-organized attempted coup leads to mass arrests and mass murder; large numbers of Mano and Gio flee to neighboring countries.
1986	Samuel Doe is inaugurated president of Liberia.
1988	United States withdraws "operational experts" provided to support the Doe regime and ends military assistance.
1989	NPFL under Charles Taylor invades Liberia from Côte d'Ivoire.
1990	INPFL of Prince Johnson splits from parent NPFL. InterFaith Mediation Committee tries to broker peace among AFL, NPFL, and INPFL and provides core proposal adopted later as ECOWAS peace proposal. First ECOWAS-sponsored peace conference is held in Banjul; Interim Government of National Unity (IGNU) is formed. ECOMOG intervenes. UN Security Council imposes arms embargo. Samuel Doe is captured and killed by INPFL forces.
1991	All-Liberia Conference is held in Monrovia. NPFL invades Sierra Leone and sponsors formation of RUF. ULIMO is organized in Sierra Leone ostensibly as resistance to NPFL/RUF. Yamoussoukro peace conferences are sponsored by President Houphouët-Boigny of Côte d'Ivoire.
1992	NPFL launches invasion of Monrovia, code-named Operation Octopus.
1993	Cotonou peace agreement is signed by IGNU, NPFL, and ULIMO.
1994	New Liberia National Transitional Government (LNTG), dominated by three armed groups (NPFL, ULIMO-K, and ULIMO-J), is installed.
1995	Accra Clarification is signed. Second LNTG is installed.

1996	Month-long violent conflict takes place among armed groups in Monrovia. Abuja Agreement is signed. Third LNTG is installed.
1997	Partial disarmament, demobilization, and elections take place. National elections are held; Charles Taylor is declared winner of contest for president.
1998	Hostilities resume in Monrovia between ULIMO-J and forces associated with Taylor's government.
1999	LURD initiates hostilities against government forces in northwestern Liberia.
2001	UN Security Council accuses Charles Taylor of involvement in Sierra Leonean conflict.
2003	MODEL launches attack on government forces in southeastern Liberia. LURD and MODEL close in on Monrovia. Special Court of Sierra Leone unseals indictment against Charles Taylor, charging him with war crimes and crimes against humanity committed in Sierra Leone. Charles Taylor is exiled to Nigeria. Accra Peace Conference is convened; National Transitional Government of Liberia (NTGL) is established.
April 2004	Disarmament of armed groups begins.
December 2004	Electoral law is passed by Transitional Assembly after much controversy.
February 7, 2005	Elections Commission announces October 11, 2005, as date for presidential and legislative elections.
April 25, 2005	Voter registration begins.

Appendix 2: Internally Displaced Persons and Refugees

Liberians as Internally Displaced Persons (IDPs) and Refugees, 1991–2003 (estimates)

Year	Internally Displaced	Refugees	Total
1991	500,000	661,000	1.16 million
1992	600,000	600,000	1.20 million
1993	1 million	740,000	1.74 million
1994	1.1 million	780,000	1.88 million
1995	1 million	750,000	1.75 million
1996	1 million	755,000	1.755 million
1997	500,000	475,000	975,000
1998	75,000	310,000	385,000
1999	50,000	250,000	300,000
2000	20,000	190,000	210,000
2001	80,000	215,000	295,000
2002	100,000	280,000	380,000
2003	150,000	280,000	430,000

Source: World Refugee Survey (www.refugees.org).

Internal Displacement in Select African Countries (2002)

Country	Number (estimate)
Sudan	Up to 4 million
Angola	1.2 million
Democratic Republic of Congo	Up to 1 million
Burundi	500,000
Liberia	Up to 500,000
Sierra Leone	Up to 500,000
Uganda	Up to 500,000
Nigeria	Up to 400,000
Somalia	350,000
Congo Brazzaville	250,000
Guinea Bissau	200,000
Rwanda	Up to 150,000
Ethiopia	100,000
Kenya	100,000
Ghana	Up to 20,000
Senegal	5,000 to 10,000
Mali	Up to 10,000

Source: U.S. Committee for Refugees (www.refugees.org).

Appendix 3:
Representative Lists of
Liberian Networks and NGOs

Clan-, District-, and County-Based Development Associations That Functioned Before and During Period of Conflict

Name	Location	Activity
Bokeza Development Association	Bokeza, Lofa County	Community development
Gbandi Farmers Cooperative Development Association	Kolahun, Lofa County	Crop production, marketing
Kalayezia Development Organization	Voinjama, Lofa County	Community development
Luyeama Development Association	Zorzor, Lofa County	Community development
Bokomo Development Association	Bokomo, Gbarpolu County	School, clinic projects
Bopolu Development Association	Bopolu, Gbarpolu County	Road repairs, school, clinic projects
Kle Development Association	Kle, Bomi County	Crafts, microcredit
Kokoyah Development Association	Kokoyah, Bong County	Community development
Sanoyea Development Association	Sanoyea, Bong County	Road repairs
Kpanyan Development Association	Kpanyan, Sinoe County	School, road repairs
Tarjuarzon Development Association	Tarjuarzon, Sinoe County	Political advocacy (statutory district status)
Dugbe River Union	Borkon Jedae, Sinoe County	Schools, clinics, road repairs
Butaw Development Association	Butaw, Sinoe County	School, clinic project
Maryland Development Association	Harper, Cape Palmas	Schools, clinics, road repairs

Self-Organized Networks and NGOs

Name	Type of Organization	Activities	Operational Location	Year Establised
Action for Greater Harvest	NGO	Agriculture/ community development	Montserrado, Bong, Margibi, Lofa	1998
Agricultural Relief Services	NGO	Agriculture	Nimba	1995
Catholic Justice and Peace Commission	NGO	Human rights	National	1991
Center for Democratic Empowerment	NGO	Governance	National	1994
Christian Association of the Blind	NGO	Special education	National	1985
Christian Humanitarian Services	NGO	Health/ agriculture	Grand Kru	1993
Community Project Services	NGO	Water/sanitation	Grand Bassa	1993
Community Union for Sustainable Development	Community-based	Community development	Nimba	2000
Dempeloi Cooperative Society	Community-based	Agriculture	Montserrado	
Environment Enhancement Through Ants and Pest Protection	NGO	Environment/ health	Montserrado	1995
Farmers Against Hunger	Community-based	Agriculture training/trauma counseling	Montserrado	1999
Grand Bassa Agricultural Group	NGO	Agriculture	Grand Bassa	1995
Human Development Foundation	NGO	Water/sanitation	Montserrado	1999
Inter-Religious Council	Faith-based	Peace/ reconciliation	National	1990
Liberia Annual Conference/ United Methodist Church	Faith-based	Human services	National	1934
Liberia Agro-Systems	NGO	Agriculture/ water/ sanitation	Sinoe	2000
Liberia Islamic Union for Reconstruction and Development	Faith-based	Community development	National	1991
Measuagoon	NGO	Agriculture/ community development	National	1997
Medical Emergency and Relief Cooperation International	NGO	Health	National	1990
Multi-Agrisystems Promoters	NGO	Agriculture/ community development	Grand Gedeh	2000
New African Research and Development Associates	NGO	Community development	National	1987
New Family Empowerment for Development	NGO	Community development	Grand Cape Mount	1994
Susukuu, Inc.	NGO	Community development	National	1974

Women's Development Organizations

Name	Location/County	Activity
Association of Female Lawyers of Liberia	National	Gender equity
Cavalla Women's Development Association	Rural/Maryland County	Women's microcredit
Gbandi Women's Development Association	Rural/Lofa County	Agriculture
Jallah Town Women's Development Association	Urban/Monrovia	Craft/mutual assistance
Kakata Women's Development Association	Periurban	Horticulture/microcredit
Kongee Konwroh Women's Development Association	Urban/Monrovia	Mutual assistance/ community development
Liberian Women Initiative	National	Literacy/civic education/ peacebuilding
Plunkor Women's Development Association	Urban/Monrovia	Craft/mutual assistance
Saye Town Women's Development Association	Urban/Montserrado	Craft/tie-dyeing
Sinoe Women's Development Association	Countywide/Sinoe	All purpose
Southeastern Women's Association	Rural/Maryland	Agriculture
Zorzor District Women's Care	Rural/Lofa County	Agriculture/skills training/HIV/AIDS awareness

U.S.-Based Branches of Alumni Associations of Liberian Educational Institutions

Name of U.S.-Based Organization	Name of Liberian Educational Institution	Location of Educational Institution	Type of Educational Institution
Bishop Julwe High School Alumni Association	Bishop Julwe High School	Zwedru, Grand Gedeh County	Secondary school
B.W.I. Alumni Association	Booker Washington Institute	Kakata, Margibi County	Technical/secondary school
B. W. Harris Alumni Association	B. W. Harris Episcopal High School	Monrovia	Secondary school
Cape Palmas High School Alumni Association	Cape Palmas High School	Harper, Maryland County	Secondary school
Cathedral School Alumni Association	Cathedral High School	Monrovia	Secondary school
College of West Africa Alumni Association, USA	College of West Africa	Monrovia	Junior college
Cuttington University College, USA	Cuttington University College	Suacoco, Bong County	University
Lutheran Training Institute Alumni Association	Lutheran Training Institute	Salayea, Lofa County	Secondary school
Ricks Institute Alumni Association, USA	Ricks Institute	Virginia, Montserrado County	Secondary school/ junior college
Association of Former Students and Alumni of the Muslim Congress High School	Muslim Congress High School	Monrovia	Secondary school
Suehn Alumni Association	Suehn Industrial Training Mission	Suehn, Bomi County	Secondary/vocational school
University of Liberia Alumni Association, USA	University of Liberia	Monrovia	University
National Alumni Association of Laboratory and Tubman High School in the Americas	Tubman High School	Monrovia	Secondary/technical school

U.S.-Based Affiliates of Community Organizations in Liberia

Name	U.S. Headquarters	Affiliation in Liberia	Activity
Barrolle Association	Trenton, NJ	Monrovia	Sports
Federation of Lofa Associations in the Americas	Detroit, MI	Lofa County	All-purpose countywide support
Grand Gedeh Associations in the Americas	Philadelphia, PA	Grand Gedeh	All-purpose countywide support
Islamic Union for Reconstruction and Development	Philadelphia, PA	Sectarian (Islam)	All-purpose community support
Maryland County Development Association		Maryland County	All-purpose countywide support, especially microcredit
National Association of Bong County Citizens	New York, NY	Bong County	All-purpose countywide support
St. Paul River District, Inc.	Cleveland, OH	Montserrado County	All-purpose community support
Tappita Development Association		Tappita District, Nimba County	Health support
Liberian Mandingo Association of New York	Brooklyn, NY	Ethnic	Peacebuilding/community development
United Nimba Citizens Council	Minneapolis, MN	Nimba County	All-purpose countywide support
Women's Care International Foundation	Tucker, GA	Orphanages in Liberia and Sierra Leone	Educational support

Acronyms

ACP	African Caribbean Pacific
ACS	American Colonization Society
AFRC	Armed Forces Revolutionary Council (Sierra Leone)
AU	African Union
CBO	community-based organization
CEDE	Center for Democratic Empowerment
CRS	Catholic Relief Services
CSIS	Canadian Security and Intelligence Service
CSO	civil society organization
DRC	Democratic Republic of Congo
ECOMOG	ECOWAS Monitoring Group
ECOWAS	Economic Community of West African States
FDA	Forestry Development Authority
FLY	Federation of Liberian Youth
IAD	Institutional Analysis and Development
IANSA	International Action Network on Small Arms
ICG	International Crisis Group
ICRC	International Committee of the Red Cross
IDPs	internally displaced persons
IGNU	Interim Government of National Unity
IGO	intergovernmental organization
IMF	International Monetary Fund
INGO	international nongovernmental organization
IRC	International Rescue Committee
LNTG	Liberia National Transitional Government
LPC	Liberia Peace Council
LURD	Liberia United for Reconciliation and Democracy
LWS/WF	Lutheran World Service/World Federation
MODEL	Movement for Democracy in Liberia

MOJA	Movement for Justice in Africa
MSF	Médecins Sans Frontières
NEPAD	New Partnership for African Development
NGO	nongovernmental organization
NPFL	National Patriotic Front of Liberia
NTGL	National Transitional Government of Liberia
OAU/AU	Organization of African Unity/African Union
OTC	Oriental Timber Company
PAL	Progressive Alliance of Liberia
PDG	Democratic Party of Guinea
PPP	Progressive People's Party
RDTF	Rural Development Task Force
RUF	Revolutionary United Front (Sierra Leone)
SAP	structural adjustment program
SCF	Save the Children Fund
SCOGO	Special Commission on Government Operations
SELF	Special Emergency Life Fund
TRC	truth and reconciliation commission
TWP	True Whig Party
ULAA	Union of Liberian Associations in the Americas
ULIMO-J	United Liberation Movement for Democracy in Liberia (Johnson wing)
ULIMO-K	United Liberation Movement for Democracy in Liberia (Kromah wing)
UNDP	United Nations Development Programme
UNECA	United Nations Economic Commission for Africa
UNHCR	United Nations High Commissioner for Refugees
UNICEF	United Nations Children's Fund
UPP	United People's Party
WAEC	West African Examination Council

References

Abdullah, Ibrahim. 1998. "Bush Path to Destruction: The Origin and Character of the Revolutionary United Front/Sierra Leone." *Journal of Modern African Studies* 36, no. 2 (June): 203–235.

Abdullah, Ibrahim, and Patrick Muana. 1998. "The Revolutionary United Front of Sierra Leone: A Revolt of the Lumpenproletariat." In Christopher Clapham, ed., *African Guerrillas.* Oxford: James Currey, pp. 172–193.

Abraham, Arthur. 1978. *Mende Government and Politics Under Colonial Rule: A Historical Study of Political Change in Sierra Leone, 1890–1937.* Freetown: Sierra Leone University Press.

———. 2001. "Dancing with the Chameleon: Sierra Leone and the Elusive Quest for Peace." *Journal of Contemporary African Studies* 19, no. 2: 165–183.

Adebajo, Adekeye. 2002. *Liberia's Civil War: Nigeria, ECOMOG, and Regional Security in West Africa.* Boulder, CO: Lynne Rienner Publishers.

Adedeji, Adebayo. 1999. "Comprehending African Conflicts." In Adebayo Adedeji, ed., *Comprehending and Mastering African Conflicts: The Search for Sustainable Peace and Good Governance.* London: Zed Press, pp. 3–21.

Afolayan, Adebisi. 1976. "The Six Year Primary Project in Nigeria." In Ayo Bamgbose, ed., *Mother-Tongue Education: The West African Experience.* London: Hodder & Stoughton.

Agrawal, Arun, and Jesse Ribot. 1999. "Accountability in Decentralization: A Framework with South Asian and African Cases." *Journal of Developing Areas* 33 (Summer): 473–502.

Ake, Claude. 1993. "The Unique Case of African Democracy." *International Affairs* 69, no. 2: 239–244.

———. 1996. *Democracy and Development in Africa.* Washington, DC: Brookings Institution.

Akerlof, George. 1970. "The Market for 'Lemons': Uncertainty and the Market Mechanism." *Quarterly Journal of Economics* 84 (August).

Akpan, Monday B. 1968. "The African Policy of the Liberian Settlers, 1841–1932." Ph.D. diss., University of Ibadan, Nigeria.

Anderson, Benjamin J. K. 1971. *Narrative of a Journey to Musardu, the Capital of the Western Mandingo, Together with Narrative of the Expedition Despatched to Musardu in 1874.* London: Cass.

219

Anning, Emmanuel Kwesi. 1994. "Managing Regional Security in West Africa: ECOWAS, ECOMOG, and Liberia." Working Paper No. 94, Centre for Development Research, Copenhagen, February 2.

Ayee, Joseph R. A. 1997. "The Adjustment of Central Bodies to Decentralization: The Case of the Ghanaian Bureaucracy." *African Studies Review* 40, no. 2 (September): 37–57.

Ayo, S. Bamidele. 2002. *Public Administration and the Conduct of Community Affairs Among the Yoruba in Nigeria.* Oakland, CA: ICS Press and Workshop in Political Theory and Policy Analysis.

Azango, Bertha B. 1968. "The Historical and Philosophical Development of Liberian Education, Viewed from the Education Laws." *Liberian Historical Review* 1: 28–37.

Bangura, Yusuf. 2000. "Strategic Policy Failure and Governance in Sierra Leone." *Journal of Modern African Studies* 38, no. 4: 551–577.

Barkan, Joel D., ed. 1998. *Five Monographs on Decentralization and Democratization in Sub-Saharan Africa.* Iowa City: Center for International and Comparative Studies, with the University of Iowa Libraries.

Barkan, Joel D., Michael L. McNulty, and M. A. O. Ayeni. 1991. "Hometown Voluntary Associations, Local Development, and the Emergence of Civil Society in Western Nigeria." *Journal of Modern African Studies* 29, no. 3: 457–480.

Berdal, Mats, and David M. Malone, eds. 2000. *Greed and Grievance: Economic Agendas in Civil Wars.* Boulder, CO: Lynne Rienner Publishers.

Berkeley, Bill. 2001. *The Graves Are Not Yet Full: Race, Tribe, and Power in the Heart of Africa.* New York: Basic Books.

Bettis, L. W., and D. G. Imig. 1969. *Government Organization Training and Management.* USAID Mission to Liberia, www.dec.org/content.cfm?rec_no=19754.

Blair, H. 2000. "Participation and Accountability in Periphery: Democratic Local Governance in the Periphery." *World Development* 28, no. 1: 21–39.

Boahen, A. Adu. 1964. *Britain, the Sahara, and the Western Sudan, 1788–1861.* Oxford: Clarendon Press.

———. 1987. *African Perspectives on Colonialism.* Baltimore: Johns Hopkins University Press.

Boyden, Jo. 1994. "Children's Experience of Conflict Related Emergencies: Some Implications for Relief Policy and Practice." *Disasters* 18, no. 3: 254–267.

Bracken, Patrick J. 1998. "Hidden Agendas: Deconstructing Post Traumatic Stress Disorder." In P. Bracken and C. Petty, eds., *Rethinking the Trauma of War.* London: Free Association Books.

Bratton, Michael. 1989. "Beyond the State: Civil Society and Associational Life in Africa." *World Politics* 41, no. 3 (April): 407–430.

———. 1994. "Neopatrimonial Regimes and Political Transitions in Africa." *World Politics* 46, no. 4: 453–489.

Brown, George W. [1941] 1981. *The Economic History of Liberia.* Washington, DC: Associated Publishers.

Buchanan, James M. 1977. *Freedom in Constitutional Contract: Perspective of a Political Economist.* College Station: Texas A&M University Press.

Burrowes, Carl Patrick. 2004. *Power and Press Freedom in Liberia 1830–1970: The Impact of Globalization and Civil Society on Media-Government Relations.* Trenton, NJ: Africa World Press.

Caine, Kenneth L. 1999. "The Rape of Dinah: Human Rights, Civil War in Liberia and Evil Triumphant." *Human Rights Quarterly* 21, no. 2 (May): 265–307.

Catholic JPC (Justice and Peace Commission). 1994. Gbarnga Report, p. 4. Catholic Diocese of Monrovia, Liberia.

Chaudhuri, J. Pal. 1985. "An Analysis of the Recent Developments in Liberia." *Liberia Forum* 1, no. 1: 45–54.

Cheema, G. Shabbir, and Dennis A. Rondinelli, eds. 1983. *Decentralization and Development: Policy Implementation in Developing Countries.* Beverly Hills: Sage Publications.

Cilliers, Jakkie, and Peggy Mason, eds. 1999. *Peace, Profit, or Plunder? The Privatisation of Security in War-Torn African Societies.* Halfway House, South Africa: Institute for Security Studies.

Clapham, Christopher. 1976. *Liberia and Sierra Leone: An Essay in Comparative Politics.* Cambridge: Cambridge University Press.

Clegg, Claude A., III. 2004. *The Price of Liberty: African Americans and the Making of Liberia.* Chapel Hill: University of North Carolina Press.

Clower, Robert W., George Dalton, Mitchell Harwitz, and A. A. Walters. 1966. *Growth Without Development: An Economic Survey of Liberia.* Evanston, IL: Northwestern University Press.

Cohen, John M., and Stephen B. Peterson. 1999. *Administrative Decentralization: Strategies for Developing Countries.* West Hartford, CT: Kumarian Press.

Coleman, James S. 2003. "Norms as Social Capital." In Elinor Ostrom and T. K. Ahn, eds., *Foundations of Social Capital.* Cheltenham, UK: Edward Elgar, pp. 136–158.

———. 1988. "Social Capital in the Creation of Human Capital." *American Journal of Sociology* 94 (supplement): 95–120.

Collier, Paul. 2000. "Doing Well Out of War: An Economic Perspective." In Mats Berdal and David M. Malone, eds., *Greed and Grievance: Economic Agendas in Civil Wars.* Boulder, CO: Lynne Rienner Publishers, pp. 91–111.

———. 2003. *Breaking the Conflict Trap: Civil War and Development Policy.* Washington, DC: World Bank and Oxford University Press.

Conteh-Morgan, Earl, and Mac Dixon-Fyle. 1999. *Sierra Leone at the End of the Twentieth Century: History, Politics and Society.* New York: Peter Lang.

Cooper, Neil. 2001. "Conflict Goods: The Challenges for Peacekeeping and Conflict Prevention." *International Peacekeeping* 8, no. 3 (August): 21–38.

Crawford, Sue E. S., and Elinor Ostrom. 2000. "A Grammar of Institutions." In Michael D. McGinnis, ed., *Polycentric Games and Institutions: Readings from the Workshop in Political Theory and Policy Analysis.* Ann Arbor: University of Michigan Press, pp. 114–155.

Crocker, Chester A. 1999. *Herding Cats: Multiparty Mediation in a Complex World.* Washington, DC: United States Institute of Peace Press.

Crowder, Michael. 1968. *West Africa Under Colonial Rule.* Evanston, IL: Northwestern University Press.

Crummell, Alexander. [1862] 1969. *The Future of Africa: Being Addresses, Sermons, Etc., Etc., Delivered in the Republic of Liberia.* New York: Scribner. Republished by Negro History Press, Detroit, MI.

CSIS (Canadian Security Intelligence Service). 2000. *Conflict Between and Within States.* Report No. 2000/06, August. Available at www.csis-scrs.gc.ca.

d'Azevedo, Warren L. 1962. "Some Historical Problems in the Delineation of a Central West Atlantic Region." *Annals of the New York Academy of Sciences* 96: 512–538.

———. 1969–1971. "A Tribal Reaction to Nationalism." Parts 1–4. *Liberian Studies Journal* 1 (Spring 1969): 1–21; 2 (1969): 43–63; 3 (1970): 99–115; 4 (1970–1971): 1–19.

da Costa, Peter. 1994. "Counseling Victims of the Civil War." *Africa Report* 39, no. 2 (March–April): 30–31.

Derman, William. 1973. *Serfs, Peasants, and Socialists: Former Serf Village in the Republic of Guinea.* Berkeley: University of California Press.

de Soto, Hernando. 2000. *The Mystery of Capital: Why Capitalism Triumphs in the West and Fails Everywhere Else.* New York: Basic Books.

Duffield, Mark. 2000. "Globalization, Transborder Trade, and War Economies." In Mats Berdal and David M. Malone, eds. *Greed and Grievances: Economic Agendas in Civil Wars.* Boulder, CO: Lynne Rienner Publishers, pp. 69–89.

Dunn, D. Elwood. 1979. *The Foreign Policy of Liberia During the Tubman Era, 1944–1971.* London: Hutchinson Benham.

Dunn, D. Elwood, and S. Byron Tarr. 1988. *Liberia: A National Polity in Transition.* Metuchen, NJ: Scarecrow Press.

Dupraz, Emily. 2002. "The Oils of War." *Harvard International Review* 24, no. 1: 10–11.

Eavis, Paul. 1999. "Awash with Light Weapons." *The World Today* 55, no. 4: 19–21.

The Economist, March 8, 2003.

Ekeh, Peter. 1975. "Colonialism and the Two Publics in Africa: A Theoretical Statement." *Comparative Studies in Society and History: An International Quarterly* 17, no. 1: 91–112.

Elazar, Daniel J. 1987. *Exploring Federalism.* Tuscaloosa: University of Alabama Press.

Ellis, Stephen. 1999. *The Mask of Anarchy: the Destruction of Liberia and the Religious Dimension of an African Civil War.* New York: New York University Press.

Ensminger, Jean. 1990. "Co-opting the Elders: The Political Economy of State Incorporation in Africa." *American Anthropologist* 92: 662–675.

Evans, Peter. 1992. "The State as Problem and Solution." In S. Haggard and R. R. Kaufman, eds., *The Politics of Economic Adjustment.* Princeton: Princeton University Press, pp. 139–181.

Evans-Pritchard, Edward. 1940. *The Nuer: A Description of the Modes of Livelihood and Political Institutions of a Nilotic People.* Oxford: Clarendon Press.

Fahnbulleh, H. Boima, Jr. 1985. *The Diplomacy of Prejudice: Liberia in International Politics, 1945–1970.* New York: Vantage Press.

Fanthorpe, Richard. 2001. "Neither Citizen Nor Subject? 'Lumpen' Agency and the Legacy of Native Administration in Sierra Leone." *African Affairs* 100: 363–386.

Fatton, Robert, Jr. 1992. *Predatory Rule: State and Civil Society in Africa.* Boulder, CO: Lynne Rienner Publishers.

Fieldhouse, D. K. 1999. *The West and the Third World: Trade, Colonialism, Dependence and Development.* Oxford: Blackwell.

Firmin-Sellers, Kathryn. [1995] 1999. "The Concentration of Authority: Constitutional Creation in the Gold Coast, 1950." In Michael D. McGinnis, ed., *Polycentric Governance and Development: Readings from the Workshop in Political Theory and Policy Analysis.* Ann Arbor: University of Michigan Press, pp. 186–208.

Fishman, Joshua. 1985. *The Rise and Fall of Ethnic Revival: Perspectives on Language and Ethnicity.* Berlin: Mouton.

Fisman, Raymond, and Roberta Gatti. 2002. "Decentralization and Corruption: Evidence Across Countries." *Journal of Public Economics* 83, no. 3 (March): 325–345.

Fofana, Lansana. 1998. "Politics-Sierra Leone: Exposing the Hidden Hand of Libya." Inter Press Service, October 16, 1998.

Folke, Carl, Steve Carpenter, Thomas Elmqvist, Lance Gunderson, C. S. Holling, Brian Walker, et al. 2002. *Resilience and Sustainable Development: Building*

Adaptive Capacity in a World of Transformation. Scientific Background Paper on Resilience for the Process of the World Summit on Sustainable Development on Behalf of the Environmental Advisory Council to the Swedish Government.

Fortes, Meyer, and E. E. Evans-Pritchard, eds., 1940. *African Political Systems*. London: Oxford University Press, for the International African Institute.

Fox, Jonathan, and Josefina Aranda. 1996. *Decentralization and Rural Development in Mexico: Community Participation in Oaxaca's Municipal Funds Program*. La Jolla, CA: Center for U.S.-Mexican Studies, University of California, San Diego.

Freire, Paulo. 1970. *Pedagogy of the Oppressed*. New York: Continuum International Publishing Group.

———. 1998. *Politics and Education*. Los Angeles: UCLA Latin American Center Publications.

Frey, Bruno, and Reiner Eichenberger. 1999. *The New Democratic Federalism for Europe: Functional, Overlapping, and Competing Jurisdictions*. Cheltenham, UK: Edward Elgar.

Fukuyama, Francis. 1992. *The End of History and the Last Man*. New York: Free Press.

Gable, Eric. 2000. "The Culture Development Club: Youth, Neo-Tradition, and the Construction of Society in Guinea Bissau." *Anthropological Quarterly* 73, no. 4: 195–204.

Garbarino, James, Kathleen Kostelny, and Nancy Dubrow. 1991. "What Children Can Tell Us About Living in Danger." *American Psychologist* 46, no. 4: 376–383.

Gellar, Sheldon. 2005. *Democracy in Senegal: Tocquevillian Analytics in Africa*. New York: Palgrave Macmillan.

Gibson, Clark, Margaret A. McKean, and Elinor Ostrom, eds. 2000. *People and Forests: Communities, Institutions, and Governance*. Cambridge: MIT Press.

Global IDP. 2001, 2004. www.idpproject.org.

Global Witness. 2001. "Taylor Made: The Pivotal Role of Liberia's Forests and Flag of Convenience in Regional Conflict." www.globalwitness.org.

———. 2002. "Logging Off: How the Liberian Timber Industry Fuels Liberia's Humanitarian Disaster and Threatens Sierra Leone." www.globalwitness.org.

———. 2003. "The Usual Suspects: Liberia's Weapons and Mercenaries in Côte d'Ivoire and Sierra Leone—Why It's Still Possible, How It Works and How to Break the Trend." www.globalwitness.org.

GOL (Government of Liberia). 2000a. *Challenges and Opportunities for Fulfilling the Rights of Children in War-Torn Liberia: A Situation Analysis*. A Report Jointly Commissioned by the Eminent Persons' Group On Advocacy for Children and UNICEF, synthesized by Professor Ahmed Mohiddin. November 2000.

———. 2000b. *Impact of Under-Development, Debt and Armed Conflict on Children in Liberia: A Situational Assessment and Analysis*. A Report Jointly Commissioned by the Government of Liberia, the Eminent Persons Group on Advocacy for Children and UNICEF, draft.

Guannu, Joseph S. 1983. *Liberian History Up to 1847*. Smithtown, NY: Exposition Press.

Gyimah-Boadi, E. 1996. "Civil Society in Africa." *Journal of Democracy* 7, no. 2: 118–132.

Habermas, Jurgen. 1992. "Further Reflections on the Public Sphere." In Craig Calhoun, ed., *Habermas and the Public Sphere*. Cambridge: MIT Press, pp. 421–461.

Hamilton, Alexander, John Jay, and James Madison [1788] n.d. *The Federalist*. Edited by Edward M. Earle. New York: Modern Library.

Harbeson, John, Donald Rothchild, and Naomi Chazan, eds. 1994. *Civil Society and the State in Africa*. Boulder, CO: Lynne Rienner Publishers.

Harshe, Rajen. 1984. *Pervasive Entente: France and Ivory Coast in African Affairs*. Atlantic Highlands, NJ: Humanities Press.

Hartzell, Caroline A. 1999. "Explaining the Stability of Negotiated Settlements to Intrastate Wars." *Journal of Conflict Resolution* 43, no. 1: 3–22.

Henries, A. Doris Banks. [1966] 1980. *Civics for Liberian Schools*. New York: Collier-Macmillan International.

Henries, Richard, and A. Doris Banks Henries. 1966. *Liberia, the West African Republic*. New York: St. Martin's Press.

Holsoe, Svend E. 1971. "A Study of Relations Between Settlers and Indigenous Peoples in Western Liberia, 1821–1847." *African Historical Studies* 2: 331–362.

———. 1974. "The Manipulation of Traditional Political Structures Among Coastal Peoples in Western Liberia During the Nineteenth Century." *Ethnohistory* 21: 158–167.

———. [1994] 2002. "Locally Empowering Rural Political Institutions in Liberia." Manuscript.

Hooghe, Liesbet, and Gary Marks. 2003. "Unraveling the Central State, but How? Types of Multi-Level Governance." *American Political Science Review* 97, no. 2: 233–244.

Howell, Jude, and Jenny Pearce. 2001. *Civil Society and Development: A Critical Exploration*. Boulder, CO: Lynne Rienner Publishers.

Huband, Mark. 1998. *The Liberian Civil War*. London: Frank Cass.

Huberich, Charles Henry. 1947. *The Political and Legislative History of Liberia*. 2 vols. New York: Central Book Company.

Human Development Report. 1995. New York: UNDP, p. 1.

Human Rights Watch. 2003. *Sudan, Oil and Human Rights*. New York: Human Rights Watch.

Hutchful, Eboe. 1997. "Political Parties and Civil Societies in Sub-Saharan Africa: Conflicting Objectives?" In Marina Ottaway, ed., *Democracy in Africa: The Hard Road Ahead*. Boulder, CO: Lynne Rienner Publishers.

Hutchful, Eboe, and Abdulaye Bathily, eds. 1998. *The Military and Militarism in Africa*. Dakar: CODESRIA.

IANSA (International Action Network on Small Arms). 2001. www.iansa.org/regions.

ICG (International Crisis Group). 2003a. *Sierra Leone: The State of Security and Governance*. Africa Report No. 67, September. www.crisisweb.org.

———. 2003b. *Guinea: Uncertainties at the End of an Era*. Africa Report No. 74. December 19. www.crisisweb.org.

ICRC (International Committee of the Red Cross) News. 2000. 14, no. 20 (April).

IRC (International Rescue Committee). 2004. "Mortality in the Democratic Republic of Congo: Results from a Nation-Wide Survey." December. www.theirc.org.

Jackson, Robert, and Carl Rosberg. 1982. *Personal Rule in Black Africa: Prince, Autocrat, Prophet, Tyrant*. Berkeley: University of California Press.

Jaye, Thomas. 2003. *Issues of Sovereignty, Strategy, and Security in the Economic Community of West African States (ECOWAS) Intervention in the Liberian Civil War*. Lewiston, NY: Edwin Mellen Press.

Jones, Hannah Abeodu Bowen. 1962. "The Struggle for Political and Cultural Unification in Liberia, 1847–1930." Ph.D. diss., Department of History, Northwestern University, Evanston, IL.

Kamara, Siapha. 1987. "Food Production and Availability Trends in Liberia." M. Phil. thesis, Institute of Social Studies, The Hague.

Karnga, Abayomi. 1926. *History of Liberia*. Liverpool: Tyte.

Kasfir, Nelson, ed. 1998. *Civil Society and Democracy in Africa: Critical Perspectives*. London: Frank Cass.

Kiser, Larry L., and Elinor Ostrom. [1982] 2000. "Three Worlds of Action: A Metatheoretical Synthesis of Institutional Approaches." In Michael D. McGinnis, ed., *Polycentric Games and Institutions: Readings from the Workshop in Political Theory and Policy Analysis*. Ann Arbor: University of Michigan Press.

Ki-Zerbo, Joseph. 1978. *Histoire de l'Afrique noire d'hier à demain*. Paris: A. Hatier.

Krishna, Anirudh. 2002. *Active Social Capital: Tracing the Roots of Development and Democracy*. New York: Columbia University Press.

Kuhnert, Stephan. 2001. "An Evolutionary Theory of Collective Action: Schumpeterian Entrepreneurship for the Common Good." *Constitutional Political Economy* 12: 13–29.

Kulah, Arthur F. 1999. *Liberia Will Rise Again: Reflections on the Liberian Civil Crisis*. Nashville, TN: Abingdon Press.

Lal, Deepak. 1984. *The Political Economy of the Predatory State*. Washington, DC: World Bank (Development Research Department).

Lamin, Abdul. 2003. *Peace and Justice in Sierra Leone: The Truth and Reconciliation Commission and the Special Court*. Ph.D. diss., Howard University, Washington, DC.

Lederach, John Paul. 1997. *Building Peace: Sustainable Reconciliation in Divided Societies*. Washington, DC: United States Institute of Peace Press.

Lemarchand, René. 1992. "Uncivil States and Civil Societies: How Illusion Became Reality." *Journal of Modern African Studies* 30, no 2: 177–192.

Levitt, Jeremy. 2005. *The Evolution of Deadly Conflict in Liberia: From Paternaltarianism to State Collapse 1822–2003*. Durham, NC: Carolina Academic Press.

Lewis, Peter, ed. 1998. *Africa: Dilemmas of Development and Change*. Boulder, CO: Westview Press.

Liberia National Transitional Government, United Nations/World Bank. 2004. *Joint Needs Assessment*.

Liberty, Clarence E. Zamba. 2002. *Growth of the Liberian State: An Analysis of Its Historiography*. Northridge, CA: New World African Press, in association with the Liberian Studies Association.

Liebenow, J. Gus. 1969. *Liberia: The Evolution of Privilege*. Ithaca, NY: Cornell University Press.

———. 1987. *Liberia: The Quest for Democracy*. Bloomington: Indiana University Press.

Little, Kenneth L. 1966. *The Mende of Sierra Leone: A West African People in Transition*. Rev. ed. New York: Routledge & Kegan Paul.

Livingstone, Ivan, and Roger Charlton. 2001. "Financing Decentralized Development in a Low-Income Country: Raising Revenue for Local Government in Uganda." *Development and Change* 31, no. 1: 77–100.

Lizza, Ryan. 2005. "White House Watch: Charles at Large." *New Republic,* April 25, pp. 10–11.

Locke, John. 1952. *The Second Treatise of Government*. Edited by Thomas P. Peardon. New York: Liberal Arts Press.

Lonsdale, John. 1986. "Political Accountability in African History." In Patrick Chabal. ed., *Political Domination in Africa: Reflections on the Limits of Power.* Cambridge: Cambridge University Press, pp. 126–157.

Lutheran World Federation (Liberia). 1999. *Fourth Quarter Report, Liberia Programme*. October–December.

Maine, Henry Sumner. 1960. *Ancient Law.* London: J. M. Dent.

Mamdani, Mahmood. 1996. *Citizen and Subject: Contemporary Africa and the Legacy of Late Colonialism.* Princeton: Princeton University Press.

———. 2001. *When Victims Become Killers: Colonialism, Nativism, and the Genocide in Rwanda.* Princeton: Princeton University Press.

Maren, Michael. 1997. *The Road to Hell: The Ravaging Effects of Foreign Aid and International Charity.* New York: Free Press.

Martin, Jane J. 1968. *The Dual Legacy: Government Authority and Mission Influence Among the Glebo of Eastern Liberia, 1834–1910."* Ph.D. diss., Department of History, Boston University.

Matloff, Judith. 1996. "France Clings to Lost Glory in Ex-Colonies." *Christian Science Monitor,* January 2.

Mattes, Hanspeter. 1995. "The Rise and Fall of the Revolutionary Committees." In Dirk Vandewalle, ed. *Qadhafi's Libya, 1969–1994.* New York: St. Martin's Press.

McGinnis, Michael D., ed. 1999a. *Polycentric Governance and Development: Readings from the Workshop in Political Theory and Policy Analysis.* Ann Arbor: University of Michigan Press.

———, ed. 1999b. *Polycentricity and Local Public Economies: Readings from the Workshop in Political Theory and Policy Analysis.* Ann Arbor: University of Michigan Press.

———, ed. 2000. *Polycentric Games and Institutions: Readings from the Workshop in Political Theory and Policy Analysis.* Ann Arbor: University of Michigan Press.

McIntosh, Susan Keech, ed. 1999. *Beyond Chiefdoms: Pathways to Complexity in Africa.* Cambridge: Cambridge University Press.

McKinnon, Ronald, and Thomas Nechyba. 1997. "Competition in Federal Systems: The Role of Political and Financial Constraints." In John Ferejohn and Barry R. Weingast, eds., *The New Federalism: Can the States Be Trusted?* Stanford, CA: Hoover Institution Press, Stanford University, pp. 3–61.

Michels, Robert. [1911] 1966. *Political Parties: A Sociological Study of the Oligarchical Tendencies of Modern Democracy.* Edited by S. M. Lipset. New York: Free Press.

Middleton, John, and David Tait, eds. 1958. *Tribes Without Rulers: Studies in African Segmentary Systems.* London: Routledge & Kegan Paul.

Ministry of Education, Republic of Liberia National Mass Literacy Program. 1999–2000.

Ministry of Education, Republic of Liberia Annual Reports. 2000.

Montesquieu, Charles Louis de Secondat. [1748] 1966. *The Spirit of the Laws.* New York: Hafner.

Nagbe, K. Moses. 1996. *Bulk Challenge.* Cape Coast, Ghana: Champion Publications.

Naldi, Gino J. 1999. *The Organization of African Unity: An Analysis of Its Role.* London: Mansell.

Ndegwa, Stephen. 1996. *The Two Faces of Civil Society: NGOs and Politics in Africa.* West Hartford, CT: Kumarian Press.

Neuffer, Elizabeth. 2000. "Kigali Dispatch: It Takes a Village." *New Republic,* April 10, pp. 18–19.

North, Douglass. 1990. *Institutions, Institutional Change, and Economic Performance.* New York: Cambridge University Press.

Nzongola-Ntalaja, Georges. 1998. *From Zaire to the Democratic Republic of the Congo.* Uppsala: Nordiska Afrikainstitutet.

Oakerson, Ronald J. 1999. *Governing Local Public Economies: Creating the Civic Metropolis.* Oakland, CA: ICS Press.

Obeng, Samuel. 2002. "'For the Most Part, They Paid No Attention to Our Native Languages': The Politics About Languages in Sub-Saharan Africa." In Samuel Gyasi Obeng and Beverly Hartford, eds., *Political Independence with Linguistic Servitude: The Politics About Languages in the Developing World*. New York: Nova Science Publishers, pp. 75–96.

Olowu, Dele, and James S. Wunsch. 2004. *Local Governance in Africa: The Challenge of Democratic Decentralization*. Boulder, CO: Lynne Rienner Publishers.

Orvis, Stephen. 2001. "Civil Society in Africa or African Civil Society." *Journal of Asian and African Studies* 36, no. 1: 17–38.

Osmani, S. R. 2001. "Participatory Governance, People's Empowerment and Poverty Reduction." Conference Paper Series, UNDP/SEPED, and the World Summit for Social Development (Copenhagen), www.undp.org/seped/publications/conf_pub.

Ostrom, Elinor. 1990. *Governing the Commons: The Evolution of Institutions for Collective Action*. Cambridge: Cambridge University Press.

———. 1992. *Crafting Institutions for Self-Governing Irrigation Systems*. San Francisco: Institute for Contemporary Studies Press.

———. 2005. *Understanding Institutional Diversity in Open Societies*. Princeton: Princeton University Press.

Ostrom, Elinor, and T. K. Ahn. 2003. "Introduction." In Elinor Ostrom and T. K. Ahn, eds., *Foundations of Social Capital*. Cheltenham, UK: Edward Elgar, pp. xi–xxxix.

Ostrom, Elinor, Roy Gardner, and James Walker. 1994. *Rules, Games and Common-Pool Resources*. Ann Arbor: University of Michigan Press.

Ostrom, Elinor, Clark Gibson, Sujai Shivakumar, and Krister Andersson. 2002. *Aid, Incentive, and Sustainability: An Institutional Analysis of Development Cooperation*. SIDA Studies in Evaluation 02/1. Stockholm: Swedish International Development Cooperation Agency.

Ostrom, Elinor, and Marco A. Janssen. 2002. "Multi-Level Governance and Resilience of Social and Ecological Systems." Working Paper, Workshop in Political Theory and Policy Analysis, Indiana University.

Ostrom, Elinor, Roger B. Parks, and Gordon P. Whitaker. [1974] 1999. "Defining and Measuring Structural Variations in Interorganizational Arrangements." In Michael D. McGinnis, ed., *Polycentricity and Local Public Economies: Readings from the Workshop in Political Theory and Policy Analysis*. Ann Arbor: University of Michigan Press, pp. 265–283.

Ostrom, Elinor, and Gordon P. Whitaker. [1973] 1999. "Does Local Community Control of Police Make a Difference?" In Michael D. McGinnis, ed., *Polycentricity and Local Public Economies: Readings from the Workshop in Political Theory and Policy Analysis*. Ann Arbor: University of Michigan Press, pp. 176–202.

Ostrom, Vincent. [1973] 1974. *The Intellectual Crisis in American Public Administration*. Rev. ed. Tuscaloosa: University of Alabama Press.

———. [1971] 1987. *The Political Theory of a Compound Republic: Designing the American Experiment*. 2nd ed. Lincoln: University of Nebraska Press.

———. [1990] 1995. "The Problem of Sovereignty in Human Affairs." In James S. Wunsch and Dele Olowu, eds., *The Failure of the Centralized State: Institutions and Self-Governance in Africa*. San Francisco: ICS Press. pp. 228–244.

———. 1997. *The Meaning of Democracy and the Vulnerability of Democracies: A Response to Tocqueville's Challenge*. Ann Arbor: University of Michigan Press.

———. 1999. "Polycentricity" (2 parts). In Michael D. McGinnis, ed., *Polycentricity and Local Public Economies: Readings from the Workshop in Political Theory and Policy Analysis.* Ann Arbor: University of Michigan Press, pp. 52–74; 119–138.

Ostrom, Vincent, and Elinor Ostrom. [1977] 1999. "Public Goods and Public Choices." In Michael D. McGinnis, ed., *Polycentricity and Local Public Economies: Readings from the Workshop in Political Theory and Policy Analysis.* Ann Arbor: University of Michigan Press, pp. 75–103.

Ostrom, Vincent, Charles Tiebout, and Robert Warren. 1999. "The Organization of Government in Metropolitan Areas: A Theoretical Inquiry. In Michael D. McGinnis, ed., *Polycentricity and Local Public Economies: Readings from the Workshop in Political Theory and Policy Analysis.* Ann Arbor: University of Michigan Press, pp. 31–51.

O'Toole, Thomas. 1986. *The Central African Republic: The Continent's Hidden Heart.* Boulder, CO: Westview Press.

Oxfam Report. 2002. *Rigged Rules and Double Standards: Trade, Globalisation and the Fight Against Poverty.* www.oxfam.org/eng/policy.htm.

Peters, Pauline. 1994. *Dividing the Commons: Politics, Policy and Culture in Botswana.* Charlottesville: University of Virginia Press.

Pham, John-Peter. 2004. *Liberia: The Portrait of a Failed State.* New York: Reed Press.

Popkin, Samuel L. 1988. "Public Choice and Peasant Organization." In Robert H. Bates, ed., *Toward a Political Economy of Development: A Rational Choice Perspective.* Berkeley: University of California Press.

Popper, Karl. 1952. *The Open Society and Its Enemies.* London: Routledge & Kegan Paul.

Putnam, Robert D. 1993. *Making Democracy Work: Civic Traditions in Modern Italy.* Princeton: Princeton University Press.

Pye, Lucian. 1971. *Warlord Politics: Conflict and Coalition in the Modernization of Republican China.* New York: Praeger.

Reno, William. 1995. *Corruption and State Politics in Sierra Leone.* Cambridge: Cambridge University Press.

———. 2000. "Shadow States and the Political Economy of Civil Wars." In Mats Berdal and David M. Malone, eds., *Greed and Grievance: Economic Agendas in Civil Wars.* Boulder, CO: Lynne Rienner Publishers, pp. 43–68.

Renou, Xavier. 2002. "A New French Policy for Africa?" *Journal of Contemporary African Studies* 20, no. 1: 5–27.

Ribot, Jesse C. 1999. "Decentralisation, Participation and Accountability in Sahelian Forestry: Legal Instruments of Political-Administrative Control." *Africa* 69, no. 1: 23–65.

———. 2003. "Democratic Decentralisation of Natural Resources: Institutional Choice and Discretionary Power Transfers in Sub-Saharan Africa." *Public Administration and Development* 23, no. 1: 53–65.

Rodney, Walter. 1973. *How Europe Underdeveloped Africa.* London: Bogle-L'Ouverture Publications.

Rondinelli, Dennis A., John R. Nellis, and Shabbir G. Cheema. 1984. *Decentralization in Developing Countries: A Review of Recent Experience.* Staff Working Paper No. 581. Washington, DC: World Bank.

Rondinelli, Dennis A., James S. McCullough, and Ronald W. Johnson. 1989. "Analyzing Decentralization Policies in Developing Countries: A Political-Economy Framework." *Development and Change* 20, no. 3–4: 57–87.

Rufin, Jean-Christophe. 1996. *Le dossier: Les conflits en Afrique.* Paris: Institut de Relations Internationales et Stratégiques (IRIS).

Sawyer, Amos. 1987a. *Effective Immediately—Dictatorship in Liberia, 1980–1986: A Personal Perspective.* Bremen: Liberia Working Group.

———. 1987b. "The Making of the 1984 Liberian Constitution." *Liberian Studies Journal* 12, no. 1.

———. 1992. *The Emergence of Autocracy in Liberia: Tragedy and Challenge.* San Francisco: ICS Press.

———. [1998] 1993a. "The Putu Development Association: A Missed Opportunity." In Vincent Ostrom, David Feeny, and Hartmut Picht, eds., *Rethinking Institutional Analysis and Development: Issues, Alternatives, and Choices.* San Francisco: ICS Press, pp. 247–278.

———. [1998] 1993b. "The Development of Autocracy in Liberia." In Vincent Ostrom, David Feeny, and Hartmut Picht, eds., *Rethinking Institutional Analysis and Development: Issues, Alternatives, and Choice.* San Francisco: ICS Press, pp. 279–313.

———. 1995. "Proprietary Authority and Local Administration in Liberia." In James S. Wunsch and Dele Olowu, eds., *The Failure of the Centralized State: Institutions and Self-Governance in Africa.* San Francisco: ICS Press, pp. 148–173.

———. 2004. "Violent Conflicts and Governance Challenges in West Africa: The Case of the Mano River Basin Area." *Journal of Modern African Studies* 42, no. 3: 437–463.

Sawyer, Amos, and Conmany Wesseh. 2000. *Exiting War: From Disarmament to Elections in Liberia: Proceedings of Workshops and Other Activities on Disarmament, Elections and Reconciliation.* Monrovia: Center for Democratic Empowerment.

Sawyer, Amos, Conmany Wesseh, and Samuel Ajavon Jr. 2000. *Sharing the Kola Nut: Understanding Ethnic Conflict and Building Peace in Liberia—Experiences from Lofa and Nimba.* Monrovia: Sabanoh Printing Press, for Center for Democratic Empowerment.

Sawyer, Amos, Conmany Wesseh, Richard Panton, and Tiswen Synyenlentu. 2000. "Ethnic-Based Conflict in Sinoe: Challenges and Opportunities for Conflict Management and Reconciliation: A Report from Research and Reconciliation Interventions." Center for Democratic Empowerment, Monrovia. Manuscript.

SCF (Save the Children Fund). 1999. Annual Report, Liberia. www.savethechildren .org.

Scholnick, Ellin Kofsky. 2002. "Language, Literacy, and Thought: Forming a Partnership." In Eric Amsel and James P. Byrnes, eds., *Language, Literacy, and Cognitive Development: The Development and Consequences of Symbolic Communication.* Mahwah, NJ: Lawrence Erlbaum, pp. 3–25.

Schraeder, Peter. 1997. "France and the Great Game in Africa." *Current History* 96 (May): 206–211.

Schroder, Gunter, and Dieter Seibel. 1974. *Ethnographic Survey of Southeastern Liberia: The Liberian Kran and the Sapo.* Newark: Department of Anthropology, University of Delaware.

Schwab, Peter. 2001. *Africa: A Continent Self-Destructs.* New York: Palgrave Macmillan.

———. 2004. *Designing West Africa: Prelude to Twenty-First Century Calamity.* New York: Palgrave Macmillan.

Scott, James C. 1998. *Seeing Like a State: How Certain Schemes to Improve the Human Condition Have Failed.* New Haven: Yale University Press.

Scribner, Sylvia, and Michael Cole. 1981. *The Psychology of Literacy.* Cambridge: Harvard University Press.

Seely, Jennifer. 2001. "A Political Analysis of Decentralisation: Coopting the Tuareg Threat in Mali." *Journal of Modern African Studies* 39, no. 3: 499–525.

Selassie, Bereket H. 1974. *The Executive in African Governments.* London: Heinemann.

Sen, Amartya. 1999. *Development as Freedom.* New York: Anchor Books.

Seyon, Patrick. 1998. "Quick-Fixing the State in Africa: The Liberian Case." Working Paper in African Studies No. 217, African Studies Center, Boston University.

Sheridan, James. 1966. *Chinese Warlord: The Career of Feng Yu-hsiang.* Palo Alto: Stanford University Press.

Sherman, Mary Antoinette Brown. 1982. "Education in Liberia." In A. Babs Fafunwa and J. U. Aisiku, eds. *Education in Africa: A Comparative Study.* London: Allen & Unwin, pp. 162–187.

———. 1989. "Perspective on Education in Liberia." Paper presented at the Twenty-first Annual Conference, Liberian Studies Association, Glassboro State College, Glassboro, NJ, March 24–26.

Shick, Tom. 1977. *Behold the Promised Land: A History of Afro-American Settler Society in Nineteenth Century Liberia.* Baltimore: Johns Hopkins University Press.

Shivakumar, Sujai. 2005. *The Constitution of Development: Crafting Capabilities for Self-Governance.* New York: Palgrave Macmillan.

Simons, Geoff. 1993. *Libya: The Struggle for Survival.* New York: St. Martin's Press.

Smoke, Paul, 2003. "Decentralization in Africa: Goals, Dimensions, Myths and Challenges." *Public Administration and Development* 23, no. 1: 7–16.

Southall, Aiden., ed. 1961. *Social Change in Modern Africa: Studies Presented and Discussed.* London: Oxford University Press, for the International African Institute.

Spence, Rebecca. 1999. "The Centrality of Community-Led Recovery." In Geoff Harris, ed., *Recovery from Armed Conflict in Developing Countries.* London: Routledge, pp. 204–222.

Stedman, Stephen John. 1991. "Conflict and Conflict Resolution in Africa: A Conceptual Framework." In Francis M. Deng and I. William Zartman, eds., *Conflict Resolution in Africa.* Washington, DC: Brookings Institution.

Suret-Canale, Jean. 1964. *French Colonialism in Tropical Africa, 1900–1945.* London: C. Hurst.

Szeftel, Morris. 2000. "'Eat with Us': Managing Corruption and Patronage Under Zambia's Three Republics, 1964–99." *Journal of Contemporary African Studies* 18, no. 2: 207–219.

Taryor, Nya Kwiawon, ed. 1985. *Justice, Justice: A Cry of My People—The Struggle for Economic Progress and Social Justice in Liberia.* Chicago: Strugglers' Community Press.

Thompson, Vincent B. 1970. *Africa and Unity: The Evolution of Pan-Africanism.* New York: Humanitarian Press.

Tocqueville, Alexis de. [1835–1840] 1969. *Democracy in America.* Edited by J. P. Mayer. Garden City, NY: Anchor Books.

Tutu, Desmond. 1999. *No Future Without Forgiveness.* New York: Doubleday.

UN Population Division. 2000. *World Population Prospect: 2000.* http://esa.un.org/unpp.

UN Security Council. 2001. *Report of the Panel of Experts Appointed Pursuant to Security Council Resolution 1306 (2000).* New York: United Nations.

UNDP, *Human Development Reports.* 2000, 2001. New York: UNDP. http://hdr.undp.org.

UNECA. 1990. *African Charter for Popular Participation in Development*. Addis Ababa: UNECA.

UNICEF. 1980–2004. *State of the World's Children*. New York: UNICEF. www.unicef .org/publications.

van der Kraaij, F. P. M. 1983. *The Open Door Policy of Liberia: An Economic History of Modern Liberia*. Vol. 1. Bremen: Bremer Afrika Archi Bank, im Selbstverlag des Museums.

Wafula, Richard M. 2003. "My Audience Tells Me in Which Tongue I Should Sing: The Politics About Languages in African Literatures." In Samuel Gyasi Obeng and Beverly Hartford, eds., *Political Independence with Linguistic Servitude: The Politics About Languages in the Developing World*. New York: Nova Science Publishers, pp. 97–111.

Walker, Brian, Stephen Carpenter, John Anderies, Nick Abel, Graeme Cumming, Marco Janssen, et al. 2002. "Resilience Management in Social-Ecological Systems: A Working Hypothesis for a Participatory Approach." *Conservation Ecology* 6, no. 1. www.consecol.org/vol6/iss1/art14.

Walter, Barbara F. 1999. "Designing Transitions from Civil War: Demobilization, Democratization and Commitments to Peace." *International Security* 24, no. 1 (Summer): 127–155.

wa Thiong'o, Ngugi. 1986. *Decolonising the Mind*. London: James Currey.

Weh-Dorliae, Yarsuo. 2004. *Proposition 12 for Decentralized Governance in Liberia: Power Sharing for Peace and Progress*. Philadelphia: Bushfire Ventures.

Weiss, Herbert. 2000. *War and Peace in the Democratic Republic of the Congo*. Uppsala: Nordiska Afrikainstitutet.

West, Harry G. 2000. "Girls with Guns: Narrating the Experience of War of FRELIMO's 'Female Detachment.'" *Anthropological Quarterly* 73, no. 4 (October): 80–204.

Williams, Gabriel. 2002. *Liberia: The Heart of Darkness*. Victoria, BC, Canada: Trafford Publishing.

Wunsch, James S. 2001. "Decentralization, Local Governance and Recentralization in Africa." *Public Administration and Development* 21, no. 4: 277–288.

Wunsch, James S., and Dele Olowu, eds. [1990] 1995. *The Failure of the Centralized State: Institutions and Self-Governance in Africa*. San Francisco: Institute for Contemporary Studies Press.

Yansane, Aguibou Y. 1980. *Decolonization and Dependency: Problems of Development*. Westport, CT: Greenwood Press.

Yoder, John Charles. 2003. *Popular Political Culture, Civil Society and State Crisis in Liberia*. Lewiston, NY: Edward Mellen Press.

Young, Crawford. 1994. *The African Colonial State in Comparative Perspective*. New Haven: Yale University Press.

Zack-Williams, Alfred. 1995. *Tributors, Supporters and Merchant Capital: Mining and Underdevelopment in Sierra Leone*. Aldershot, UK: Avebury.

Zartman, I. William, ed. 1995. *Elusive Peace: Negotiating an End to Civil Wars*. Washington, DC: Brookings Institution.

Zolberg, Aristide. 1966. *Creating Political Order: The Party-States of West Africa*. Chicago: Rand McNally.

Index

233

About the Book

C AN A STABLE POLITICAL ORDER BE ESTABLISHED IN LIBERIA IN THE AFTERMATH OF the collapse of governance and a horrendous period of pillage and carnage? Amos Sawyer argues that the task can indeed be accomplished—but only in the context of new constitutional arrangements and governing institutions that differ markedly from those of the past.

Sawyer draws deeply on his experience as head of state as he explores new ways of establishing constitutional foundations for democratic governance. Though he focuses on Liberia (and to some extent Sierra Leone and Guinea), his work speaks profoundly to the many other parts of Africa where the governing systems established at independence have broken down with often tragic consequences.

Amos Sawyer, president of Liberia in 1990–1994, is associate director and research scholar at the Workshop in Political Theory and Policy Analysis, Indiana University. He is also coordinator of the Consortium for Self Governance in Africa.